Career Changing
The Worry-free Guide

Career Changing
The Worry-free Guide

by
Linda Kline
and
Lloyd L. Feinstein

Little, Brown and Company   Boston ▪ Toronto

LIBRARY OF CONGRESS CATALOG CARD NO.

Third Printing

The authors are grateful to the following companies for permission to quote as noted:

American Management Association for excerpts from *COMPFLASH*, March 1981.

Dow Jones & Company, Inc., for excerpts on pages 12, 36, and 117 from *The Wall Street Journal*. Reprinted by permission of The Wall Street Journal © Dow Jones & Company, Inc. 1980, 1974. All rights reserved.

Fox Morris Associates for the chart on page 42. Copyright © 1980 by Fox Morris Associates. Reprinted by permission.

HOMEQUITY, Inc., for excerpts from *Relocation Issues and Trends*, April 1981. Copyright © 1981 by HOMEQUITY, Inc.

Pitman Learning, Inc., for excerpts from *Preparing Instructional Objectives*, Second Edition, by Robert F. Mager. Copyright © 1975 by Pitman Learning, Inc., Belmont, California.

Women Business Owners of New York, Inc., for excerpts from *Womanventure*, May 1981. Edited by Connie Sternberg.

LIBRARY OF CONGRESS CATALOGING IN PUBLICATION DATA

Kline, Linda, 1944–
   Career changing.

   Bibliography: p.
   1. Career changes. I. Feinstein, Lloyd L.
II. Title.
HF5384.K54 1982   650.1′4   82–20344
   ISBN 0–316–49858–0 (pbk.)

VB

Published simultaneously in Canada
by Little, Brown & Company (Canada) Limited

PRINTED IN THE UNITED STATES OF AMERICA

DEDICATION

Career Changing is dedicated to all of you in the workforce (and those of you who contemplate entering or reentering the world of work) who are realistic and do not accept the often-held assumption that your job or career situation will improve through the goodwill of others (be it a friend, relative, co-worker, supervisor, department head, or top executive).

Career-minded people know that their rate of advancement is directly related to personal effort expended, not efforts of others.

If you are like most people in the workforce, you may not be fully cognizant of how the job market really functions and where the many pitfalls exist. Our book's objective is to assist you in advancing your career as quickly and painlessly as possible. Our goal is to help you recognize and select the correct methods that will allow you to take complete charge of your next job change and all subsequent career moves. It's quite possible that our advice, if taken seriously, could increase your total future earning power by hundreds of thousands of dollars, perhaps millions.

Enjoy the book!

Preface

Why Another Book on Changing Jobs?

Many books, some pretty good, some not so good, have been written in recent years on how to change jobs and/or career fields. Why another one?

Because, in our estimation as professionals from both sides of the human resources field (personnel), not one of these other books has ever told the true story of how trying it is to effect a truly meaningful change and how long it can sometimes take you to do so. Most other books either simplify an experience that can be fraught with anxiety or they highlight only one or two areas of the change process, such as résumé writing or performing a skills analysis.

We know that the process of changing jobs, and certainly of changing careers, can be an uncomfortable one. What we hope to accomplish with this book is to increase your comfort level while you are looking for new work and learning to work smarter, not necessarily harder. Although it is hard work if you're serious, *smart* work is the key.

Career Changing will provide you with a total marketing approach to job hunting, not a piecemeal one. For *you* are the product that is being marketed, not your résumé or Brooks Brothers suit. Not that packaging isn't important—it is—but in the end, an organization hires *you*.

We feel that if you follow the precepts discussed in our book, the organizations you seek out and who seek you out *will* want to hire you. For you will have learned how to outmarket your competition.

Throughout, we have provided you with "Insiders' Tips," information that we, the authors, one an executive search consultant, the other a director of human resources at a Fortune 1000 company, have experienced over the years in the hiring and placing of applicants.

Who Should Read This Book?

If you are in the initial stages of contemplating either a change or your first job and you aren't in extreme pain or panic, you should read the entire volume, as it will orient you onto the correct track and save valuable time and effort when the day dawns that you decide to look for a position.

If you have written or updated your résumé and if you are employed or between jobs but have not yet sent out the résumé, look first at chapter 4 if you are staying within your established career area, and then at chapter 3. If you haven't interviewed in a while, also read chapter 8, then the rest of the book.

If you are changing career areas, read chapters 5 and 2 first, then chapters 3 and 4, then the rest of the book, particularly chapter 11, the glossary of jargon.

If your résumé has been sent out but has not gained you interviews, check out chapters 3 and 4, then chapter 7 (for a new approach), then the rest.

If your résumé or letter campaign has been getting you interviews but no offers (or no meaningful ones), read chapters 8 and 1 first, then the rest of the book.

If you have limited your search to using employment agencies and reviewing the want ads (without much success), read chapter 9 first to enlarge your options. Then review chapters 1, 3, 4, and 7.

If you're returning to the work force after a substantial absence, or if you've determined that you may need more or different education to obtain your next job, start with chapter 10, then read chapter 1, then the rest of the book.

If you're just plain hesitant to change, even if you know you would be happier in a different job, read chapter 6, then chapter 1 first.

Career Changing has been written for college graduates, currently employed or unemployed, for career changers, people returning to the work force, anyone who wants a second career instead of retirement. It will also be very useful for students in graduate school or undergraduates who will be trying to get that first job in a year's time or less.

We, the authors, are very interested in your reaction to *Career Changing*. If you'd like to send us your comments, via our publisher, we would be very pleased (even if you hate it, we'd like to know why). We would be particularly interested in hearing from those of you who have read some of the other books available on job hunting. Let us know how ours stacks up.

Good luck, be prepared, relax, and enjoy the experience of changing. You will meet some wonderful people along the way.

Contents

Career Changing
The Worry-free Guide

1. You're Better than You Think You Are

"You will never amount to much."

—A MUNICH SCHOOLMASTER TO ALBERT
EINSTEIN, AGED 10.

Our adult self-images were shaped when we were children, through the way we interacted with and were treated by our parents, siblings, other relatives, teachers, and friends. Any negative components can (and usually do) follow us into our adult lives and may cause feelings of inferiority or of never being quite "good" enough to obtain what we want.

When we are adults, this negative self-image is often reinforced in the world of work. A typical example is of the boss who points out any mistakes you make but never praises your successes. What is the usual result of this negative reinforcement? We magnify our bad points totally out of proportion and minimize our strengths. This holds true for all aspects of our lives, particularly in the workplace.

Do You Work "Out of Title"?

We all tend to limit the reporting of our work lives, both on the job or off. When someone you meet socially asks you what you do, you may say, "I'm in personnel," even if you are the director of human resources for a major company. Or, "I'm a secretary," when in truth you are the mainstay of your department and do many things other than typing your manager's memos and answering the telephone. We minimize and downplay our achievements, partly to appear humble (we were all trained that it's not nice to boast) and partly because we don't feel *we* deserve to have what we do.

Have you ever read a résumé that was so boring (because the writer downplayed his/her accomplishments) you had to reread it three times to remember what was said? Unfortunately, most résumés, cover letters, and general correspondence are written this way. Most people will take credit for only those tasks that are covered by the titles and descriptions forced upon them by their companies or organizations, even if their day-to-day work has little or no relation to their company job descriptions. Many of us "work out of title" but fail to take credit for these experiences when we review our work and put it on paper.

And we often let others take credit for things that are rightfully ours.

Example: Barbara Wilkinson worked for one of the major banks in Chicago as an administrative assistant in the International Finance Division and reported directly to the v.p. in charge of the division. She had a B.A. and M.A. in modern languages, was working on an M.B.A. in marketing at night, had lived in France for two years, and spoke French, Spanish, and German fluently. Needless to say, her boss (the vice president) utilized her background and skills in many areas other than clerical. However, when Barbara attempted

3

BARBARA R. WILKINSON
2351 Michigan Avenue, #12B
Chicago, Illinois 60612
(312)492-6468

PREVIOUS EDUCATION

SCHOOL	MAJOR	ATTENDANCE	DEGREE
University of Chicago (Evening Division) Chicago, Illinois	Marketing Management	9/78 - Present	M.B.A.
Fordham University Bronx, New York	French	2/75 - 2/76	M.A.
Faculté des Lettres Université de Nancy Nancy, France	Modern Languages: French, Spanish German	9/72 - 6/74	Licence ès lettres
Hunter College New York, New York	French--Major Education--Minor	9/69 - 6/73	B.A.

PREVIOUS EXPERIENCE

COMPANY	POSITION	EMPLOYED	REASON FOR LEAVING
Continental Illinois National Bank & Trust Co. Chicago, Illinois	Administrative assistant	2/76 - Present	To find position in Lending or Financial Marketing

Duties: Research in International Finance Division, reports, balance sheet and
      income statement reviews, follow-up correspondence, providing background
      (financial and historical) information on pending loans; and bank
      syndication financing (research and reports done in English, French
      and Spanish).

Chemical Construction Corp. 1 Penn Plaza New York, New York	Technical translator	2/74 - 2/75	Company folded

Duties: Technical translating and interpreting engineering reports, operating
      manuals, blueprints, brochures.
         Subject matter: Chemical, civil, electrical engineering
         Supervised: Clerical staff

Embassy of Pakistan 8, rue Lord Byron Paris, France	Interpreter to ambassador	10/73 - 6/74	Returned to States

Duties: Interpreting for ambassador (French-English), coordinating programs,
      extensive traveling.

to transfer into the bank's training program to become a lending officer, she found herself blocked. Her job description, as written by her boss and by Personnel, showed her as having a position only two steps above a nondegreed secretary. And, as Barbara never mentioned her work projects at all in the interview for the position in the training program, she was not selected.

Opposite is Barbara's résumé before she took credit for work performed.

In counseling Barbara we discovered some interesting things. She'd actually worked on some very important projects for the division but hadn't taken credit for them. Why not? The answers are typical: (1) her boss, the v.p. of the International Finance Division, had always signed *his* name to *her* reports (a very common occurrence), so Barbara figured no one would believe she'd written them, and (2) the reports had been typed by different typing pool secretaries and she didn't have copies (only her boss did), (3) Barbara's job description, as furnished by the bank for level, title, et cetera, never mentioned project research or report writing. As you can see, many parts of our jobs that are highly successful and important are never recorded. We take them for granted. After all, if *we* do them, how important can they really be?

After several sessions with us we assigned Barbara some homework: to describe to us in *action*-oriented language her research, data-collection, and report-writing projects. We then had her take the paragraphs she'd written, helped her tighten them up, and after several tries she came up with an action letter that said it all! We'll discuss in chapter 7 the very specific way an action letter is designed, but meanwhile, in reading Barbara's original résumé and then reading her action letter on page 4, you can see that she was, indeed, better than she thought she was.

Taking Credit

Another area where we find you may minimize yourself is in *taking credit* for work completed when *you* did not do every bit of it. *Example:* you are a member of a four-person team assigned to an important project that has to be completed in three and a half months. All of you on this team have specific areas of expertise and you must gather the information necessary to put the report together in a comprehensive way. *Your* part, Part A, has to mesh comfortably with the other three parts. Even though you didn't work directly on the other three areas, chances are you *know* what they're all about. If Part B, C, or D had been assigned to you instead of Part A, you could just as easily have done your report on B, C, or D. *If* you really understand B, C, and D, *even though you didn't do B, C, or D*, take all or partial credit for the project if a future employer asks if you have knowledge of B, C, or D. *If* you can replicate B, C, and D, take credit for them. If you cannot replicate B, C, or D, DO NOT take credit—you will be found out.

This is stated by Dr. Adele M. Scheele in *Skills for Success:* "If we feel that we must be *totally* prepared before we enter an experience, we will be forever trapped by the dangerous model of the 'good student.'"

"Other" Kinds of Work

The validity of "other" kinds of work, not just your on-the-job experiences, needs to be considered. People rarely realize, let alone take credit for, the fact that all work, paid or not, is valuable and often teaches skills and develops behavior as important as what is learned while working from 9 A.M. to 5 P.M. Those with military experience have learned skills and know how to work as team members, and as managers if they have been officers. If you were

Dear

As Assistant to the Vice President for International Finance at a major Chicago bank, I conducted an extensive survey of the reactions of the European press to the 1977 Spanish elections. To assess the financial implications of the elections and their impact on the bank's investments, the articles were organized by date and country, and within each country by political reaction. I wrote up individual reports for each country and translated pertinent articles as appendices to the report, which was submitted to the bank's Board of Directors.

I am writing because your organization may be in need of a person with my background and experience for your Management Training Program in International Corporate Lending. If so, the following accomplishments may be of interest:

--I produce financial reviews for extending a line of credit, joining a syndication, increasing or decreasing a line of credit, or letting the credit line lapse. I analyze balance sheets and income statements, following institutional guidelines. To add depth to the analysis, I consult credit file data, dispatch telexes in both French and English to our six shareholders for their assessment and approval, and obtain recommendations from other key financial institutions. Completed reviews were submitted to the Vice President.

--As Project Coordinator for a photocopying survey, I interfaced with management and line staff to explain the bank's need to evaluate current copy demand. I supervised employee compliance with the survey's guidelines. I produced daily reports evaluating the use of various types of photocopying jobs. I monitored discrepancies between machine metering and employee logs. I prepared a summary report for the Purchasing Director recommending the most potentially profitable investment in photocopying services. This resulted in yearly savings of approximately $9,000 for our department alone.

--Using information supplied by the Vice President, I compose and supervise the preparation of all correspondence (produced in both French and English). I translate correspondence, reports and telexes for dissemination among various members of the International Finance Division.

I graduated from Hunter College in New York in 1973 with a B.A., speak French and Spanish fluently, and am presently matriculated at the University of Chicago's graduate evening division to obtain my M.B.A. in marketing. My salary requirements are competitive. I would be glad to discuss my experience further in a personal interview and will call you within 10 days to set up a convenient time to meet.

Sincerely yours,

Barbara R. Wilkinson

an officer you managed and motivated your subordinates, often large numbers of people, a skill that's not to be minimized, particularly if your current 9 to 5 job has no one for you to manage. If you're trying to convince your boss to give you a staff to manage, you can prove by describing your military experiences that you've supervised and motivated others.

Women often tell us apologetically, "I was only a volunteer"—well, let us tell you something!

Volunteer work, often stated as "only volunteer work," can be highly demanding and can be the source of much learning, including the development of management and leadership skills. So don't shy away from using that kind of experience in evaluating and discussing your talents. When you are working and being paid to do a job, a subordinate who promises to do something for you and doesn't come through can be fired. If, however, a volunteer promises something and reneges, you're stuck. You cannot fire someone who doesn't work for you. You may have to remotivate this person, put someone else on the project and hope *they* will come through for you, or do it yourself.

The same is true of homemaking. So much emphasis lately has been put on women working outside the home that many women who enjoy and/or can afford to be homemakers are embarrassed to say they don't have a $35,000-a-year job in addition to running a house and caring for three kids, a husband, two dogs, three cats, six gerbils, and a king snake. However, the level of organization required to perform successfully all aspects of homemaking is staggering. (The newest term, by the way, is not homemaker, but *domestic engineer*.) Homemaking, or domestic engineering, if you will, has been put down too long. And who's to say this should only be a woman's domain? Men should be able to stay home if they desire and their wives should work if that's what they want to do. *Choice* is the key word. But again, whether you're a male or female domestic engineer, the *work*, the *organization of that work*, and its *results* are what you should look at and be able to discuss.

If the job is described accurately, you are the chief purchasing agent, budget manager, investor of excess funds, resident doctor, nurse and therapist, cook, chauffeur, carpenter, painter, etc. The validity of your work is incredible although our society rewards only paid work. But recognize this fact and get around it. A properly understood and evaluated experience will be very positive if you express it correctly in an interview.

Tooting Your Own Horn

The Bible notwithstanding, the meek so far have not inherited the earth. It's necessary to understand the importance of promoting yourself because, with few exceptions, no one will do it for you. To go back to Barbara Wilkinson, even though her boss signed his name to all her research reports, she should have kept copies of "befores" and "afters" and had other colleagues read them. She should have talked about them within her department, she should have become friendly with people in the International Lending area where she wanted to be and shown them her work, and she should have had the reports with her at outside interviews in case they were needed. But—and this is a very important "but"—she (and this applies to you, too) must first recognize the work she does as being important and to articulate its importance to others, particularly people in positions *above* her.

Powerful Thought

Perception of your abilities is the key. You may be the best engineer/secretary/actuary/social worker in the country, but if you don't tell anyone what you've done, no one's going to know (except your boss, and he or she certainly won't tell anybody—he or she might lose you).

The extent of one's power is largely determined by perception. "If you think you have it, then you have it. If you think you don't have it (even if you do) then you don't have it," says Herbert A. Cohen, author of *You Can Negotiate Anything*.

Please don't run around flapping your gums at anyone who'll listen about how terrific you are. That quickly grows tedious. But—you must *judiciously* spread the gospel of your worth. As stated, *perception* of your abilities is the key. You may be not much above average, but if you market your skills properly, you'll do a lot better than someone who may be better skilled than you, but who never says a word about himself. *Actual* ability doesn't count as much as *perceived* ability, and most people, whether they work in corporations at high levels or in the world's governments, are average in abilities. But they've convinced others that they're better than they think they are. If they can, you can too.

Don't feel that you are a failure or an underachiever if you have not yet found your life's work. Even if you are a college graduate you may not be happier on your job than other people. A late 1970s study by the College Placement Council shows that some of the widely held assumptions about college education and job satisfaction have been brought into question. The study concluded that finding a job related to one's college major is not essential for job satisfaction, and that most graduates who consider their jobs to be nonprofessional can be happy in their work. Many college students who prepare early for a specific career are not more satisfied with their work than those who choose later. "Attempting to create a perfect fit between college education and careers is a wasted effort because a perfect fit doesn't matter to the consumer of education—the students," the study reported.

So, if you're not certain what it is you want to do, where you want to do it, or how much you should get paid for doing it, you're in good company! Go on to chapter 2, "Job Facts of Life for the 1980s." It should help ease your mind somewhat as well as tell you how you might examine fields other than those you are presently considering.

2. Job Facts of Life for the 1980s

"Don't look back. Something may be gaining on you."

—SATCHEL PAIGE, FORMER PITCHER FOR
THE CLEVELAND INDIANS

Where Will the Jobs Be in the 1980s?

Where are the jobs going to be in this peculiar decade of the 1980s and maybe into the 1990s? How can you make educated guesses as to which fields will be the safest from the ravages of inflation and which ones are more or less recession-proof? What if the answers are unpleasant for you (you'd rather be an urban planner than a bank manager)—how do you reconcile these things? Can you?

According to the spring 1980 *Occupational Outlook Quarterly*, a publication of the U.S. Department of Labor, the 1980s job market will be improved in several areas, one of which may surprise you: teachers of elementary students!

According to recent projections by the National Center for Education Statistics (NCES) and the Bureau of Labor Statistics, the 1980s will be good for new graduates prepared to teach elementary school. Equilibrium between the demand for and the supply of these teachers is expected to occur around 1984 or 1985, and a shortage of such teachers is predicted by the end of the eighties. However, teachers of secondary school will still exceed demand. Keep in mind, though, that elementary educators with specialties in mathematics, special education, science, etc., will fare better in job getting than teachers of art and music.

What has caused this prediction? The number of births, while declining for twenty years, began to go back up in the late 1970s. Not that people are having larger families; they're not. There are just more people in our general population, and many are of childbearing age. The Bureau of the Census expects a moderate rise in births through the mid-1980s but another decline beginning around 1987. That means elementary-school teachers will not have problems getting jobs until the early to mid-1990s, when the decline will affect them. Total *new* growth in elementary-school teacher employment during the 1980s is expected to be about 280,000, a 21 percent increase. If predictions are wrong and the pupil-teacher ratio remains at its 1980 level, the growth of new jobs (not replacement) will be only 150,000, or 11 percent. However, it's still an increase! Total elementary-school teacher jobs are predicted to be 840,000. Secondary-school teachers will lose approximately 160,000 jobs between 1980 and 1990 as a result of the projected decline in the secondary-school-age population. However, regions with rapidly rising populations, such as the South and Southwest, will employ more new teachers than the Northeast, which is losing population.

Since competition for most jobs has stiffened in recent years, planning a career requires careful research, as the elementary teacher outlook makes clear. You don't want to pick a field where you spend most of your life in the unemployment line. The number of people employed in any occupation depends on the demand for the goods and services provided by these workers. If the demand for a product or service grows, employment will increase. But there are exceptions to this.

Changes in the technology used to make products or provide services enable businesses to increase output while decreasing the numbers of people hired. Example: mechanized book binding has limited the job opportunities in binderies, although there are more books being bound than ever before. And, despite the rising use of credit for shopping, the number of credit managers has decreased because retail stores have computerized their credit operations.

Since the 1950s, service-producing industries have grown faster than goods-producing industries; consequently, employment in white-collar and service occupations has grown more rapidly than employment in blue-collar occupations. In 1978, 80 percent of all white-collar workers and over 90 percent of all service workers were employed in service-producing industries such as wholesale and retail trade, transportation, utilities, insurance, real estate, finance, and government, as against 60 percent of blue-collar workers employed in goods-producing industries such as manufacturing, agriculture, construction, and mining.

Between 1978 and 1990 total employment is expected to rise 21 percent, from 94.4 million to 114.0 million workers. One way to view this increase is that economic expansion will create nearly 20 million *new* jobs plus 47 million others as people leave the labor force because of retirement, illness, death, or family duties. But the key is to know where the jobs will be. The fastest growing group of occupations during the 1980s will be in the *service* areas such as cleaning, food, health, personal and protective services.

The accompanying tables show the fastest expanding and most available job areas projected to 1990.

Winners and Losers of 1980

Starting salaries for people with little or no work experience:

Management consultants: if you are getting an M.B.A. degree from a highly regarded Ivy League university such as Harvard, University of Pennsylvania (Wharton), Stanford, or Chicago, and are in the top 10 percent of your class, have a B.S. or B.A. degree from another prestigious college or university, if you are willing to travel 50 to 75 percent of your time, and are very outgoing and physically attractive, you can command up to $46,000 *to start* if you are hired by one of the major management consulting firms such as McKinsey & Co. or Booz Allen & Hamilton (1981 figures).

However, for the 99.9 percent of us who don't have these credentials, let's stop contemplating hara-kiri; there are other areas of employment.

Another big winner is *computer programming*, an area that's going to be in great demand for years; average 1980 starting salary nationwide, $16,000. *Systems analysts* make even more.

Losers: *newspaper reporters*. In a field that has been overcrowded for several years, only about 50 percent of all people seeking reporting jobs found one in 1980. Starting salary? A paltry $10,000.

Another job category, often maligned and very underpaid for years, will finally begin to equalize out in pay and promotional opportunities: *secretarial work*. The current national shortage of secretaries is about 80,000 annually and this deficit is expected to pass the 250,000 mark by or before 1985. The women's movement is usually held accountable for the fact that fewer women seek secretarial jobs.

FASTEST GROWING JOBS, 1978–90		JOBS WITH THE MOST OPENINGS, 1978–90	
Occupation	Annual openings	Occupation	Annual openings
Bank clerks	45,000	Secretaries and stenographers	305,000
Bank officers and financial managers	28,000	Retail sales workers	226,000
Business machine repairers	4,200	Building custodians	180,000
City managers	350	Cashiers	119,000
Computer service technicians	5,400	Bookkeeping workers	96,000
Construction inspectors	2,200	Nursing aides, orderlies, and attendants	94,000
Dental assistants	11,000	Cooks and chefs	86,000
Dental hygienists	6,000	Kindergarten and elementary teachers	86,000
Dining room attendants and dishwashers	37,000	Registered nurses	85,000
Flight attendants	4,800	Assemblers	77,000
Guards	70,000	Waiters and waitresses	70,000
Health service administrators	18,000	Guards	70,000
Homemaker-home health aides	36,000	Blue-collar-worker supervisors	69,000
Industrial machinery repairers	58,000	Local truck drivers	64,000
Landscape architects	1,100	Accountants	61,000
Licensed practical nurses	60,000	Licensed practical nurses	60,000
Lithographers	2,300	Typists	59,000
Nursing aides, orderlies, and attendants	94,000	Carpenters	58,000
Occupational therapists	2,500	Industrial machinery repairers	58,000
Occupational therapy assistants	1,100	Real estate agents and brokers	50,000
Physical therapists	2,700	Construction laborers	49,000
Podiatrists	600	Engineers	46,500
Respiratory therapy workers	5,000	Bank clerks	45,000
Speech pathologists and audiologists	3,900	Private household workers	45,000
Teacher aides	26,000	Receptionists	41,000
Travel agents	1,900	Wholesale trade sales workers	40,000

Note: For these occupations, employment in 1990 is projected to be at least 50 percent higher than it was in 1978.

Note: Replacement needs and growth are projected to cause these occupations to offer the largest number of openings. Competition for openings will vary by occupation.

Source: U.S. Department of Labor, Bureau of Labor Statistics, *Occupational Outlook Quarterly* (Spring 1980).

The movement was and is a factor, but major complaints about secretarial work pertain to undercompensation and lack of upward mobility. Many terribly paid secretaries actually run businesses. Low salaries are really the problem. Starting salaries for beginners average $9,500 in the South and Midwest and $12,000 on the East and West coasts.

But secretarial salaries are on the rise, with ranges of $1,200 to $1,500 per month being offered in Los Angeles and, like any field, specialists such as legal or executive secretaries command the highest pay.

For experienced nonlegal and nonexecutive secretaries the range is $14,000 to $17,000, though some make more than $20,000. A few "executive" secretaries earn in excess of $30,000. Those who take shorthand can earn up to $2,000 more than ones who don't, and a skilled secretary with a B.A. degree may get $3,000 more to start than a high-school graduate.

Oil companies are among the highest paying employers. Atlantic Richfield in California starts secretaries at $13,000 to $15,000 (1980 data); after only three years, many earn $19,000. Conversely, advertising agencies, "glamorous" places to work, pay only $10,400 to $11,000 per year in New York City! Since demand is up and supply is down, qualified secretaries can soon look forward to better pay scales.

But as it's viewed as a "woman's" field, fewer than 1 percent of all secretaries are men. The few men who are in the field usually do very well. Herbert Nelson, himself secretary to the publisher of the *Bergen Record*, a suburban New Jersey daily newspaper, said, "The word *secretary* turns men off. It's a label that means 'woman's job.'" Nelson, fifty, got into the work twenty-six years ago when he was called on to replace another male secretary, as he had studied shorthand and typing. Nelson still spends a large part of his time taking dictation and typing, but has been named secretary to the board of directors and draws an imposing salary of $60,000. He thinks young men miss a bet by passing up secretarial work. "It gives you great visibility, because you often go to work directly for the top executives," he points out.

What Is Marketing?

It's a favorite catchall term for everything from sales positions, whose occupants are often called marketing representatives, to product management to marketing research, which includes the utilization of SAMI and Nielsen reports for data collection. One popular aspect of marketing is found in the advertising fields and with their clients. A *Wall Street Journal* article appearing in April 1982 shows where to find the best pay.

Who pays higher salaries, the advertisers or the advertising agencies? A survey of 154 executives at 35 corporations and 457 executives at 25 of the nation's largest advertising agencies found that the advertisers usually offer better compensation.

The survey, done by a New York executive search firm, was made on behalf of a major ad agency that wanted to know if it was paying its executives enough. The search firm compared the average pay of people in five agency job levels and their peer positions at client companies. The table below shows their findings.

Most bona fide *marketing* jobs require an M.B.A. these days. This is mostly true of the two categories below, of advertiser and agency. It also helps considerably if your M.B.A.

Advertiser	Salary + bonus	Agency	Salary + bonus
Assistant product manager (1–3 years' experience)	$ 31,000 + 2,000	Assistant acount executive (1–2 years' experience)	$19,000 + 0
Product manager (3–5 years' experience)	46,300 + 10,000	Account executive (3–6 years' experience)	31,000 + 2,500
Group product manager (5–8 years' experience)	59,600 + 15,000	Vice president/ account supervisor (6–8 years' experience)	43,800 +12,500
Marketing director (8–10 years' experience)	70,000 + 20,000	Vice president/ management supervisor (8 years' or more experience)	55,000 +16,000
Vice president — marketing (10 years' or more experience)	100,000 + 25,000	Senior vice president/ management supervisor (12 years' or more experience)	78,000 +31,300

Source: *Wall Street Journal,* April 22, 1982.

degree is from a top-rated business school (for example, in the Ivy League). Snobby? Certainly—but this is the real world, boys and girls!

Thirteen Major Occupational Categories

The following information is from "The Job Outlook in Brief," a reprint from the spring 1980 *Occupational Outlook Quarterly,* the career guidance magazine of the U.S. Department of Labor. This is by no means a complete list of occupations, but it will give you a pretty good idea about where the jobs will be through 1990. Information such as this is very valuable if you are thinking of switching careers or if you are about to embark on special education or training in college or a technical school with an eye toward getting a good position upon completion.

Example: If you've decided to become a political scientist, the annual job projections nationwide through the year 1990 are for 500 new political scientists per year. That's only 10 per state! Somehow this doesn't seem like the most promising place to begin a career.

Keep in mind, too, that when job vacancies are few and competition for them is steep, salaries *decrease.* So if making money appeals to you, this field of endeavor and others with low projections of annual employment will not help you accumulate great wealth in any rapid fashion. The best possible thing to do is to select an area of employment that not only appeals to you but where the demand for people exceeds the supply. Then you have what is called a seller's market instead of a buyer's market, as in the case of our political scientist. If you can't or won't do that, I hope you have a wealthy family, husband, or wife (or like to live very simply)!

KEY WORDS . . .

Changing Employment between 1978 and 1990

If the statement reads . . .	Employment is projected to . . .
Much faster than average growth	Increase more than 50 percent
Faster than average growth	Increase 25 to 49.9 percent
Growth about as fast as average	Increase 15 to 24.9 percent
Growing more slowly than average	Increase 5 to 14.9 percent
Little change	Increase or decrease no more than 4.9 percent
Decline	Decrease 5 percent or more

Opportunities and Competition for Jobs

If the statement reads . . .	The demand for workers may be . . .
Excellent opportunities	Much greater than the supply
Very good opportunities	Greater than the supply
Good or favorable opportunities	About the same as the supply
May face competition	Less than the supply
Keen competition	Much less than the supply

Source: *Occupational Outlook Quarterly,* Spring 1980.

**PROJECTED CHANGE IN EMPLOYMENT BY
MAJOR OCCUPATIONAL GROUP, 1978-90**
(in thousands)

Occupational Group	Employment			Openings		
	1978	Projected 1990	Percent Change[1]	Total	Growth	Replace- ments[2]
White-collar workers	47,205	58,400	23.6	36,800	11,200	25,600
Professional and technical workers	14,245	16,900	18.3	8,300	2,600	5,700
Managers and adminis- trators, except farm	10,105	12,200	20.8	7,100	2,100	5,000
Sales workers	5,951	7,600	27.7	4,800	1,700	3,100
Clerical workers	16,904	21,700	28.4	16,600	4,800	11,800
Blue-collar workers	31,531	36,600	16.1	16,200	5,100	11,100
Craft workers	12,386	14,900	20.0	7,000	2,500	4,500
Operatives, except transport	10,875	12,500	15.0	5,600	1,600	4,000
Transport operatives	3,541	4,100	16.2	1,700	600	1,100
Nonfarm laborers	4,729	5,100	8.1	2,000	400	1,600
Service workers	12,839	16,700	29.9	12,200	3,800	8,400
Private household workers	1,162	900	-23.2	500	-300	800
Other service workers	11,677	15,800	35.2	11,700	4,100	7,600
Farm workers	2,798	2,400	-15.9	1,300	-400	1,700
Total	**94,373**	**114,000**	**20.8**	**66,400**	**19,600**	**46,800**

[1] Calculated from unrounded figures.
[2] Due to deaths, retirements, and other separations from the labor force. Does not include transfers out of occupations.
Source: *Occupational Outlook Quarterly,* Spring 1980.

Occupational Employment Outlook

Occu-pation	Estimated employ-ment, 1978	Average annual openings 1978-90[1]	Employment prospects
INDUSTRIAL PRODUCTION AND RELATED OCCUPATIONS			
Foundry occupations			
Pattern-makers	3,700	135	Employment expected to grow more slowly than average. Use of durable metal patterns will offset increases in foundry production.
Molders	21,000	500	Employment expected to increase more slowly than average. Although large demand likely for metal castings, laborsaving innovations will moderate employment growth.
Core-makers	12,000	350	Employment expected to increase more slowly than average as growing use of machine coremaking limits the need for additional workers.
Machining occupations			
All-round machinists	484,000	22,500	Employment expected to increase about as fast as average due to growing demand for machined metal parts. Many openings likely in maintenance shops of manufacturing plants.
Instrument makers (mechanical)	6,000	300	Employment expected to grow about as fast as average in response to the need for new and custom made instruments. Laborsaving innovations may limit growth somewhat.
Machine tool operators	542,000	19,600	Employment expected to increase about as fast as average as metalworking industries expand. Although advances in machine tools may affect some jobs, opportunities should be very good.
Setup workers (machine tools)	65,000	3,000	Employment expected to increase about as fast as average as demand for machined goods grows. Automatically controlled machine tools may limit need for additional workers.

Occu-pation	Estimated employ-ment, 1978	Average annual openings 1978-90[1]	Employment prospects
Tool-and-die makers	170,000	8,600	Employment expected to increase about as fast as average as need for tools and dies continues. However, advances in tool making processes may limit growth.
Printing occupations			
Compos-itors	181,000	3,900	Employment expected to decline as trend to high-speed photo-typesetting and typesetting computers continues. Best prospects for graduates of post-secondary school programs in printing technology.
Lithog-raphers	28,000	2,300	Employment expected to increase much faster than average in response to continued growth of offset printing. Best job prospects for graduates of post-secondary school programs in printing technology.
Photo-engravers	8,000	150	Employment expected to decline as firms switch from letterpress to offset printing. Job opportunities will be scarce.
Electro-typers and stereo-typers	2,000	(2)	Employment expected to decline due to greater use of offset printing and other laborsaving equipment. Job opportunities will be scarce.
Printing press operators and assistants	167,000	5,000	Employment expected to increase more slowly than average as faster and more efficient presses limit growth. Applicants will face competition for jobs.
Book-binders and bindery workers	69,000	2,600	Employment expected to increase more slowly than average due to increasing mechanization of bindery operations

Notes

[1] Due to growth and replacement needs. Does not include transfers out of occupations. Estimates of replacement openings on working life tables developed by Bureau of Labor Statistics.

[2] Estimate not available.

[3] Excludes part-time junior instructors.

[4] For the Nation as a whole, projected decrease in employment is expected to be greater than number of openings resulting from deaths and retirements.

[5] Total does not equal sum of individual estimates because all branches of engineering are not covered separately in *The Occupational Outlook Handbook*.

Occupation	Estimated employment, 1978	Average annual openings 1978-90[1]	Employment prospects
Other industrial production and related occupations			
Assemblers	1,164,000	77,000	Employment expected to increase faster than average due to growing demand for consumer products and industrial equipment. Since most jobs are in durable goods industries, however, economic changes and national defense spending often affect job opportunities.
Automobile painters	42,000	2,000	Employment expected to increase about as fast as average due to growing number of vehicles and traffic accidents. Job opportunities are best in heavily populated areas.
Blacksmiths	11,000	300	Employment expected to decline as blacksmiths are replaced by welders and machines in large shops. Slight increase in employment of farriers due to growing popularity of horseracing and recreational horseback riding.
Blue-collar worker supervisors	1,671,000	69,000	Employment expected to increase about as fast as average. Large part of increase in nonmanufacturing industries. Because competition for supervisory jobs is keen, the best opportunities are for workers with leadership ability and some college.
Boilermaking occupations	37,000	3,100	Employment expected to increase much faster than average due to construction of electric powerplants and expansion of manufacturing industries. Job opportunities are sensitive to economic conditions.
Boiler tenders	71,000	2,800	Little change in employment expected as more boilers are equipped with automatic controls.
Electroplaters	40,000	800	Little change in employment expected as increasing use of automated plating equipment restricts growth.

Occupation	Estimated employment, 1978	Average annual openings 1978-90[1]	Employment prospects
Forge shop occupations	77,000	2,000	Although forge shop production should expand considerably, little change in employment expected as improved forging techniques and equipment allow greater output per worker.
Inspectors (manufacturing)	771,000	35,000	Employment expected to increase about as fast as average as output of industry increases and manufactured goods become more complex. Some industries that employ inspectors are sensitive to economic conditions.
Millwrights	95,000	4,700	Employment expected to increase about as fast as average due to construction of new plants, improvements in existing plants, and installation and maintenance of increasingly complex machinery.
Motion picture projectionists	11,000	750	Little change in employment expected. Growth in number of multi-screen theaters and use of laborsaving equipment will limit openings, thus creating keen competition for jobs.
Ophthalmic laboratory technicians	26,400	1,400	Employment expected to grow about as fast as average as more people use corrective lenses. Graduates of postsecondary school training programs will have the best job opportunities.
Photographic laboratory occupations	57,000	2,700	Employment expected to grow about as fast as average due to increasing use of photography in business, government, and research and rising popularity of amateur photography.
Power truck operators	363,000	14,000	Employment expected to increase about as fast as average as more firms use power trucks in place of hand labor. Job opportunities depend upon demand for manufactured goods.
Production painters	133,000	5,200	Employment expected to grow about as fast as average. Although manufacturing output is rising rapidly, increased use of automatic painting processes and other laborsaving innovations will moderate demand for painters.

Notes

[1] Due to growth and replacement needs. Does not include transfers out of occupations. Estimates of replacement openings on working life tables developed by Bureau of Labor Statistics.

[2] Estimate not available.

[3] Excludes part-time junior instructors.

[4] For the nation as a whole, projected decrease in employment is expected to be greater than number of openings resulting from deaths and retirements.

[5] Total does not equal sum of individual estimates because all branches of engineering are not covered separately in *The Occupational Outlook Handbook*.

Occupation	Estimated employment, 1978	Average annual openings 1978-90[1]	Employment prospects
Stationary engineers	179,000	7,700	Employment expected to change little because of trend to more powerful and more centralized equipment.
Waste water treatment plant operators (sewage plant operators)	112,000	(2)	Employment expected to grow much faster than average as new treatment plants are built and existing ones are expanded to cope more effectively with water pollution.
Welders	679,000	35,000	Employment expected to grow faster than average due to expansion of metalworking industries. Very good opportunities except during economic downturns.

OFFICE OCCUPATIONS

Clerical occupations

Occupation	Estimated employment, 1978	Average annual openings 1978-90[1]	Employment prospects
Bookkeeping workers	1,830,000	96,000	Employment expected to grow more slowly than average due to increasing use of bookkeeping machines and computers. Due to high replacement needs, job opportunities are expected to be numerous.
Cashiers	1,403,000	119,000	Plentiful job opportunities expected as employment grows faster than average and replacement needs remain high. However, widespread adoption of automatic checkout systems could slow future growth.
Collection workers	78,000	4,600	Employment expected to grow about as fast as average as an increasing use of credit results in a greater number of delinquent accounts. Good job opportunities for aggressive and personable people, particularly in collection agencies and retail trade firms.
File clerks	273,000	16,500	Employment expected to grow about as fast as average as business expansion creates a need for more and better recordkeeping. Jobseekers with typing and other office skills should have the best opportunities.

Occupation	Estimated employment, 1978	Average annual openings 1978-90[1]	Employment prospects
Hotel front office clerks	79,000	5,400	Employment expected to grow as fast as average. The use of computerized reservation systems may limit growth.
Office machine operators	160,000	9,700	Employment expected to grow about as fast as average. The spread of centralized and computerized recordkeeping and processing systems will limit growth somewhat. Most openings will result from replacement needs.
Postal clerks	260,000	2,000	Employment expected to decline due to increasing automation of mail processing.
Receptionists	588,000	41,000	Employment expected to grow faster than average as business, personal, and professional services expand. Some opportunities for part-time work.
Secretaries and stenographers	3,684,000	305,000	Skilled persons seeking secretarial positions should find numerous opportunities. Part-time secretarial jobs should also remain plentiful. Use of dictation machines will continue to limit demand for stenographers.
Shipping and receiving clerks	461,000	22,000	Employment expected to rise about as fast as average as business expansion results in a greater volume of goods to be distributed. Use of computers to store and retrieve shipment records may limit growth somewhat.
Statistical clerks	377,000	23,500	Employment expected to grow faster than average as need for collection and processing of data increases. Knowledge of computers may be helpful for some jobs.
Stock clerks	507,000	23,000	Employment expected to increase about as fast as average. Use of computers to manage storage space and automated equipment to move stock may limit growth somewhat.

Notes

[1] Due to growth and replacement needs. Does not include transfers out of occupations. Estimates of replacement openings on working life tables developed by Bureau of Labor Statistics.

[2] Estimate not available.

[3] Excludes part-time junior instructors.

[4] For the nation as a whole, projected decrease in employment is expected to be greater than number of openings resulting from deaths and retirements.

[5] Total does not equal sum of individual estimates because all branches of engineering are not covered separately in *The Occupational Outlook Handbook.*

Occu-pation	Estimated employ-ment, 1978	Average annual openings 1978-90[1]	Employment prospects
Typists	1,044,000	59,000	Good opportunities expected as business expansion increases the amout of paperwork and replacement needs remain high. Demand particularly strong for typists who can handle a variety of office duties and operate word processing equipment.

Computer and related occupations

Occu-pation	Estimated employ-ment, 1978	Average annual openings 1978-90[1]	Employment prospects
Computer operating personnel	666,000	12,500	Employment of console and peripheral equipment operators expected to rise about as fast as average as use of computers expands. Employment of keypunch operators expected to decline, however, due to more efficient direct data entry techniques.
Programmers	247,000	9,200	Employment expected to grow faster than average as computer usage expands, particularly in accounting, business management, and research and development. Brightest prospects for college graduates with degree in computer science or related field.
Systems analysts	182,000	7,900	Employment expected to grow faster than average as computer capabilities are increased and computers are used to solve a greater variety of problems. Excellent prospects for graduates of computer-related curriculums.

Banking occupations

Occu-pation	Estimated employ-ment, 1978	Average annual openings 1978-90[1]	Employment prospects
Bank clerks	505,000	45,000	Employment expected to grow much faster than average as banking services expand. Job opportunities should be good, especially for persons trained to operate peripheral computer equipment.
Bank officers and managers	330,000	28,000	Employment expected to grow faster than average as expansion of bank services and increasing dependence on computers add to the need for officers and managers. Good opportunities for college graduates as management trainees.
Bank tellers	410,000	17,000	Employment expected to grow more slowly than average. High replacement needs and expansion of bank services should create good opportunities for jobs.

Insurance occupations

Occu-pation	Estimated employ-ment, 1978	Average annual openings 1978-90[1]	Employment prospects
Actuaries	9,000	500	Employment expected to rise faster than average as insurance sales increase. However, a large number of qualified applicants are likely to create keen competition for jobs.
Claim representatives	169,000	10,250	Employment expected to grow faster than average due to increasing insurance claims.
Underwriters, insurance agents, and brokers	568,000	30,000	Employment expected to grow about as fast as average as insurance sales continue to expand. Favorable opportunities for agents and brokers who are ambitious and enjoy saleswork.

Administrative and related occupations

Occu-pation	Estimated employ-ment, 1978	Average annual openings 1978-90[1]	Employment prospects
Accountants	985,000	61,000	Employment expected to increase faster than average as managers rely more on accounting information to make business decisions. College graduates will be in greater demand than applicants who lack this training.
Buyers	115,000	7,400	Employment expected to grow about as fast as average. But keen competition anticipated because merchandising attracts large numbers of college graduates.
City managers	3,300	350	Employment expected to grow much faster than average. Competition will be keen, however, even for persons with graduate degrees in public administration.
College student personnel workers	55,000	(2)	Competition for jobs expected as tighter budgets in public and private colleges and universities limit employment growth. Best opportunities in junior and community colleges.

Notes

[1] Due to growth and replacement needs. Does not include transfers out of occupations. Estimates of replacement openings on working life tables developed by Bureau of Labor Statistics.

[2] Estimate not available.

[3] Excludes part-time junior instructors.

[4] For the nation as a whole, projected decrease in employment is expected to be greater than number of openings resulting from deaths and retirements.

[5] Total does not equal sum of individual estimates because all branches of engineering are not covered separately in *The Occupational Outlook Handbook.*

Occupation	Estimated employment, 1978	Average annual openings 1978-90[1]	Employment prospects
Credit managers	49,000	2,200	Employment expected to grow more slowly than average as use of computers and telecommunications equipment allows centralization of credit offices.
Hotel managers and assistants	168,000	8,900	Employment expected to grow more slowly than average. Best opportunities for persons with degrees in hotel administration.
Lawyers	487,000	37,000	Employment expected to grow faster than average in response to increased population, business activity, and government regulation. But keen competition likely for salaried positions. Best prospects for establishing new practices will be in small towns and expanding suburbs, although starting a practice will remain a risky and expensive venture.
Marketing research workers	24,000	(2)	Employment expected to grow much faster than average as demand for new products stimulates marketing activities. Best opportunities for applicants with graduate training in marketing research or statistics.
Personnel and labor relations workers	405,000	17,000	Employment expected to grow faster than average as new standards for employment practices in areas of occupational safety and health, equal employment opportunity, and pensions stimulate demand. Best opportunities with State and local governments.
Purchasing agents	185,000	13,400	Employment expected to increase faster than average as businesses try to reduce purchasing costs. Excellent job opportunities, especially for persons with a master's degree in business administration.
Urban and regional planners	17,000	800	Employment expected to grow faster than average. Oversupply of graduates may cause competition for jobs.

Occupation	Estimated employment, 1978	Average annual openings 1978-90[1]	Employment prospects
SERVICE OCCUPATIONS			
Cleaning and related occupations			
Building custodians	2,251,000	180,000	Employment expected to grow about as fast as average as rising number of office buildings, hospitals, and apartment houses increases demand for maintenance services. Good opportunities for full-time, part-time and evening work.
Hotel housekeepers and assistants	20,000	2,000	Employment expected to grow faster than average. Best opportunities in newly built hotels and motels.
Pest controllers	31,500	2,500	Employment expected to grow faster than average in effort to control rapidly reproducing pest population.
Food service occupations			
Bartenders	282,000	21,600	Employment expected to increase faster than average as many new restaurants, hotels, and bars open.
Cooks and chefs	1,186,000	86,000	Employment expected to increase faster than average as population grows and people spend more money on dining out. Most starting jobs available in small restaurants, school cafeterias, and other eating places where food preparation is simple.
Dining room attendants and dishwashers	455,000	37,000	Plentiful openings expected due to high turnover and substantial employment growth. Many opportunities for students in part-time jobs.
Food counter workers	463,000	34,000	Employment expected to grow faster than average due to increasing business in eating places. Job openings will be plentiful.
Meatcutters	204,000	5,200	Employment expected to decline because of practice of cutting and wrapping meat for several stores at one location.

Notes

[1] Due to growth and replacement needs. Does not include transfers out of occupations. Estimates of replacement openings on working life tables developed by Bureau of Labor Statistics.

[2] Estimate not available.

[3] Excludes part-time junior instructors.

[4] For the nation as a whole, projected decrease in employment is expected to be greater than number of openings resulting from deaths and retirements.

[5] Total does not equal sum of individual estimates because all branches of engineering are not covered separately in *The Occupational Outlook Handbook.*

Occupation	Estimated employment, 1978	Average annual openings 1978-90[1]	Employment prospects	Occupation	Estimated employment, 1978	Average annual openings 1978-90[1]	Employment prospects
Waiters and waitresses	1,383,000	70,000	Employment expected to grow about as fast as average as restaurant business increases. Job openings should be plentiful.	Fire-fighters	220,000	7,500	Employment expected to increase about as fast as average as need for fire protection grows and professionals replace volunteers. Keen competition for jobs in urban areas; better opportunities in smaller communities.
Personal service occupations							
Barbers	121,000	9,700	Employment expected to grow about as fast as average due to increasing demand for barbershop services. Better opportunities for hairstylists than for conventional barbers.	Guards	550,000	70,000	Employment expected to grow faster than average due to increased concern over crime and vandalism. Best opportunities in guard and security agencies and in night-shift jobs.
Bellhops and bell captains	20,000	600	Employment is expected to decline because of increasing popularity of economy motels. Best opportunities in motels, small hotels, and resort areas open only part of the year.	Police officers	450,000	16,500	Employment expected to rise about as fast as average as law enforcement needs increase. Keen competition expected with best prospects for applicants with some college training in law enforcement.
Cosmetologists	542,000	28,500	Employment expected to grow about as fast as average in response to rising demand for beauty shop services. Keen competition for jobs is likely.	State police officers	47,000	1,800	Employment expected to grow faster than average primarily due to demand for officers to work in highway patrol.
Funeral directors and embalmers	45,000	2,200	Little employment change expected since existing funeral homes and their employees should be able to meet any additional demand for funeral services.	Construction inspectors (government)	20,000	2,200	Employment expected to grow faster than average as concern about safe construction of new housing and commercial buildings increases. Best opportunities for college graduates and persons experienced as carpenters, electricians, or plumbers.
Private household service occupations							
Private household workers	1,162,000	45,000	Despite expected decline in employment, job opportunities will be plentiful.	Health and regulatory inspectors (government)	100,000	5,800	Employment expected to grow about as fast as average as a result of public concern for quality and safety of consumer products.
Protective and related service occupations							
Correction officers	110,000	13,000	Employment expected to increase faster than average as correctional facilities expand and the number of persons in them increases. Also, replacement needs will create a substantial number of job openings.	Occupational safety and health workers	80,000	(2)	Employment expected to grow faster than average as new safety and health programs are started and existing ones upgraded and expanded. Best prospects for graduates of curriculums related to occupational safety and health.
FBI special agents	8,000	(2)	Employment expected to rise as FBI responsibilities grow. Few replacement needs because of low turnover rate.				

Notes

[1] Due to growth and replacement needs. Does not include transfers out of occupations. Estimates of replacement openings on working life tables developed by Bureau of Labor Statistics.

[2] Estimate not available.

[3] Excludes part-time junior instructors.

[4] For the nation as a whole, projected decrease in employment is expected to be greater than number of openings resulting from deaths and retirements.

[5] Total does not equal sum of individual estimates because all branches of engineering are not covered separately in *The Occupational Outlook Handbook*.

Occupation	Estimated employment, 1978	Average annual openings 1978-90[1]	Employment prospects
Other service occupations			
Mail carriers	245,000	7,000	Employment expected to increase more slowly than average due to anticipated cutbacks in frequency of mail deliveries. Many openings will result due to replacement needs.
Telephone operators	311,000	9,900	Employment expected to decline due to increased direct dialing and technological improvements. Many openings will result from replacement needs.

EDUCATION AND RELATED OCCUPATIONS

Teaching occupations

Occupation	Estimated employment, 1978	Average annual openings 1978-90[1]	Employment prospects
Kindergarten and elementary school teachers	1,322,000	86,000	Although employment is expected to grow about as fast as average, applicants may face competition for jobs. The number of people qualified to teach is expected to approximate the number of openings.
Secondary school teachers	1,087,000	7,200	Keen competition expected due to declining enrollment coupled with large increases in supply of teachers. More favorable opportunities will exist for persons qualified to teach special education, vocational subjects, mathematics, and the natural and physical sciences.
College and university faculty	673,000[3]	11,000	Employment expected to decline due to decreasing enrollments and budgetary constraints. Keen competition among doctoral and master's degree holders.
Teachers aides	342,000	26,000	Employment expected to rise much faster than average as more aides are hired to lessen teachers' clerical duties.

Library occupations

Occupation	Estimated employment, 1978	Average annual openings 1978-90[1]	Employment prospects
Librarians	142,000	8,000	Employment expected to grow more slowly than average. Keen competition for jobs is likely. Best opportunities for librarians with a scientific or technical background.
Library technicians and assistants	172,000	7,700	Employment expected to grow more slowly than average. Public and college and university libraries will offer the best job opportunities.

SALES OCCUPATIONS

Occupation	Estimated employment, 1978	Average annual openings 1978-90[1]	Employment prospects
Automobile parts counter workers	97,000	4,200	Employment expected to grow about as fast as average due to increasing demand for new accessories and replacement parts.
Automobile sales workers	158,000	10,400	Employment expected to grow faster than average as demand for automobiles increases. Job openings may fluctuate, however, because sales are affected by changing economic conditions.
Automobile service advisors	25,000	1,100	Employment expected to grow about as fast as average as automobiles increase in number and complexity. Most job openings in large dealerships in heavily populated areas.
Gasoline service station attendants	340,000	5,200	Employment expected to decline because of anticipated slow growth of gasoline consumption and the trend to self-service stations. Many job openings will result from replacement needs.
Manufacturers sales workers	402,000	21,700	Employment expected to grow about as fast as average. Good opportunities for persons with product knowledge and sales ability.
Models	60,000	(2)	Employment expected to increase due to rising advertising expenditures and greater sales of clothing and accessories. Nevertheless, because the glamour of modeling attracts many persons, competition for openings should be keen.
Real estate agents and brokers	555,000	50,000	Employment expected to rise about as fast as average in response to growing demand for housing and other properties. However, field is highly competitive. Best prospects for college graduates and transfers from other sales jobs.

Notes

[1] Due to growth and replacement needs. Does not include transfers out of occupations. Estimates of replacement openings on working life tables developed by Bureau of Labor Statistics.

[2] Estimate not available.

[3] Excludes part-time junior instructors.

[4] For the nation as a whole, projected decrease in employment is expected to be greater than number of openings resulting from deaths and retirements.

[5] Total does not equal sum of individual estimates because all branches of engineering are not covered separately in *The Occupational Outlook Handbook*.

Occupation	Estimated employment, 1978	Average annual openings 1978-90[1]	Employment prospects
Retail trade sales workers	2,851,000	226,000	Employment expected to grow faster than average. High turnover should create excellent opportunities for full-time, part-time, and temporary work.
Route drivers	195,000	3,600	Employment expected to change little, but several thousand openings will result annually from replacement needs. Best opportunities for applicants who have sales experience and good driving records and who are seeking wholesale routes.
Securities sales workers	109,000	5,500	Employment expected to grow more slowly than average. Job opportunities fluctuate with economic conditions.
Travel agents	18,500	1,900	Employment expected to grow much faster than average. Because travel expenditures often depend on business conditions, job opportunities are very sensitive to economic changes.
Wholesale trade sales workers	840,000	40,000	Employment expected to grow about as fast as average as wholesalers sell wider variety of products and improve customer services. Good opportunities for persons with product knowledge and sales ability.

CONSTRUCTION OCCUPATIONS

Occupation	Estimated employment, 1978	Average annual openings 1978-90[1]	Employment prospects
Bricklayers, stonemasons, and marble setters	205,000	6,200	Employment expected to grow more slowly than average. Job openings should be plentiful except during economic downturns.
Carpenters	1,253,000	58,000	Plentiful job opportunities except during economic downturns. Employment expected to grow due to increasing construction of new structures and alteration and maintenance of old ones. Carpenters with all-round training will have best prospects.

Occupation	Estimated employment, 1978	Average annual openings 1978-90[1]	Employment prospects
Cement masons and terrazzo workers	83,000	4,400	Employment expected to increase faster than average due to growing construction activity and greater use of concrete as a building material. Job opportunities should be favorable.
Construction laborers	860,000	49,000	Employment expected to grow about as fast as average due to increasing construction activity. Job openings should be plentiful except during economic downturns.
Drywall installers and finishers	82,000	(2)	Employment expected to grow faster than average as drywall is increasingly used in place of plaster.
Electricians (construction)	290,000	12,900	Employment expected to increase about as fast as average as more electricians are needed to install electrical fixtures and wiring in new and renovated buildings.
Elevator constructors	17,000	(2)	Employment expected to grow about as fast as average as number of high-rise apartments and commercial buildings increases.
Floor covering installers	88,000	3,200	Employment expected to increase faster than average due to expanding construction activity and widespread use of resilient floor coverings and carpeting. Best opportunities for persons able to install carpeting and resilient flooring.
Glaziers	19,000	1,000	Employment expected to increase faster than average as use of glass in construction increases.
Insulation workers	51,000	2,600	Employment expected to grow faster than average as energy saving insulation is installed in homes and businesses.
Ironworkers	78,000	4,100	Employment expected to increase faster than average for all occupations due to growing use of structural steel. Job opportunities are more abundant during early spring.

Notes

[1] Due to growth and replacement needs. Does not include transfers out of occupations. Estimates of replacement openings on working life tables developed by Bureau of Labor Statistics.

[2] Estimate not available.

[3] Excludes part-time junior instructors.

[4] For the nation as a whole, projected decrease in employment is expected to be greater than number of openings resulting from deaths and retirements.

[5] Total does not equal sum of individual estimates because all branches of engineering are not covered separately in *The Occupational Outlook Handbook*.

Occupation	Estimated employment, 1978	Average annual openings 1978–90[1]	Employment prospects
Lathers	23,000	[2]	Employment expected to change little due to increased use of drywall and other substitute materials.
Operating engineers	581,000	36,000	Employment expected to grow faster than average due to increasing construction activity. Job opportunities should be plentiful except during economic downturns.
Painters	484,000	26,000	Although some growth will result from new construction, employment expected to increase more slowly than average. The number of job openings fluctuates with amount of construction activity.
Paperhangers	20,000	1,500	Although the popularity of wall paper and vinyl wallcoverings is rising, employment of paperhangers is expected to grow more slowly than average.
Plasterers	28,000	1,100	Employment will grow more slowly than average as drywall materials are used in place of plaster. Some openings will result from replacement needs.
Plumbers and pipefitters	428,000	20,000	Employment expected to grow about as fast as average as a result of increased construction activity and the need to repair and modernize existing plumbing and piping.
Roofers	114,000	4,500	Employment expected to grow about as fast as average due to new construction and need to repair existing roofs. Demand for dampproofing and waterproofing also will stimulate need for more roofers. Because construction activity fluctuates, however, openings may be plentiful in some years, scarce in others.
Sheet-metal workers	70,000	3,500	Employment expected to increase faster than average due to use of air conditioning and heating ducts and other sheet-metal products in homes, stores, offices, and other buildings.

Occupation	Estimated employment, 1978	Average annual openings 1978–90[1]	Employment prospects
Tilesetters	33,000	1,800	Employment expected to increase faster than average due to a trend toward two or more tile bathrooms in houses and apartments.

OCCUPATIONS IN TRANSPORTATION ACTIVITIES

Air transportation occupations

Occupation	Estimated employment, 1978	Average annual openings 1978–90[1]	Employment prospects
Air traffic controllers	21,000	700	Although employment expected to grow about as fast as average, applicants are likely to face keen competition for available jobs. Best opportunities for college graduates with experience as controllers, pilots, or navigators.
Airplane mechanics	132,000	3,500	Employment expected to grow more slowly than average, but opportunities in various areas of aviation may differ. Good opportunities in general aviation; keen competition for airline jobs; opportunities in Federal Government dependent upon defense spending.
Airplane pilots	76,000	3,800	Employment expected to grow faster than average, but applicants are likely to face keen competition for available jobs. Best opportunities for recent college graduates with flying experience.
Flight attendants	48,000	4,800	Employment expected to grow much faster than average as airline travel increases. Competition for jobs likely to be keen.
Reservation, ticket, and passenger agents	56,000	2,200	Employment expected to grow about as fast as average as airline travel increases. Nevertheless, popularity of airline jobs will result in keen competition.

Merchant marine occupations

Occupation	Estimated employment, 1978	Average annual openings 1978–90[1]	Employment prospects
Merchant marine officers	13,500	700	Little change in employment expected as size of Nation's fleet remains fairly constant.
Merchant marine sailors	24,800	[4]	Employment expected to decline as smaller crews operate new ships. Keen competition likely for those openings created by replacement needs.

Notes

[1] Due to growth and replacement needs. Does not include transfers out of occupations. Estimates of replacement openings on working life tables developed by Bureau of Labor Statistics.

[2] Estimate not available.

[3] Excludes part-time junior instructors.

[4] For the nation as a whole, projected decrease in employment is expected to be greater than number of openings resulting from deaths and retirements.

[5] Total does not equal sum of individual estimates because all branches of engineering are not covered separately in *The Occupational Outlook Handbook*.

Occupation	Estimated employment, 1978	Average annual openings 1978-90[1]	Employment prospects
Railroad occupations			
Brake operators	66,000	1,600	Little change in employment expected as laborsaving innovations in freight hauling moderate growth. Some openings will result from replacement needs.
Conductors	37,000	1,700	Employment expected to grow more slowly than average as technological advances increase freight hauling efficiency.
Locomotive engineers	34,000	2,000	Despite expected increase in demand for railroad services, slower than average employment growth likely as larger and better designed freight cars improve freight hauling efficiency.
Shop trades	76,000	2,100	Employment expected to decline as shop efficiency increases and railroad cars require less maintenance.
Signal department workers	12,800	450	Employment expected to grow more slowly than average as new signal systems require less maintenance.
Station agents	5,900	(4)	Employment expected to decline as centrally located stations handle more customer orders and billings and as mobile agents service smaller stations.
Telegraphers, telephoners, and tower operators	9,700	50	Employment expected to decline due to wider use of mechanized yard operations, centralized traffic control, and automatic signaling. Limited number of openings will arise due to replacement needs.
Track workers	59,000	1,400	Employment expected to change little due to use of laborsaving machines and installation of improved track control systems requiring less track.
Driving occupations			
Intercity busdrivers	23,500	500	Employment expected to change little. Keen competition likely for job openings.
Local transit busdrivers	77,000	3,100	Employment expected to grow about as fast as average as many cities improve local bus service.
Local truck-drivers	1,720,000	64,000	Employment expected to increase faster than average due to growth in amount of freight. Best opportunities for applicants with a good driving record.
Long distance truck-drivers	584,000	21,500	Employment expected to grow about as fast as average. Keen competition is likely for jobs in this high-paying occupation.
Parking attendants	44,000	3,200	Employment expected to grow more slowly than average as trend to self-parking systems continues. High turnover rate, however, will create many job opportunities, especially in large commercial parking facilities in urban areas.
Taxicab drivers	94,000	4,300	Although employment expected to change little, high turnover should create many job opportunities.

SCIENTIFIC AND TECHNICAL OCCUPATIONS

Occupation	Estimated employment, 1978	Average annual openings 1978-90[1]	Employment prospects
Conservation occupations			
Foresters	31,200	1,400	Employment expected to grow about as fast as average as environmental concern and need for forest products increase. But, applicants likely to face keen competition for jobs.
Forestry technicians	13,700	700	Employment expected to grow faster than average as technicians increasingly do tasks formerly handled by foresters. Even applicants with specialized postsecondary school training may face competition, however.
Range managers	3,700	200	Employment expected to grow faster than average. Good employment prospects likely as use of rangelands for grazing, recreation, and wildlife habitats increases.

Notes

[1] Due to growth and replacement needs. Does not include transfers out of occupations. Estimates of replacement openings on working life tables developed by Bureau of Labor Statistics.

[2] Estimate not available.

[3] Excludes part-time junior instructors.

[4] For the Nation as a whole, projected decrease in employment is expected to be greater than number of openings resulting from deaths and retirements.

[5] Total does not equal sum of individual estimates because all branches of engineering are not covered separately in *The Occupational Outlook Handbook.*

Occupation	Estimated employment, 1978	Average annual openings 1978-90[1]	Employment prospects
Soil conservationists	9,300	450	Employment expected to increase as fast as average as organizations try to preserve farmland and comply with recent conservation and antipollution laws. Competition may be keen.
Engineers			
Engineers	1,136,000[5]	46,500[5]	Employment expected to grow slightly faster than average. Good employment opportunities for graduates with an engineering degree.
Aerospace engineers	60,000	1,900	Employment expected to grow about as fast as average due to limited increase in Federal expenditures on space and defense programs.
Agricultural engineers	14,000	600	Employment expected to grow faster than average in response to increasing demand for agricultural products, modernization of farm operations, and increasing emphasis on conservation of resources.
Biomedical engineers	4,000	175	Employment expected to grow faster than average, but actual number of openings will be small. Increased research funds could create new jobs in instrumentation and systems for delivery of health services.
Ceramic engineers	14,000	550	Employment expected to grow faster than average as a result of need to develop and improve ceramic materials for nuclear energy, electronics, defense, and medical science.
Chemical engineers	53,000	1,800	Employment expected to grow about as fast as average. Growing complexity and automation of chemical processes will require additional chemical engineers to design, build, and maintain plants and equipment.
Civil engineers	155,000	7,800	Employment expected to increase about as fast as average as result of growing need for housing, industrial buildings, electric power generating plants, and transportation systems. Work related to environmental pollution and energy development will also cause growth.
Electrical engineers	300,000	10,500	Employment expected to increase about as fast as average due to growing demand for computers, communications equipment, military electronics, and electrical and electronic consumer goods. Increased research and development in power generation also should create openings.
Industrial engineers	185,000	8,000	Employment expected to grow faster than average due to industry growth, increasing complexity of industrial operations, expansion of automated processes, and greater emphasis on scientific management and safety engineering.
Mechanical engineers	195,000	7,500	Employment expected to increase about as fast as average due to growing demand for industrial machinery. Need to develop new energy systems and to solve environmental pollution problems will also cause growth.
Metallurgical engineers	16,500	750	Employment expected to grow faster than average due to need to develop new metals and alloys, adapt current ones to new needs, solve problems associated with efficient use of nuclear energy, and develop new ways of recycling solid waste materials.
Mining engineers	6,000	600	Employment expected to grow much faster than average due to efforts to attain energy self-sufficiency and to develop better mining systems
Petroleum engineers	17,000	900	Employment expected to grow faster than average as demand for petroleum and natural gas requires increased drilling and more sophisticated recovery methods.

Notes

[1] Due to growth and replacement needs. Does not include transfers out of occupations. Estimates of replacement openings on working life tables developed by Bureau of Labor Statistics.

[2] Estimate not available.

[3] Excludes part-time junior instructors.

[4] For the nation as a whole, projected decrease in employment is expected to be greater than number of openings resulting from deaths and retirements.

[5] Total does not equal sum of individual estimates because all branches of engineering are not covered separately in *The Occupational Outlook Handbook.*

Occupation	Estimated employment, 1978	Average annual openings 1978-90[1]	Employment prospects
Environmental scientists			
Geologists	31,000	1,700	Employment expected to grow faster than average as domestic mineral exploration increases. Good opportunities for persons with degrees in geology or earth science.
Geophysicists	11,000	600	Employment expected to grow faster than average as petroleum and mining companies need additional geophysicists who are able to use sophisticated electronic techniques in exploration activities. Very good opportunities for graduates in geophysics or related areas.
Meteorologists	7,300	300	Employment expected to increase about as fast as average. Favorable opportunities for persons with advanced degrees in meteorology. Others expected to face competition.
Oceanographers	3,600	150	Although employment expected to grow about as fast as average, competition for openings is likely. Best opportunities for persons who have a Ph.D.; those who have less education may be limited to research assistant and technician jobs.
Life science occupations			
Biochemists	20,000	900	Employment expected to grow faster than average due to increase in funds for biochemical research and development. Favorable opportunities for advanced degree holders.
Life scientists	215,000	11,200	Employment expected to grow faster than average due to increasing expenditures for medical research and environmental protection. Good opportunities for persons with advanced degrees.
Soil scientists	3,500	180	Little employment growth expected. Applicants may face competition for jobs.

Occupation	Estimated employment, 1978	Average annual openings 1978-90[1]	Employment prospects
Mathematics occupations			
Mathematicians	33,500	1,000	Slower than average employment growth is expected to lead to keen competition for jobs. Opportunities expected to be best for advanced degree holders in applied mathematics seeking jobs in government and private industry.
Statisticians	23,000	1,500	Employment expected to grow faster than average as use of statistics expands into new areas. Persons combining knowledge of statistics with a field of application, such as economics, may expect favorable job opportunities.
Physical scientists			
Astronomers	2,000	40	Little change in employment is expected as only slight increases in funds for basic research in astronomy are expected. Competition for jobs is likely to be keen.
Chemists	143,000	6,100	Employment expected to grow about as fast as average as a result of increasing demand for new products and rising concern about energy shortages, pollution control, and health care. Good opportunities should exist, except for academic positions.
Physicists	44,000	1,000	Although employment will grow more slowly than average, generally favorable job opportunities are expected for persons with advanced degrees in physics. However, persons seeking college and university positions, as well as graduates with only a bachelor's degree, will face keen competition.
Other scientific and technical occupations			
Broadcast technicians	40,000	(2)	Employment expected to increase about as fast as average as new radio and television stations are licensed and as cable television stations broadcast more of their own programs. Job competition is keen, however, and prospects are best in small cities.

Notes

[1] Due to growth and replacement needs. Does not include transfers out of occupations. Estimates of replacement openings on working life tables developed by Bureau of Labor Statistics.

[2] Estimate not available.

[3] Excludes part-time junior instructors.

[4] For the nation as a whole, projected decrease in employment is expected to be greater than number of openings resulting from deaths and retirements.

[5] Total does not equal sum of individual estimates because all branches of engineering are not covered separately in *The Occupational Outlook Handbook*.

Occupation	Estimated employment, 1978	Average annual openings 1978–90[1]	Employment prospects
Drafters	296,000	11,000	Employment expected to grow about as fast as average due to increasing complexity of designs of modern products and processes. Best prospects for graduates with associate degrees in drafting.
Engineering and science technicians	608,000	23,000	Employment expected to grow faster than average as more technicians will be needed to assist the growing number of engineers and scientists. Favorable job opportunities, particularly for graduates of postsecondary school training programs.
Food technologists	15,000	500	Employment expected to grow about as fast as average due to increasing demand for food technologists in research and development, quality control, and production. Favorable opportunities for persons with food technology degrees.
Surveyors and surveying technicians	62,000	2,300	Employment expected to grow about as fast as average due to increased construction activity. Job opportunities are affected by economic conditions.

MECHANICS AND REPAIRERS

Telephone craft occupations

Occupation	Estimated employment, 1978	Average annual openings 1978–90[1]	Employment prospects
Central office craft occupations	135,000	1,000	Little change is expected in employment as more efficient electronic switching systems replace electromechanical ones.
Central office equipment installers	21,400	(4)	Employment expected to decline as most new central office equipment is manufactured in components that come partially assembled.
Line installers and cable splicers	59,000	600	Little change in employment as technological improvements limit growth. Job openings may be found more easily in small cities.
Telephone and PBX installers and repairers	115,000	3,000	Employment expected to increase about as fast as average due to growing number of telephone and PBX and CENTREX systems.

Other mechanics and repairers

Occupation	Estimated employment, 1978	Average annual openings 1978–90[1]	Employment prospects
Air-conditioning, refrigeration, and heating mechanics	210,000	8,200	Employment expected to increase about as fast as average. Beginning mechanics may face competition for the highest paying jobs.
Appliance repairers	145,000	6,900	Employment expected to grow about as fast as average due to increasing use of appliances as population and incomes rise.
Automobile body repairers	185,000	7,800	Employment expected to increase faster than average due to increasing number of vehicles and traffic accidents.
Automobile mechanics	860,000	37,000	Employment expected to increase about as fast as average due to growing number of automobiles. Job opportunities will be plentiful.
Boat-engine mechanics	20,000	1,000	Employment expected to grow about as fast as average due to increasing number of boats. Job opportunities particularly favorable for mechanics with knowledge of electricity and electronics.
Bowling-pin-machine mechanics	6,200	(2)	Employment expected to increase more slowly than average due to limited growth in number of bowling facilities.
Business machine repairers	63,000	4,200	Employment expected to grow much faster than average as number of machines increases. Employment prospects will be good.
Computer service technicians	63,000	5,400	Employment expected to grow much faster than average as more computer equipment is used. Good opportunities for persons with postsecondary school training in electronics.
Electric sign repairers	15,000	700	Employment expected to increase as fast as average due to need to maintain growing number of electric signs.

Notes

[1] Due to growth and replacement needs. Does not include transfers out of occupations. Estimates of replacement openings on working life tables developed by Bureau of Labor Statistics.

[2] Estimate not available.

[3] Excludes part-time junior instructors.

[4] For the nation as a whole, projected decrease in employment is expected to be greater than number of openings resulting from deaths and retirements.

[5] Total does not equal sum of individual estimates because all branches of engineering are not covered separately in The Occupational Outlook Handbook.

Occu-pation	Estimated employ-ment, 1978	Average annual openings 1978-90[1]	Employment prospects
Farm equipment mechanics	62,000	3,500	Employment expected to increase about as fast as average as more complex farm equipment requires greater maintenance. Best opportunities for persons familiar with farms and farm machinery.
Furniture uphol-sterers	29,000	1,100	Little change in employment expected as people buy new furniture instead of reupholstering the old.
Industrial machinery repairers	655,000	58,000	Employment expected to increase much faster than average as more repairers will be needed to maintain machinery used in increasingly complex manufacturing, coal mining, oil exploration, and other industries.
Jewelers	32,000	(2)	Employment expected to grow about as fast as average as the demand for jewelry increases. Because of a shortage of skilled jewelers, opportunities for people with training in jewelry design, construction, or repair should exist throughout the industry.
Lock-smiths	15,000	(2)	Employment expected to grow about as fast as average as public becomes more security conscious. Favorable opportunities for persons able to install and service electronic security systems.
Mainte-nance electricians	300,000	15,500	Employment expected to increase faster than average in response to increased use of electrical and electronic equipment in industry.
Motor-cycle mechanics	13,000	500	Employment expected to grow about as fast as average due to rising number of motorcycles. Best opportunities for persons with experience and their own tools.
Piano and organ tuners and repairers	8,000	700	Employment is expected to grow more slowly than average as use of pianos and organs is limited by competition from other forms of entertainment and recreation. Opportunities for beginners will be best in piano and organ dealerships and large repair shops.

Occu-pation	Estimated employ-ment, 1978	Average annual openings 1978-90[1]	Employment prospects
Shoe repairers	22,000	1,600	Despite little change in employment, job prospects should be very good because of replacement needs. Because training is difficult to obtain, many openings are not filled.
Television and radio service technicians	131,000	6,100	Employment expected to grow faster than average as number of home electronic products such as televison sets, radios, phonographs, and tape recorders increases.
Truck mechanics and bus mechanics	165,000	6,800	Employment of truck mechanics expected to grow faster than average due to increasing use of trucks for transporting freight. Employment of bus mechanics expected to increase about as fast as average.
Vending machine mechanics	23,000	(2)	Employment expected to increase about as fast as the average as more vending machines are put in service.
Watch repairers	19,000	(2)	Although employment expected to grow more slowly than average, trained workers should find jobs readily available. Opportunities should be good for persons trained in repairing electronic watches.

HEALTH OCCUPATIONS

Dental occupations

Occu-pation	Estimated employ-ment, 1978	Average annual openings 1978-90[1]	Employment prospects
Dentists	120,000	5,500	Employment expected to grow faster than average due to population growth, increased awareness of importance of dental care, and expansion of prepayment arrangements. Opportunities for jobs should be very good.
Dental assistants	150,000	11,000	Employment expected to grow much faster than average as dentists increasingly use assistants in their practice. Excellent opportunities for full- and part-time jobs, especially for graduates of approved programs.

Notes

[1] Due to growth and replacement needs. Does not include transfers out of occupations. Estimates of replacement openings on working life tables developed by Bureau of Labor Statistics.

[2] Estimate not available.

[3] Excludes part-time junior instructors.

[4] For the nation as a whole, projected decrease in employment is expected to be greater than number of openings resulting from deaths and retirements.

[5] Total does not equal sum of individual estimates because all branches of engineering are not covered separately in *The Occupational Outlook Handbook*.

Occupation	Estimated employment, 1978	Average annual openings 1978-90[1]	Employment prospects
Dental hygienists	35,000	6,000	Employment expected to grow much faster than average because of expanding population and growing awareness of importance of regular dental care. Opportunities for jobs should be good.
Dental laboratory technicians	47,000	2,800	Employment expected to grow faster than average due to expansion of dental prepayment plans and increasing number of older persons who require dentures. Excellent opportunities for graduates of approved programs.

Medical practitioners

Occupation	Estimated employment, 1978	Average annual openings 1978-90[1]	Employment prospects
Chiropractors	18,000	1,500	New chiropractors may have difficulty establishing a practice due to dramatic increases in number of chiropractic graduates. Best opportunities in small towns and areas with few practitioners.
Optometrists	21,000	1,600	Employment expected to grow faster than average due to increase in population and greater recognition of importance of good vision. Employment prospects will be favorable.
Physicians and osteopathic physicians	405,000	19,000	Employment outlook expected to be favorable. New physicians should have little difficulty in establishing new practices.
Podiatrists	8,000	600	Employment expected to grow faster than average as expanding population demands more health services. Opportunities for graduates to establish new practices or to enter salaried positions should be favorable.
Veterinarians	33,500	1,700	Employment expected to grow faster than average because of growth in number of pets. New veterinarians may face competition in some areas.

Medical technologist, technician, and assistant occupations

Occupation	Estimated employment, 1978	Average annual openings 1978-90[1]	Employment prospects
Electrocardiograph technicians	20,000	(2)	Employment expected to grow faster than average as greater reliance placed on electrocardiographs to diagnose heart diseases and to examine older patients. Best opportunities for those with postsecondary school training.
Electroencephalographic technologists and technicians	7,000	500	Employment expected to grow faster than average due to increased use of EEG's in surgery and in diagnosing and monitoring patients with brain disease.
Emergency medical technicians	115,000	(2)	Employment expected to grow faster than average due to increasing public awareness of need for emergency medical service. Keen competition for jobs likely.
Medical laboratory workers	210,000	14,800	Employment expected to grow faster than average as physicians make more use of laboratory facilities. Job opportunities should be favorable.
Medical records technicians and clerks	50,000	4,900	Employment expected to grow faster than average as the number of health insurance, Medicare, and Medicaid claims increases the need for more complete medical records. Excellent opportunities for those with specialized training.
Operating room technicians	35,000	2,600	Employment expected to increase faster than average as technicians assume more of the routine nursing tasks in operating rooms. Graduates of postsecondary school training programs will have the best job opportunities.
Optometric assistants	15,000	1,200	Employment expected to grow faster than average as demand for eye care services increases and more optometrists hire assistants. Excellent opportunities for persons who have completed postsecondary school training.
Radiologic (X-ray) technologists	100,000	9,000	Employment expected to expand faster than average as X-ray equipment is increasingly used to diagnose and treat diseases. But applicants may face competition for jobs.

Notes

[1] Due to growth and replacement needs. Does not include transfers out of occupations. Estimates of replacement openings on working life tables developed by Bureau of Labor Statistics.

[2] Estimate not available.

[3] Excludes part-time junior instructors.

[4] For the nation as a whole, projected decrease in employment is expected to be greater than number of openings resulting from deaths and retirements.

[5] Total does not equal sum of individual estimates because all branches of engineering are not covered separately in *The Occupational Outlook Handbook*.

Occupation	Estimated employment, 1978	Average annual openings 1978–90[1]	Employment prospects
Respiratory therapy workers	50,000	5,000	Employment expected to grow much faster than average due to new applications of respiratory therapy in treating diseases. Job opportunities should be excellent for graduates of accredited programs.

Nursing occupations

Occupation	Estimated employment, 1978	Average annual openings 1978–90[1]	Employment prospects
Registered nurses	1,060,000	85,000	Employment expected to grow faster than average. Favorable opportunities, especially in some southern States and many inner-city locations. Nurses may find competition for higher paying jobs and for jobs in some urban areas with large training facilities.
Licensed practical nurses	518,000	60,000	Employment expected to grow much faster than average as population increases and demand for health care rises. Job prospects are very good.
Nursing aides, orderlies, and attendants	1,037,000	94,000	Employment expected to grow much faster than average due to increased demand for medical care. Most job openings will be in nursing homes, convalescent homes, and other long-term care facilities.

Therapy and rehabilitation occupations

Occupation	Estimated employment, 1978	Average annual openings 1978–90[1]	Employment prospects
Occupational therapists	15,000	2,500	Employment expected to grow much faster than average due to public interest in rehabilitation of disabled persons and growth of established occupational therapy programs. Job prospects should be favorable.
Occupational therapy assistants	10,000	1,100	Employment expected to grow much faster than average due to increased need for assistants in health care institutions. Opportunities should be very good, especially for graduates of approved programs.
Physical therapists	30,000	2,700	Employment expected to grow much faster than average because of increased public recognition of importance of rehabilitation.

Occupation	Estimated employment, 1978	Average annual openings 1978–90[1]	Employment prospects
			Employment opportunities should be best in suburban and rural areas.
Physical therapist assistants and aides	12,500	400	Employment expected to increase about as fast as average. Jobseekers may face competition for best positions. Assistants should have better employment prospects than aides.
Speech pathologists and audiologists	32,000	3,900	Employment expected to increase much faster than average due to growing public concern over speech and hearing disorders. Persons with only a bachelor's degree will face considerable competition for jobs.

Other health occupations

Occupation	Estimated employment, 1978	Average annual openings 1978–90[1]	Employment prospects
Dietitians	35,000	3,300	Employment expected to grow faster than average in response to increasing concern for proper nutrition and food management. Favorable full- and part-time opportunities for those with a bachelor's degree and persons with specialized training.
Dispensing opticians	17,600	1,200	Employment expected to increase faster than average as demand for eyeglasses rises. Opportunities should be excellent for persons with an associate degree in opticianry.
Health service administrators	180,000	18,000	Employment expected to grow much faster than average as quantity of patient services increases and health services management becomes more complex. Advanced degree required for best positions in hospitals.
Medical record administrators	12,500	900	Employment expected to grow as fast as average due to increasing use of health facilities. Good opportunities for graduates of approved programs.
Pharmacists	135,000	7,800	Employment expected to grow faster than average due to establishment of new pharmacies and increasing use of pharmacists in health care institutions. Applicants may face competition for jobs.

Notes

[1] Due to growth and replacement needs. Does not include transfers out of occupations. Estimates of replacement openings on working life tables developed by Bureau of Labor Statistics.

[2] Estimate not available.

[3] Excludes part-time junior instructors.

[4] For the nation as a whole, projected decrease in employment is expected to be greater than number of openings resulting from deaths and retirements.

[5] Total does not equal sum of individual estimates because all branches of engineering are not covered separately in *The Occupational Outlook Handbook*.

Occupation	Estimated employment, 1978	Average annual openings 1978-90[1]	Employment prospects

SOCIAL SCIENTISTS

Anthropologists — 7,000 — 350 — Employment expected to increase about as fast as average. Nearly all new jobs will be in nonacademic areas. Even persons with a Ph.D. in anthropology can expect keen competition for jobs.

Economists — 130,000 — 7,800 — Employment expected to grow faster than average. Master's and Ph.D. degree holders may face keen competition for academic positions but can expect good opportunities in nonacademic areas, particularly for those trained in quantitative methods. Persons with bachelor's degrees likely to face keen competition.

Geographers — 10,000 — 500 — Employment expected to grow about as fast as average. Advanced degree holders likely to face keen competition for academic positions, but good prospects in nonacademic areas. Bachelor's degree holders will face competition.

Historians — 23,000 — 700 — Little change in employment expected. Keen competition anticipated, particularly for academic positions. Best opportunities for Ph.D.'s with a strong background in quantitative research methods.

Political scientists — 14,000 — 500 — Employment expected to increase more slowly than average. Keen competition likely, especially for academic positions. Best opportunities for advanced degree holders with training in applied fields such as public administration or public policy.

Psychologists — 130,000 — 6,700 — Employment expected to grow faster than average. Graduates face increasing competition, particularly for academic positions. Best prospects for doctoral degree holders trained in applied areas, such as clinical, counseling, and industrial psychology.

Occupation	Estimated employment, 1978	Average annual openings 1978-90[1]	Employment prospects

Sociologists — 19,000 — 600 — Employment expected to grow more slowly than average. Ph.D.'s may face competition, particularly for academic positions. Best opportunities for Ph.D.'s trained in quantitative research techniques. Very keen competition below Ph.D. level.

SOCIAL SERVICE OCCUPATIONS

Counseling occupations

School counselors — 45,000 — 1,700 — Employment expected to grow more slowly than average as declining school enrollment coupled with financial constraints limits growth.

Employment counselors — 6,100 — (2) — Employment growth is highly dependent on the level of Federal and State funding. Applicants are expected to face some competition in both public and private employment agencies.

Rehabilitation counselors — 19,000 — (2) — Employment growth dependent upon government funding for rehabilitation agencies. Some openings expected with insurance and other private companies to help in equal employment opportunity efforts.

College career planning and placement counselors — 5,000 — (2) — Little change expected in employment although some growth may occur in community and junior colleges where there are no career planning and placement programs at present. Keen competition likely for jobs.

Clergy

Protestant ministers — 190,000 — (2) — Competition is expected for positions in individual congregations. Some ministers will find work in youth, family relations, and welfare programs and as chaplains in hospitals, universities, or the Armed Forces.

Notes

[1] Due to growth and replacement needs. Does not include transfers out of occupations. Estimates of replacement openings on working life tables developed by Bureau of Labor Statistics.

[2] Estimate not available.

[3] Excludes part-time junior instructors.

[4] For the nation as a whole, projected decrease in employment is expected to be greater than number of openings resulting from deaths and retirements.

[5] Total does not equal sum of individual estimates because all branches of engineering are not covered separately in *The Occupational Outlook Handbook.*

Occu-pation	Estimated employ-ment, 1978	Average annual openings 1978-90[1]	Employment prospects
Rabbis	4,000	(2)	Reform rabbis may face some competition for available positions, and Orthodox clergy expected to encounter very keen competition. Rabbis from the Conservative branch of Judaism should have good opportunities.
Roman Catholic priests	58,000	(2)	Growing number of priests needed as supply of seminary graduates fails to keep pace with increasing Catholic population.

Other social service occupations

Occu-pation	Estimated employ-ment, 1978	Average annual openings 1978-90[1]	Employment prospects
Cooperative extension service workers	16,000	650	Employment expected to increase more slowly than average. Need for persons who can relay advances in farming practices from researchers to farmers will lead to some growth.
Home-maker-home health aides	110,000	36,000	Employment expected to grow much faster than average as public awareness of the availability of home care services increases.
Social service aides	134,000	7,500	Employment expected to grow about as fast as average as social welfare programs expand and aides perform tasks formerly handled by professional personnel. Many opportunities for part-time work.
Social workers	385,000	22,000	Employment expected to increase about as fast as average due to expansion of health services, services for the elderly, and counseling services. Best opportunities for graduates of master's and Ph.D. degree programs in social work.

ART, DESIGN, AND COMMUNICATIONS-RELATED OCCUPATIONS

Performing artists

Occu-pation	Estimated employ-ment, 1978	Average annual openings 1978-90[1]	Employment prospects
Actors and actresses	13,400	850	Employment expected to grow faster than average, but overcrowding in this field will persist. Persons finding jobs may be limited to part-time work only.

Occu-pation	Estimated employ-ment, 1978	Average annual openings 1978-90[1]	Employment prospects
Dancers	8,000	550	Although employment expected to grow about as fast as average, applicants are likely to face keen competition for jobs.
Musicians	127,000	8,900	Although employment expected to grow faster than average, job competition will be keen.
Singers	22,000	1,600	Although employment growth is expected to be faster than average, competition for long-term jobs likely to be keen. Some opportunities for part-time and short-term jobs.

Design occupations

Occu-pation	Estimated employ-ment, 1978	Average annual openings 1978-90[1]	Employment prospects
Architects	54,000	4,000	Employment expected to rise faster than average, but competition for jobs likely.
Display workers	44,000	3,300	Employment expected to grow faster than average because of the popularity of visual merchandising, the use of merchandise to decorate stores.
Floral designers	56,000	4,200	Expected increases in sales of flowers and floral arrangements will cause employment to grow faster than average. Job openings are sensitive to economic conditions.
Industrial designers	13,000	550	Employment expected to grow about as fast as average due to an increasing number of products and an emphasis on product safety.
Interior designers	79,000	3,600	Increasing use of design services in business establishments and homes expected to cause employment to grow about as fast as average. Competition for jobs likely, however. Best opportunities for talented college graduates in interior design and graduates of professional interior design schools.
Land-scape architects	14,000	1,100	Employment expected to grow faster than average due to increases in new construction and city and regional environmental planning. Job openings are sensitive to economic conditions.

Notes

[1] Due to growth and replacement needs. Does not include transfers out of occupations. Estimates of replacement openings on working life tables developed by Bureau of Labor Statistics.

[2] Estimate not available.

[3] Excludes part-time junior instructors.

[4] For the nation as a whole, projected decrease in employment is expected to be greater than number of openings resulting from deaths and retirements.

[5] Total does not equal sum of individual estimates because all branches of engineering are not covered separately in *The Occupational Outlook Handbook*.

Occu-pation	Estimated employ-ment, 1978	Average annual openings 1978-90[1]	Employment prospects
Photogra-phers	93,000	3,800	Employment expected to grow about as fast as average. Portrait and commercial photographers likely to face keen competition. Good opportunities in areas such as law enforcement and scientific and medical research photog-raphy.

Communications-related occupations

Occu-pation	Estimated employ-ment, 1978	Average annual openings 1978-90[1]	Employment prospects
News-paper reporters	45,000	2,400	Employment expected to grow about as fast as average. Best op-portunities on newspapers in small towns and suburbs and for gradu-ates who have specialized in news-editorial studies and com-pleted a newspaper internship.
Public relations workers	131,000	7,500	Employment expected to grow about as fast as average as cor-porations, associations, and other large organizations expand public

Occu-pation	Estimated employ-ment, 1978	Average annual openings 1978-90[1]	Employment prospects
			relations efforts to gain public support. Competition for jobs likely to be keen during economic downturns.
Radio and televi-sion announcers	27,000	850	Employment expected to increase about as fast as average as new stations are licensed and as cable television stations do more of their own programming. Keen competition likely for openings, however. Best prospects in small cities.
Technical writers	24,000	(2)	Employment expected to grow about as fast as average due to need for effective communication of scientific and technical infor-mation in areas such as computer science and electronics. Best op-portunities for persons with both writing ability and scientific or technical background.

Source: *Occupational Outlook Quarterly,* Spring 1980.

Notes

[1] Due to growth and replacement needs. Does not include transfers out of occupations. Estimates of replacement openings on working life tables developed by Bureau of Labor Statistics.

[2] Estimate not available.

[3] Excludes part-time junior instructors.

[4] For the Nation as a whole, projected decrease in employment is expected to be greater than number of openings resulting from deaths and retirements.

[5] Total does not equal sum of individual estimates because all branches of engineering are not covered separately in *The Occupational Outlook Handbook.*

Some Highlighted Job Areas

If you're good at it, selling can be a lucrative area. Not retail or real estate sales, which can be terrific when the economy is booming or terrible when it's not and interest rates are high...but sales of products such as chemicals, office equipment (particularly high technology "office of the future" products), and computers, and services such as time-sharing, corporate consulting, and space sales are all high-paying. Service selling can take a long time, sometimes one year or longer before a client will sign up for your services, but commissions are generally high.

Here's an example of what sales can be like, from a March 1981 article appearing in *Compflash,* a monthly newsletter published by the American Management Association. Women readers take heed!

March 1981

Some electronics and information-processing companies tell *The Wall Street Journal* that their female sales representatives are outperforming their male peers. Women's commissions were 10 to 15 percent higher than men's at Exxon's Qyx typewriter division; the company's top sales reps in the past three years were women. Semispecialists of America, an electronic products distributor, says its average saleswoman earned $31,500 last year, compared with about $25,000 for a man. A 28-year-old saleswoman at TDX Systems, a long-distance phone service supplier, is making $60,000 a year after 18 months on the job. But, says WSJ, opportunities aren't as bright in older industries, where tradition is difficult to break. A Union Carbide chemical sales executive comments, "A lot of men are reluctant to have women calling on them."

How do you know you'd like a career in or be good at sales? Does the word *sales* make you feel squeamish? Do you conjure up the image of Willy Loman in *Death of a Salesman?* If you do, you're wrong. That was the past. Most sales representatives of the 1980s will have college degrees (many of them technical) and will work for sizable companies. Starting salaries range from $9,000 to $20,000 and there will be intensive on-the-job training programs of up to two years' length. Besides salaries and company benefits, sales reps often get company cars (the 1982 value of a midsize American car is $8,500 after taxes) and/or car allowances, expense accounts, and bonuses or commissions.

QUALITIES OF A SUCCESSFUL SALES REPRESENTATIVE

Traits and Skills Factors	Intelligence Primary	Motivation Primary	Personality Primary	Knowledge and Experience Primary
	Communication skills — proper use of language and grammar	Capability for working alone without supervision	Strong competitiveness	College education preferred but not always necessary
	Organizational abilities	Strong goal-orientation	Leadership/self-confidence	Details can be learned on the job
	Good common sense if possible	Self-starting	Patience but persistence	**Secondary**
	Secondary	Ambition/success-orientation	Ability to handle pressure	Direction, motivation, and leadership of others — coaching experience desirable but not necessary
	Ability to learn quickly	People-orientation	Flexibility	
	Thoroughness	**Secondary**	Integrity	Prior sales background (may be a plus or a minus)
	Acceptance of frustration and ability to learn from it	Aggressiveness	**Secondary**	
	Creativity	Enjoyment of hard work	Friendliness	
		Acceptance of frustration and ability to learn from it		

Sales or marketing representatives have certain advantages over the traditional 9 A.M. to 5 P.M. one-workplace person. They get out of their offices a lot! If not being tied down to one spot all day except for a lunch break appeals to you, if you are an outgoing person who enjoys meeting new people, if you consider yourself relatively persuasive and are good at turning noes and maybes into yesses, and you really like money, then you should definitely consider sales. And, you can travel, although not all sales jobs require extensive travel. Finally, promotions are quicker in sales than in most other positions, as performance is usually the key factor judged, not how much the boss likes you. Many of the presidents of our country's major corporations have had experience in sales. It's a highly valued skill for top management.

Remember, too, that sales jobs are monetarily rewarding in several ways: (1) straight salary, (2) salary plus bonus or commission monthly, quarterly, or annually, (3) a "draw" against commission, (4) a straight commission, (5) expenses and/or car—it depends on the job. You must determine if you can live on a fluctuating amount of pay.

Another, *very* different area to consider is coal mining. Coal mining? The February 10, 1981, *Wall Street Journal* reported that the average pay of $19,442 attracted large numbers of young applicants to a field that will require an additional 45,000 new workers per year during this decade.

Believe it or not, women have entered the mines in this heretofore male-dominated industry. In 1960 and 1970 women represented 1.5 percent of the total employees and in 1975 only 2.5 percent. Also, they were in lower-ranking and lower-paying office jobs and routine service functions. But between 1975 and 1978, employment of women doubled. And in part, some of these gains were in production positions, both underground and in surface mines. Of approximately 8,500 women employed in the bituminous coal industry in early 1979, over 1,000 were actually working as miners. The median age of coal mine workers has dropped from forty-five years of age in 1970 to thirty-five years in 1975. Educational attainment levels also rose. Labor demands for mining personnel are expected to grow during the 1980s from an actual figure of 214,000 to about 325,000 in 1990—over a 50 percent increase in less than thirteen years.

In spite of all the gloom-and-doom predictions of many economists, military leaders, and politicians, the early 1980s appear to be pretty good for many kinds of jobs. In fact, according to a November, 1980, article in *Dun's Review*, 1980 was the best year *ever* for executive jobs. Major search firms reported that the number of openings for executives was at an all-time high despite the recession. And salaries continued to escalate because of inflation, the cost of living, and job-switching. *Dun's* own fall 1980 survey of 1,420 positions filled by 20 of the nation's leading recruiting firms showed a 16 percent increase over 1979 in all positions filled at $40,000 and above. There was also a 30 percent rise over 1979 for positions paying $100,000 or more. Part of these statistics, of course, is that boards of directors tend to fire high-level executives much more quickly now if their performance is not satisfactory. Openings for engineering executives in this study totaled 80, almost double their 1979 figures. Twenty of these jobs paid over $60,000 (as against 8 in 1979). Openings for sales and marketing execs increased 20 percent. The chart on the following page shows what salaries and perks were typical in the fall of 1980.

We predict, upon the basis of our knowledge of the employment market and our study of the business press through the first quarter of 1982, that although jobs may still be plentiful for top executives and highly specialized technical personnel, pay raises for the next several years will probably be smaller. Also, bonuses will be performance-based rather than being a percentage of salary.

TYPICAL COMPENSATION PACKAGES

	Top Management	Middle Management	Lower Management
Title	Chief Operating Officer ($1½ bil. sales manufacturer)	Division Manager	Division Controller
Base Salary	$300,000	$100,000	$40,000
Initial Bonus (To make up for benefits lost by changing jobs)	1 year's salary	25%–50% of one year's salary if giving up equity plan or deferred compensation	$10,000 maximum (usually for relocation expenses only)
Annual Bonus (expected & maximum)	50% of base salary 100% of base salary	40% of base salary 80% of base salary	25% of base salary 50% of base salary
Capital Accumulation	25,000 nonqualified stock options plus 50,000 performance units	7,500 nonqualified stock options	2,000 nonqualified stock options
Retirement Benefits	company pension plan plus supp. benefits to equal 65% of final average 5-year gross pay (salary plus bonus)	40%–50% of final average 5-year gross pay	40%–50% of final average 5-year gross pay
Life Insurance	3 times base salary	1½ times base salary	1½ times base salary
Major Medical & Dental	company group plan plus supp. benefits	company group plan	company group plan
Perks	car, luncheon club, country club, personal tax and financial planning advice	possibly car, a luncheon club or a country club	none

Source: Peat, Marwick, Mitchell & Co./*Wall Street Journal*, November 17, 1980.

Prospects for College Graduates

Between 1969 and 1978 nearly twice as many college graduates entered the work force each year, on the average, as entered between 1962 and 1969. Because many job openings traditionally sought by graduates were not available in sufficient numbers, more and more graduates entered non-traditional fields. The chart shows this change.

Jobs Entered by College Graduates, 1962–1969 and 1969–1978, by Major Occupational Group

(Percentages)	1962–1969	1969–1978
Operatives, laborers, service, farm and unemployed	1.0	11.6
Craft workers	2.6	3.1
Clerical workers	2.9	10.1
Sales workers	3.0	9.0
Managers and administrators, except farm	17.2	20.3
Professional and technical workers	73.2	45.9

Source: U.S. Bureau of Labor Statistics

In 1962 approximately 415,000 people earned bachelors' degrees; in 1972 over 900,000 earned them, and in 1982 there will be just under 1,000,000. In the last year, a small drop has occurred, which is predicted to continue through 1990; but the annual number of college graduates will still hover about the 960,000 mark. However, despite the magnitude of this job mismatch, college graduates will still be better off in the labor market than less educated people will be.

With all these upsets in the "traditional" labor force, economic and technological trends indicate that widespread job displacement will become a major problem in the 1980s and 1990s. Many workers will be reassigned at lower salaries and face loss of seniority and status (or they will face unemployment).

Competition and Mobility

Upward mobility will be more of a problem for current managers than for people just beginning in positions that will eventually qualify them for management and executive jobs.

Several anecdotes and articles appearing in the business press from 1980 through early 1982 seem to confirm this trend. In 1980 and 1981 there were several gloom-and-doom reports warning executives about the new crop of well-educated young men and women (close to 8½ million through 1986) seeking and getting high-paying managerial jobs. Naturally, this influx of talent will cause many existing people to fall off or slow down their climb up the executive ladder.

Most of us are used to competition, but many younger executives are practically obsessive about achieving success. They are willing to put in long hours and sacrifice much of their personal lives to attain their goals.

Labor-force growth as a whole should slow down during the 1980s because the present working-age population has already absorbed the 1960s and 1970s "baby boom" people. But there will be an increase in the work force of people between the ages of twenty-five to fifty-four, with women counting for much of this increase.

Keep in mind that there will be a shrinking market for some job areas, with many qualified people, as well qualified as you are, trying to get the same jobs as you. Some will get your jobs, too, unless *you* know how to outmarket your competition.

Creative Thinking for Switching Careers

Let's apply some creative thinking to finding new careers in the 1980s. If you are like most people who are discontented with their present work lives, you know you want to try another field but are afraid of losing salary level, job title, and, worst of all, perhaps discovering after making the switch that you don't like your new field of endeavor any more than the one you're in now.

How can you avoid making (perhaps) these costly and time-consuming errors? Try doing the following: (1) use our want-ad analysis technique (chapter 5) to narrow your interests to a few specific areas and job titles and then pursue these for jobs; (2) try part-time or evening work in your desired area, if possible; (3) get into an apprenticeship program (this usually requires completion of some specialized education); (4) do volunteer work; (5) take a course or two in your "possible" new field; (6) determine if you really should return to college full time or part time.

One of our friends, Steve Burke, a junior-high-school science teacher who'd been teaching for seven years, had seriously begun to consider leaving teaching two or three years ago. He recognized that the transition into a profit-oriented company would be difficult because he knew how many business people negatively perceived the education field in general and teachers in particular. Except for summer jobs as a house painter and carpenter and three years in the air force, he had had no relevant business experience.

Two years ago he took action. He wasn't exactly sure what he wanted to do, but he decided to try some part-time evening work to help him define his likes and dislikes. Steve selected an area that could offer him full-time employment if he liked the work. He chose telephone sales, selling imprinted writing instruments (pens and pencils) to small businesses. He started working for a local employer four hours a night, two nights a week, increased to three nights in only four months, found he enjoyed the work and was good at it, and when he figured out his commissions, he found he was earning in excess of $11,000 a year part-time compared to his full-time teaching salary of $16,300.

After less than a year he discovered that his teaching experience was valuable at his part-time position. Because of the high turnover rate among telephone sales representatives, he had become the "senior" representative. His manager asked him to train all newly hired employees, which he did and did well. After their training period ended, he received a small percentage of their sales, adding to his own earnings.

In fourteen or fifteen months he was thinking seriously about full-time, daytime employment and discussed it with his manager. She told him that nothing was then available but she'd let him know when an opening occurred. Within seven months the day supervisor was promoted, and Steve was offered and accepted this position. His base salary is now $16,500 plus commissions. He expects he'll be able to earn between $22,000 and $25,000 in his first year of full-time employment and have hiring, training, and supervisory responsibilities for a staff of five to eight people. Granted he gave up his union card and long summer vacations for two weeks of vacation per year, but he decided the opportunity to earn about $150 more per week was well worth it.

With the rising cost of energy, mail order and telephone sales are two areas to consider if you want part-time employment in a sales field. Or you could sell cosmetics from door to door, or work part-time at retail sales for a *major* department store during holiday season. Good part-time retail salespersons are often considered for full-time training programs to become buyers and merchandisers if they express an interest in joining the company.

Major banks with computer-run operations areas often work three or four shifts, twenty-four hours a day, processing paper such as checks and stocks and bonds.

There are part-time data-entry positions in computer software companies that pay high wages, but provide no benefits. Most have flexible hours; you may work as many or as few hours as you wish. If you decide to pursue a career in this area there are schools to attend and courses to be taken that will just about guarantee you a starting salary of $12,000 to $20,000 upon completion.

OTHER THINGS TO DO: Take a couple of courses in any field in which you have an interest. This will enable you to decide if you want to pursue a particular area further or try another field. But avoid the pitfall of becoming a permanent student. You'll be disqualified by employers as being overqualified but underexperienced.

VOLUNTEER: If you've always liked math or dealing with people and think you might like fund-raising or statistical analysis, volunteer for a job in a large charitable organization such as the United Fund or the American Cancer Society. These organizations are often partially run by local business people recruited for part-time work or on sabbatical leave from their companies for six months to a year. It's a terrific way to make business contacts. You can get involved with designing questionnaires, obtaining data, writing public relations pieces, estimating the costs of fund-raising....

Do you like to write? *Volunteer* to be a reporter for a local newspaper. Contacts are excellent, particularly if you can get to interview business people.

JOIN PROFESSIONAL ASSOCIATIONS in your area of interest. If you are not allowed to join, attend monthly meetings and develop contacts that will help you get interviews.

REENTRY WOMEN: The best single way to get a job is to acquire salable skills. This can be done in local schools or evening or weekend community adult education programs. The courses run the gamut from clerical skills to automotive repair, furniture refinishing, bookkeeping, and accounting. You can work temporary jobs as a receptionist or a clerk-typist, in a garage, as a telephone switchboard operator, filling in for the bookkeeper who had a coronary attack, or whatever.

Do you like art? Try for a part-time job in a museum or in a local gallery. If no job exists, *volunteer*. Then, if you do well, ask again for the job. Are you a good cook? Cater parties or cook for small businesses that put on catered lunches for their executives.

NOTE: Most national companies with customer service areas have a second shift to enable them to contact and to be contacted by customers two and three time zones away. This is another area to investigate for part-time work.

A True Story

One of the authors' aunts was a middle-aged housewife who was forced to go to work to pay the medical expenses of her husband's serious illness. She took a part-time job in a major Boston department store's fine-china department. She became so intrigued with the merchandise that she studied up on it in her spare time and soon became more knowledgeable than the "trained" buyers. Eventually she started working full time and became the department head, increasing sales for the store 300 to 400 percent. She had no college degree and no prior business experience and was over fifty years old!

We mentioned apprenticeship before. According to Robert L. Perry, consulting editor for the *Mechanix Illustrated Guide to Personal Computers*, in an article he wrote for *Consumers Digest*, March/April 1981:

> *Apprenticeships.* Apprenticeship training is a singular realm. Most programs are joint efforts on the part of management and labor committees in regions where jobs are concentrated, such as automobile specialties in Detroit or the apparel trade in New York.
>
> Although apprenticeships are often not required in many skilled trade jobs, they almost invariably result in higher pay and better job offers. They also lead to "master" status, which is a step up for those who wish to start their own business.
>
> However, in many areas, competition for entry into apprenticeship programs is intense. Women and minority groups have an advantage on paper in some programs, although whether discriminatory practices still occur is a matter of individual cases. The only requirements, generally, are high school or GED and age, usually 18 or 19.

Recently the Equal Employment Opportunity Commission found apprenticeship age limits and diploma requirements unlawful, but unions have not yet agreed to conciliation.

Skilled trades are also areas that many college graduates, particularly those who possess liberal arts backgrounds, are looking into. However, remember that many positions are concentrated in different geographic locations. You cannot expect to graduate from a technical school in your hometown and immediately find a job as an aircraft mechanic if you don't live within commuting distance of an airport.

Control Data Institute, one of the largest and best-known computer training schools, offers courses in computer programming, operations, service, and maintenance. The maintenance technician's course lasts seven months (853 hours of training) and enables the student to maintain and repair mainframe computers, microcomputers, and standard peripherals, such as printers, disk storage devices, card readers, and magnetic tape units.

The course costs nearly $5,000, but graduates were hired into entry-level positions at an average of nearly $13,000 per year as of the first half of 1980.

Programmers and operators trained for 680 hours at a cost below $4,500, and the average graduate found work for a salary just below $13,000 in early 1980. The realistic starting salary in 1981 was closer to $14,000. In addition, all three computer occupations can expect to yield between $17,500 and $20,000 within two years.

What do you do if you don't have a college degree but still want to earn enough money to live comfortably? You can start by looking at the list below of 25 careers that don't require a B.A. or a B.S. degree. All require some form of specialized training but some train as little as a few months.

We have provided from *Consumers Digest* a partial list of organizations and publications with information about starting a new technical or skilled trade career.

Job Title	Training	1981 Salary	1984 Salary
Aerospace plant worker	VT, PV	$17,400	$20,800
Airplane mechanic	2 yr. VT, PV	17,400	20,800
Appliance repair/service	CC, VT, PV	19,800	23,700
Blue collar supervisor	2 yr. CC, VT	21,600	26,000
Boilermaker	4 yr. AP	28,800	34,500
Computer console operator	1–2 yr. CC, VT, PV	12,500	15,000
Computer manufacturing inspector	1–2 yr. VT, PV	17,400	20,800
Computer programmer	CC, VT, PV	15,600	18,700
Computer service technician	1–2 yr. VT, PV	15,000	18,000
Dental hygienist	dental hygiene schools	15,600	18,700
Energy auditor	OTJ	15,000	18,000
Home inspector	OTJ, home study	16,200	19,500
Industrial machine service	4 yr. AP	19,200	23,000
Lithographer	4–5 yr. AP	27,400	32,800
Machine tool operator	OTJ	21,000	25,200
Manufacturing inspector	OTJ	16,200	19,500
Medical lab technician	2 yr. CC, VT, PV	13,200	15,800
Medical record technician	2 yr. associate degree	15,000	18,000
Microcomputer generalist	1–2 yr. VT, PV, OTJ	18,000	21,600
Operating engineer	3 yr. AP	15,000	18,000
Solar technician	OTJ, home study	16,800	20,100
Stationary engineer	4 yr. AP	19,800	23,700
Tool-and-die maker	4 yr. AP	21,000	25,200
Videocassette service	OTJ	17,300	20,800
Wastewater treatment plant operator	1–2 yr. VT, PV	15,000	18,000

Key: OTJ = on the job; AP = apprenticeship; CC = community college; VT = vocational technical school; PV = private vocational technical school (Ed.).

Source: *Consumers Digest,* March/April 1981.

Job Tenure

As you can see, there are all kinds of options available to you should you choose to pursue them. According to the *Occupational Outlook Quarterly* for Winter 1980:

> People are not only changing occupations...they're changing employers at a high rate. About 30% of the 91 million Americans employed in January 1978 had found their work in the previous 12 months....Job tenure is the length of time an employee has worked steadily for the same employer. In 1978, median job tenure was 3.6 years, a slight decline for the 3.8 years of 1968.

And, according to the most recent studies we've seen, in 1982, this 3.6 year tenure figure from January 1978 is declining further.

What Worries Personnel Executives the Most?

Where else is there a need for career-minded people? According to a fairly recent survey of personnel executives, finding generalists for top management jobs is a worrisome issue. They feel that "general management" positions will be the hardest to fill during the 1980s. Why is this? Because for years, most companies have rewarded their personnel for becoming specialists in only one or two areas, not in obtaining broad-based experience. Now these attitudes are going to haunt them in their quest for top managers. "Management succession planning" was also named as an important current issue. After all, if people in lower-level management jobs are so highly specialized, how can you plan to have these people succeed present top generalist managers? Hopefully, since the organizations have created this monster, they will be able to solve their problems ... somehow.

Also tough to find in the years ahead will be technical and computer specialists and engineers. Easiest jobs to fill will be in the legal, sales, and financial areas.

SOURCES OF INFORMATION*

Professional Societies and Trade Associations

National Health Council, Inc., 70 W. 40th St., New York, NY 10018.

National Association of Trade and Technical Schools, 2021 K St., NW, Washington, D.C. 20006.

American Federation of Information Processing Societies, 1815 N. Lynn St., Arlington, VA 22209.

American Management Association, 135 W. 50th St., New York, NY 10020.

Water Pollution Control Federation, 2626 Pennsylvania Ave., NW, Washington, D.C. 20037.

American Institute of Certified Public Accountants, 1211 Avenue of the Americas, New York, NY 10038.

Aviation Maintenance Foundation, P.O. Box 739, Basin, WY 84210.

Engineers' Council for Professional Development, 345 E. 47th St., New York, NY 10017.

Air Conditioning and Refrigeration Institute, 1815 N. Fort Mayer Dr., Arlington, VA 22209.

Association of Home Appliance Manufacturers, 20 N. Wacker Dr., Chicago, IL 60606.

Automotive Service Industry Association, 444 N. Michigan Ave., Chicago, IL 60611.

National Joint Apprenticeship and Training Committee for the Electrical Industry, 7315 Wisconsin Ave., NW, Washington, D.C. 20014.

Federal Agencies

Office of Information, Inquiries Unit; Employment and Training Administration; U.S. Dept. of Labor; Room 10225, 601 D St., NW, Washington, D.C. 20213.

U.S. Employment Service; Apprenticeship Information Center (listed in your phone book).

Office of Information and Consumer Affairs; Employment Standards Administration; U.S. Dept. of Labor; Room C-4331, 200 Constitution Ave., NW; Washington, D.C. 20210.

Department of Veterans Benefits; Room 232A; Veterans Administration Central Office, 810 Vermont Ave., NW; Washington, D.C. 20420.

Division of Occupational Outlook; Bureau of Labor Statistics; U.S. Dept. of Labor, Washington, D.C. 20210.

*Source: *Consumers Digest,* March/April 1981.

Speaking of personnel management (called human resources in the 1980s), here is a list of salaries paid to these professionals in 1980 and the salaries that were projected then for 1981.

Job Title	Average Years' Experience	Average Current 1980 Salaries	Projected 1981 Average Salaries (and average percentage increase over 1980 levels)
Vice President	19.5 years	$60,500	$68,900 (+14.1)
Division Personnel Manager	11.1 years	$44,750	$51,900 (+16.0)
Director, Labor Relations	14.6 years	$43,000	$49,100 (+14.1)
Director, Compensation	10.7 years	$39,300	$46,200 (+17.5)
Director, Manpower Planning	13.8 years	$38,700	$44,100 (+14.0)
Director, Benefits	11.4 years	$38,100	$43,900 (+15.2)
Plant Personnel Manager	8.6 years	$33,200	$38,400 (+15.6)
Manager, Labor Relations	8.5 years	$32,900	$37,400 (+13.7)
Employment Manager	7.3 years	$30,900	$35,300 (+14.3)
Compensation Manager	5.1 years	$30,600	$35,800 (+17.1)
Employment Supervisor	4.7 years	$26,000	$29,500 (+13.5)
Employment Recruiter	3.1 years	$23,150	$27,000 (+17.0)
M.B.A. Graduate	Entry	$18,100	$19,900 (+10.1)
B.A./B.S. Graduate	Entry	$15,700	$17,200 (+ 9.1)

Note: Salary averages shown include those from companies of all sizes. In very large companies, with sales of $1 billion or more, salary averages range higher, of course (e.g., V.P., Personnel/Industrial Relations — $115,000).

Source: Fox-Morris 1980–'81 U.S. Demand/Salary Survey

The *New York Times* National Recruitment Survey, October 1981

For the past several years, in the late fall, the Sunday *New York Times* has published a magazine insert called the National Recruitment Survey. The 1981 survey, *Careers: The Reagan Effect*, discusses the changing marketplace of the 1980s and its anticipated effects. Much of what is discussed in this insert backs up what we discuss throughout *Career Changing*.

Executives of several major companies pointed up the increased need for engineers (all kinds) and computer specialists. The number of industries seeking these people far exceeds the supply. There will also be a shortage of skilled office workers.

Stock brokerage opportunities are very plentiful and it's a great area into which to switch careers. In fact, most brokerage firms prefer people with other business experience. The average age at Bache Halsey Stuart Shields's training classes in 1981 was thirty-six (68 percent of the students had prior sales experience). Stock brokerage is also a good place for women: in 1981 about 20 percent of the trainees at Merrill Lynch were female. However, you have to pass rigorous tests to qualify for brokerage training programs, much of which are on economics and finance. So, if you decide to try the stock brokerage business, take a course or two before applying (unless your work experience is in a financial arena) and be up to date on current events and business trends.

Transportation is another good field, ground transportation in particular. Transit agencies in 350 cities are looking for people with good managerial and technical skills. Don't forget—the public transportation market hires people right out of school for accounting, planning, marketing, and statistical jobs, not just as engineers and technicians. Don't fantasize about being an air traffic controller, though; over 110,000 people applied by October 1981 to replace the 12,000 controllers fired during the summer.

Decreases are expected in the factory work force due to the expanded use of robots, particularly in the automotive industry and other businesses that perform assembly work. It's been predicted that by 1990 robots may displace 65 to 75 percent of all factory workers.

By the way, robotics is a growing field. If you're an electrical or mechanical engineer, or about to be one, investigate this field.

Decreases in job openings are also expected for lawyers. The Bureau of Labor Statistics projects that by 1985 there will be fewer than 500,000 law jobs available, with about 600,000 people seeking them. As we went to press, predictions were that 30 percent of the 1982 law school graduates wouldn't find jobs in their profession. However, if you are in the top 15 percent of your class and attend a prestigious law school such as Yale, Harvard, or Columbia, you may be eagerly snatched up and offered as much as $43,000 by a snazzy New York law firm. In 1981, Houston was paying up to $35,000 for beginning attorneys from the Ivy League. Minneapolis was the lowest payer at that time, at around $24,000. But, if your degree is not from a pedigreed school you will get less: annual beginning salaries in the minor leagues ranged in 1981 from under $10,000 to $20,000.

Unemployment is up in several major sectors of our economy, and even industries that may rebound (such as the automotive) may not significantly reduce unemployment because of the permanent displacement of many workers by machines.

Other Words of Wisdom, Some Disheartening, Some Not

WOMEN: There are presently about 97 million adult workers in the full-time labor force. By 1995 this number is expected to increase by another 25 million, with women accounting for two-thirds of this growth.

COLLEGE GRADS: You may be able to find work but not always in jobs viewed as those for college graduates. *Best advice:* take business, computer, and math courses in college even if you're a liberal arts major. Remember: companies want specialists, *not* generalists. Look for work in smaller, high-technology firms and in banking, insurance, publishing, and retailing.

HIGH-SCHOOL GRADS: If college isn't for you, think about apprenticeship programs. We mentioned apprenticeship before. There will be jobs available for dental assistants and hygienists. Military service is a terrific way to obtain technical training that will be useful in civilian life. Word-processing knowledge will increase your paycheck about $50 a week if you are a secretary or wish to become one.

Where Is the Best Place to Seek Work?

If you can be flexible about where you'll live, your job prospects are better in some parts of the country than others. We'll list some facts for you.

New England

New Hampshire and Massachusetts have low unemployment among the technically skilled. Computer and electronics companies abound in these two states, and the absence of sales and income taxes in New Hampshire makes it particularly attractive (also good if you like to ski!). Maine and Vermont have a couple of good areas but, again, mostly for technical personnel. Rhode Island, after losing a major industry (jewelry manufacturing), is expanding in commercial banking and some high-technology areas but it's still a little shaky. Connecticut, particularly southern Connecticut, is very strong in many areas.

Middle Atlantic States

New York City is still good for financial positions and retailing, but many of the technical positions have moved out to New Jersey or southern Connecticut. Upstate New York has been hard hit, with as much as 15 percent unemployment, 'way over the national figures, in places like Buffalo. Maryland has lost manufacturing jobs but there will be some increase in white-collar and in service positions. Delaware, with its major focus on the chemical industry, will probably continue to do well. Pennsylvania anticipates heavy job losses in manufacturing; New Jersey seems to be holding its own (it is big in chemical and pharmaceutical industries).

Midwest

It has been very hard hit, particularly construction and manufacturing in Ohio, Illinois, Indiana, and Michigan. Farm jobs have dropped by 30 percent in some parts of Illinois, but increases in service businesses such as health, repair, and consulting will be on the upswing. This includes an anticipated 25 percent increase in clerical support at all levels.

Southwest

Pretty good generally. Texas, particularly Houston, is still the biggest employer of high-tech types, secretaries, financial, insurance, and real estate personnel. Oklahoma's good for mining.

Southeast

Employment, at the time of this writing (winter 1981–1982), is still up, especially in Florida. Although Miami has been having some serious problems, growth in the Tampa area is rising dramatically (schoolteachers and technical people are needed). And, recently, it appears that many foreign countries are opening plants in Florida because of the low tax base.

Mountain States

The Rocky Mountain area will experience some good growth, energy development in particular. Montana's not terrific and neither is Utah, but Colorado, Wyoming, and New Mexico are holding their own.

West Coast

California's the best, and with recent increases for defense spending it'll be booming soon. So will Nevada, also because of defense. Technical personnel are needed in both these states, but California also needs preschool teachers and medical workers. Service jobs are expanding here and in Arizona and Hawaii.

Northwest

Washington State is in a slump now except for engineers with experience in energy. Oregon is expanding its electronics capability (as is Washington), but don't expect to be transferred unless you are world-famous. People in this part of the country feel that to live here is reward enough, so they won't pay you to move. You'll have to be a resident already or plan to relocate there and look for work. If interest rates come down, Oregon's expected to rebound.

Top Cities to Live and Work in, in the 1980s

Phoenix and Tucson, Arizona; Fort Lauderdale, Hollywood Beach, Tampa, Florida; Austin, Beaumont, Houston, El Paso, Texas; San Diego, California; Albuquerque, New Mexico; Denver, Boulder, Colorado; Tulsa, Oklahoma.

Places to Avoid

Cleveland, Akron, Ohio; Detroit, Michigan; Buffalo, New York City, New York; Jersey City, New Jersey; Wilkes-Barre, Scranton, Pennsylvania.

We hope that this information will help you in deciding what you do next as well as where to do it if you are mobile. Chapter 3, "Product Analysis," will help you define who you really are, what transferable skills you possess, and how best to capitalize on marketing yourself.

3. Product Analysis (Know Thyself)

"Midway in life's journey I was made aware
That I had strayed into a dark forest
And the right path appeared not anywhere."

—DANTE, THE DIVINE COMEDY

As children we were all asked at one time or another, "What would you like to be when you grow up?" Our answers varied, based upon our age, socioeconomic background, self-image, and other factors. Sometimes we wanted to be teachers, firemen, doctors, dancers, entertainers, nurses, housewives, researchers, or writers. Few, if any of us, however, ever thought about becoming salespersons. There seemed something about this occupation that people found distasteful. Salespersons didn't really help others or try to make other people happy. Instead, we tended to view them as helping themselves first and only helping others secondarily. After all, they were here today, then gone tomorrow.

However, much in life should be seen in sales terms. People are a gregarious species and, as such, strive to be accepted by individuals and groups. As children we constantly tried to sell ourselves to our peers and to our teachers to gain favor and acceptance. In our early adult years, we tried to gain acceptance into a particular college or university, or into a particular fraternity or sorority. As adults we try to sell ourselves to our love objects.

Consider the idea of obtaining a new position or a job with increased responsibility. Is trying to sell yourself to others any different from what you have been doing in the past? If a difference does exist, it is only one of degree. The stakes are high for most of us when we attempt to sell ourselves to prospective employers. Those stakes are power, money, status, and influence. Since most of us define ourselves in these terms, success or failure looms large in our minds.

It is important to understand that we are always salespersons. Through our actions we sell ourselves. But do you have enough knowledge about this product to sell it effectively? And, if so, how much consideration have you given to packaging this product?

You are selling a product—and that product is YOU.

Easy for Me, Difficult for You

People in certain job categories will have an easier time switching from one position to another. Accountants tend to be accountants no matter where they work. An accountant can change from one employer (Fortune 500 in size) to a much smaller company (fewer than 2,000 employees), and the type of work performed won't change much. This is true of some other occupations, including computer fields, tax accounting, financial analysis, market research, engineering, and certain sales fields.

There are other categories where a switch entails a greater effort and may mean a transfer of fields. This is particularly true for a highly skilled person in a specific industry. *Examples:* From the aerospace industry of the early 1970s to social work, hospital work, or public education in the early 1980s. Switching to industry is very hard.

46

We can see how this problem affects the person attempting a major change by examining one field, the hospitals, a bit closer. There are many skilled persons in this field who are faced with substantial roadblocks when attempting to secure employment outside of their area. Many of these roadblocks are created by overspecialization of skills which are not readily transferable to other industries. Some examples include those needed to be a utilization review analyst, an EKG technician, an ultrasound technician, a respiratory therapist. Even people with job titles of a general management nature experience difficulty in achieving a successful switch. The reasons lie in the prejudices toward holders of certain jobs that exist within different sectors of our economy. Examples of two such persons are the medical department administrator and the hospital training director.

One of the authors of this book, Lloyd Feinstein, was formerly director of training and assistant personnel director for Bellevue Hospital Center in New York City. He found himself confronted with the common prejudices held by many in private industry about hospital people. They believed that people working for public institutions did not meet their experience standards. Specifically they believed that employment in publicly supported jobs fosters sloppy work habits such as a spendthrift attitude, little or no concern about productivity, and no attention to making a profit. This type of widespread prejudice often works both ways. Hospital managers, when hiring, often prefer to hire candidates with past experience in the same, or similar, health care fields. For the person trying to break out of health care, the task can be difficult, though it's not impossible. It was done by Lloyd, using the techniques contained in this book, and it can also be done by you. (To find out how, read on.)

It May Have to Be outside Your Normal Field

There is a familiar saying that the only things in life that are certain are death and taxes. However, a third certainty of life exists: change. Everything is changing! The economics of our everyday living and our value systems are in a constant state of flux. In the world of work since the 1960s there has emerged the "new values worker," whose emphasis is in his or her lifestyle rather than job-centered activities. This trend is expected to continue and gather strength throughout the 1980s, and its influence on the workplace will be profound.

In a real sense, this book's main objective is to give you the mental outlook, the skills, and the ability to cope with a constantly changing workplace. To handle this changing environment of the 1980s effectively, the alert job hunter must be willing to discard old ways and attitudes and explore instead all possible avenues of employment and career advancement. Readers of this book should be concerned with advancing their careers, not just getting a new job. The observation has been made that "the difference between a career and a job is about twenty hours per week." In the 1980s great emphasis will be on changes made to careers outside traditional channels.

> "To illustrate, a national survey of entering first-year college students (conducted annually by the University of California at Los Angeles and the American Council on Education) indicated in its fall 1975 report that for every three men planning to enter so-called 'masculine' career fields, such as business, engineering, law and medicine, there is now one woman. Just ten years ago, the ratio was eight to one."
>
> (Source: Russell B. Flanders, "Work: The Prospects for Tomorrow," *Occupational Outlook Quarterly,* Spring 1977.)

JAMES L. REACHMANN
24 Richard Lane
Los Angeles, California 90143

Telephone: (213) 345-4252

EDUCATION

M.P.S. UNIVERSITY OF CALIFORNIA AT LOS ANGELES, Los Angeles, California. Received Master of Professional Studies degree, June, 1976. Major concentration in Health Services Administration.

B.A. IONA COLLEGE, NEW ROCHELLE, NEW YORK
Received Bachelor of Arts degree, May, 1971 (evenings).

EXPERIENCE

January 1979
to
Present

CENTURY CITY HOSPITAL, Beverly Hills, California

Administrator/Division of Plastic and Reconstructive Surgery
Responsible for all aspects of the management and administration of the Division. Responsible for budgeting and expenditure control of funds in excess of $1,000,000. Daily interface with 11 clerical staff, 3 nurses, 8 residents. Supervise one clerical.

January 1974
to
December 1978

ST. JOSEPH'S HOSPITAL, Los Angeles, California

Administrator/Department of Family Medicine
I integrated specialty clinics and attending physicians into a Family Health Center; supervised nursing and clerical staff. Prepared grant and foundation proposals; instructed house staff in implementation of clinical investigations; and coordinated and scheduled house staff rotations.

November 1970
to
December 1974

ST. BARNABAS MEDICAL CENTER, Livingston, New Jersey

Assistant to Director of Ambulatory Care
As administrative liaison for Ambulatory Care Services, I developed a centralized appointment system and follow-up appointment system for approximately 25 specialty clinics; prepared monthly and quarterly statistical reports; assisted in preparation of Children and Youth grant annually for HEW; supervised clinical personnel.

December 1966
to
November 1970

WESTWOOD NURSING HOME, Mt. Olive, New Jersey

Assistant Administrator
Responsible for overall coordination of 5 departments, analysis and evaluation of quality of departments' function, resolution of departmental problems relating to staffing, budgeting, union/ management relations, equipment and supplies; monitoring of departmental compliance with federal, state and internal regulations; and coordination of regulatory agency surveys.

REFERENCES: Available upon request.

The problems associated with trying to switch jobs from nonprofit to profit can be seen clearly in the example of a medical department administrator named James Reachmann. The position he holds in the health-care field is characterized by:

1. *Good salary:* can be earned in this position. (However, in it men earn more than women.)
2. *Relative autonomy:* extensive in-person dealings with the main medical center and its two affiliated hospitals elsewhere in the city. (But will the job continue to have a fairly unstructured atmosphere?)
3. *Lack of experience supervising people:* medical department administrators typically have one clerical helper, who's shared. (Can he get a responsible job in his field without having been a people manager?)
4. *Several reporting relationships:* this position is supervised by an absentee vice president and is often subject to political intrigues among the department directors whom the medical department administrator supports.
5. *Strictly "staff" nature of this position:* even though he prepares budgets and generates grant proposals, his position provides a service to only the "line" personnel (doctors and nurses) within the department, not to his superiors.

These limitations can make his change to industry difficult. The chart below illustrates how a personnel director of a large corporation might interpret Jim's résumé, which describes his past and current job responsibilities as medical department administrator.

	Industry's View (Personnel Director)	Industry Evaluation
"Staff" nature of position	1. Has some budgeting experience.	+
	2. Has research and writing experience (but only from a staff viewpoint).	+/−
	3. Is a doer of assigned tasks, but has little or no leadership experience.	−
	4. A major portion of his job *may* be clerical.	−
	5. Is not responsible for profit or loss ("bottom line").	−
	6. Has little or no decision-making responsibilities.	−
Several reporting relationships	1. May be politically astute; probably a survivor.	+
	2. Is able to prioritize well.	+
	3. Value of his references is limited. No one else knows his work well.	−
	4. Job objective has been confused through conflicting management goals.	−
Lacks supervisory/ management experience	1. Has not had to get work done through efforts of others.	−
	2. Has little or no experience delegating work to subordinates.	−
	3. Has not trained subordinates or peers.	−
	4. Has little or no interviewing experience.	−
Autonomy in position	1. Has strong interpersonal skills.	+
	2. Is independent by nature.	+/−
	3. May be unable to take close direction from future bosses.	−
High salary	1. Lacks key experience in directing people; only an entry-level job may be available here for him. This candidate may be too much of a risk, particularly where he has a high salary: i.e., "not willing to pay his dues."	−

It's obvious from the above personnel director's view that Jim would experience problems in trying to switch to a job in industry. Yet it would not be impossible for him. It can be done. Typical effects of switching outside your normal field can be illustrated by observing specific occupational groups. To see how one of the authors accomplished a successful switch, turn to the chapter on résumés. But that is getting a little ahead of ourselves. The immediate task is for you to analyze your strengths to determine the quality and depth of the "product" you will be marketing—YOU.

How to List Your Strengths

For most of us, trying to determine our strengths while job hunting has often been a frustrating and unsuccessful experience. But it is not difficult to understand why we have problems when we attempt to catalogue our good points and strengths. Many of us have had job campaigns flounder on the rocks of self-evaluation for these reasons.

- You are too close to the subject. It's hard to be objective with yourself. (This closeness prevents you from asking critical questions.)
- You overlook the obvious and ignore the significant. (*Example:* Failing to take credit for past work experience because you were part of a team effort. See chapter 1.)
- As pointed out in chapter 1, "You're Better than You Think You Are," the negative chorus you hear from your "superiors" (either at work or at home) puts blinders on you.
- The job search requires more effort than you are willing to expend. This is particularly true if your previous results were less than satisfactory. Though many of you say you're serious about changing jobs, the total of your actions takes the form of complaining to friends or family. Doing this will not better your circumstances.

HOURS SPENT LOOKING FOR WORK BY PERSONS UNEMPLOYED 4 WEEKS OR LONGER, MAY 1976[1]
(Numbers in thousands)

Hours	Total	Men	Women	Husband[2]	White	Black
Total reporting:						
Number	3,926	2,262	1,665	963	3,127	751
Percent	100	100	100	100	100	100
10 hours or less	36	29	47	23	37	34
11 to 20 hours	23	23	22	19	22	24
21 to 40 hours	19	20	17	25	19	19
41 to 75 hours	10	11	8	13	10	11
76 to 100 hours	8	10	5	13	8	7
Over 100 hours	4	6	2	7	4	4
Median hours	17	20	12	27	17	18

[1] During the 4 weeks from April 18 to May 15, 1976.
[2] Husbands in husband-wife primary families, includes a small number of men who head families and are separated, widowed, divorced, or never married.
Source: United States Department of Labor, Bureau of Labor Statistics

Job seekers unemployed for four weeks or more as of mid-May 1976 were asked how many hours they had spent looking for a job during the prior four weeks. The median answer was 17 hours. The men averaged more time looking for work than women did. Married men spent more time looking for work than all other unemployed persons; about 6 out of 10 of the married men indicated that they had looked for 21 hours or more, compared with 1 out of 3 of all other persons.

It should be noted that several factors determine the amount of time an unemployed person spends looking for work. Job seekers who primarily use the telephone, write letters, or answer newspaper ads may exhaust most job possibilities after devoting only a few hours a week. Some job seekers in relatively small cities and towns may exhaust all currently available local job sources by looking only 2 to 3 hours a week. Only by expanding their search to other areas can they fruitfully spend more time in their job quest.

However, people who feel the strong financial pinch of unemployment or who have others to support may choose to spend a greater number of hours looking for work, regardless of local prospects.

Our experience shows that many so-called serious job hunters often spend more time and effort seeking new apartments or working on their cars than looking for new positions. This is an extremely common phenomenon called *fooling oneself*. This self-delusion will leave its practitioner in an old (or new) dead-end job.

Start here to create a *do-it-at-home vocational guidance exercise*. For those of you who know you're misplaced in your present position, general aptitude testing and counseling may be a good idea. There are local sources that are usually reputable and inexpensive. Check to see if your local colleges or universities have vocational guidance clinics open to the general public. Another source may be your local YMCA or YWCA. If these efforts fail or if you are not living near a college or "Y," then contact your state's professional employment service, listed in the white pages of your telephone directory.

Do you need professional career counseling? If any of the situations listed below is characteristic of your own working career, you may be a candidate for this type of counseling.

- Your interests are very general and need to be focused.
- Your interests are narrowly defined and your area offers little or no career advancement.
- Throughout your working career you've been a job hopper: that is, you have averaged less than two years in most or all positions.
- You have found yourself stuck in a dead-end job two or more times in a row in your working career and strongly suspect you're in another one now.
- You have difficulty defining and expressing your career interests verbally and in writing (via cover letters, résumés, and "action" letters).
- You have been "involuntarily terminated" (fired) from your last two positions because of "personality" conflicts.
- Jobs have always fallen in your lap, but have failed to provide you with emotional satisfaction or a sense of accomplishment.
- Your past jobs have often conflicted with your personal goals and desires.
- Your job expectations have never been realized.

NOTE: The nine criteria above will help you decide if you need a vocational guidance center to help you assess your talents. Before committing time and money to professional career counseling, however, try using the want-ad analysis technique described in chapter 5 to define your career interests. Testing centers usually test a wide range of intellectual and other types of skills. This type of testing service, however, has serious limitations when attempting to determine a person's ability to perform in actual job situations.

A most effective and highly desirable method of supplementing any testing or vocational counseling is to get into real work situations through volunteer work, summer work, part-time work, co-op work-study programs, apprenticeship, or internships.

Caveat Emptor: "Let the Buyer Beware!"

In recent years "vocational guidance counseling" services have become big business. As many parts of the 1980s job market become more difficult to enter, we expect these services will become even more widespread. These services are usually provided by "executive job counselors." Advertisements for job counseling often appear in the display ad section, just preceding the "Help Wanted" ads in major Sunday newspapers.

It is best to proceed with great caution. Check them out with your local Better Business Bureau before signing any contracts; also check with your attorney.

You should also think twice before going to any of the numerous résumé preparation services that have become so popular lately. By using either guidance counselors or résumé preparation specialists you are making a major error: you are allowing someone else to do your work. Doing so is a crutch that deprives *you* of the opportunity to learn how to explain fully your own work history. This neglect can be particularly harmful when you have to describe your work experience in a personal interview. If you haven't written or helped write your résumé or action letter but were granted an interview on the basis of some outsider's writing expertise, you'll be a "different" person in the interview from the one in your résumé.

You must learn to depend on yourself. Since nobody can go to an interview for you, allowing someone else to prepare your résumé or cover letters is self-defeating. To sell yourself successfully, you must know the "product" and be actively, not passively, involved in *all* aspects of your switch. Again, remember that you're better than you think you are!

Represent Your Product Fairly

When you're selling yourself, be sure to represent the product fairly. Fabricating, misrepresenting, or omitting data from your background and experience on a résumé or cover letter is not only intellectually dishonest but can cause you serious problems later. Recently, an applicant for a manufacturing position in the vitamin branch of a pharmaceutical company was rejected because he failed to include a previous employer. This omission was uncovered purely by accident by the prospective employer when the candidate was discussed among management. One of the managers had previously worked with the candidate at the unmentioned company. The candidate had been caught in a "lie" and management wondered if there were other areas he was "lying" about. Because his credibility was questioned, his candidacy for the position was rejected. Job applicants often fail to realize that many industries or businesses recruit from a surprisingly small labor pool. Always represent yourself truthfully *but* to your own advantage. As any salesperson will tell you, stating the truth is just plain easier. This is particularly true when you interview for a job.

When you are selling yourself, you should follow a few simple rules:

1.   Represent your background and experience accurately.

Dos	*Don'ts*
• Account for all meaningful experience that relates to the type of position you seek. • If you worked your way through college, say so.	• Avoid gaps in your work history. • Never lie or misrepresent; sooner or later you will be found out.

2.   Cover *every related* experience in your background.

Dos	*Don'ts*
• Include experiences with community, fraternal, and educational organizations—religious and political too, as long as you don't say which party or denomination.	• If you seek a nonsecretarial position, avoid describing your work experience in secretarial terms. See chapter 1 (Barbara Wilkinson's example).

3.   Express your background and experience in ways that work for you, not against you.

Dos	*Don'ts*
• Explain your experience fully using action verbs (see chapter 4). • Turn your worst negatives (you were fired, overage, lacked a college degree) into positives. • Identify personal interests such as tennis or bridge which show you are a "people" person (competitive), particularly if applying for sales or other people-oriented jobs. • Take credit for projects you had a part in (see chapter 1). • Show a progression in job responsibilities.	• Avoid self-praise. • Avoid describing yourself as a job hopper. • Don't undersell yourself. Reach above your current position (not laterally or below it). • Never mention your salary in writing, even if an ad you are answering asks for it. If the ad doesn't mention salary but asks you to tell yours, just state in your cover letter, "My salary is competitive."

4.   Select those aspects of your background and work experience that *most closely* fit the position you are seeking. The process used to accomplish this objective is covered extensively in chapter 5.

Defining Job Tasks

So let's work on the list. What tasks (paid and/or voluntary) of a constructive nature have you done that turned out well? To answer this question adequately you need a set of simple but effective guidelines for measuring accomplishments. These guidelines have two parts: (1) the *actions* you took and (2) *results* you achieved. A typical *action* list would look like this.

- Developed special seasonal and nonseasonal promotions.
- Opened up new markets for existing products and services.
- Increased the caseload of clients.
- Selected products for major promotions.
- Established markets for overruns and irregular goods.
- Reduced personnel and labor costs.
- Reduced average order-filling, turn-around time.
- Carried out an analysis of . . .

To show the logical transition of *actions* to *results*, we have selected a number of examples from the above list and added typical results.

Actions	*Results*
• Developed special seasonal and non-seasonal promotions	A 34% increase in sales the first year
• Established markets for overruns and irregular goods	Inventories reduced by 27.4% while profits increased by 3.2%
• Reduced personnel and labor costs	Departmental production remained at a constant level but ran less expensively
• Reduced average order-filling, turn-around time	A $7,430 saving in overtime costs per quarter

In describing work experience, most people simply review the list of jobs and titles they have held, and then proceed to identify their areas of responsibility. An exceptional social worker recently reported her experience in this fashion:

1978–Present   City Department of Social Services
Social Worker   Philadelphia, Pennsylvania

- Responsible for long-term intervention with families.
- Helped organize an activity group.
- Performed client advisory role.
- Fieldwork supervisor for undergraduate social work students.
- Helped with the design of a community outreach project.
- Evaluated natural parents' grievances.
- Worked with parents to determine if they were able to resume child care.
- Provided child protective services when needed.
- Attended several maternity shelter conferences.

A second example of this approach, that of merely *describing* your responsibilities, is illustrated below. However, good "action" verbs are used.

1977–Present   ACME Foods
Sales Manager   Spokane, Washington

- Worked to increase sales.
- Helped rebuild the field sales force.
- Recruited and trained salesmen and brokers.
- With two other managers, revised the incentive program.
- Introduced new products to customers.
- Developed some new packaging ideas.
- Conducted sales and training meetings on a weekly basis.
- Contacted and maintained liaison with major chain accounts and wholesalers.
- Forecast budgets and sales for my department.
- Supervised 4 sales representatives and 18 food brokers.
- Developed sales programs for major accounts.
- Originated a plan for coverage of accounts based on sales, price, volume, potential, and expense.

If we analyze the above list of job responsibilities, we can see a pattern developing. Each item uses an action verb, such as *increased, recruited, developed, reduced, selected,* or *conducted.* Though action verbs are a very important element in describing work experience, they cannot be relied upon exclusively to carry this burden. Action verbs need to be properly introduced and explained in order to achieve their full effect. To accomplish this, we suggest using the Problem-Action-Result format described below.

These approaches are somewhat typical of the ways in which many of you would describe your work experiences in a résumé, but they contain major weaknesses.

1. They only *list* areas of responsibility rather than showing how these responsibilities were carried out. There are no conclusions, only statements. To show that you are "responsible for" a particular area does not communicate to the reader of your résumé or letter how *effectively* you carried out your responsibilities. Perhaps you were terrible and got demoted or fired!

2. A list of "responsibilities" also fails to communicate what specific problems you were hired to solve.

Improving Your "Marketing Materials"

To put it in a nutshell, to increase the effectiveness of your job hunt, you must improve the quality of your "marketing materials" (your résumé, cover letters, or action letters). Being specific is much more effective than being general. Instead of stating responsibilities in a general way, describe your experience in terms of (1) the problems you were hired to solve, (2) the actions you took to solve them, and (3) the results you were able to achieve (positive or negative).

☞ *Insiders' Tip:*   Our experience shows that even when a company advertises for a generalist, it usually hires a specialist. Therefore your written marketing materials should describe you as a specialist and as specifically as possible.

How to transform your experience from a general to a specific format:

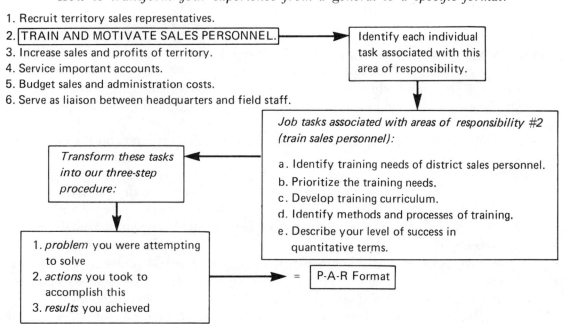

To create your list of job accomplishments so you can identify those things you enjoy doing and things you wish to avoid, it is necessary to follow the next four-step procedure.

Step 1   List *all* your experience chronologically. Cover all your paid business experience, your military experience as well as your nonjob or unpaid experience, including religious organizations, fraternal organizations, community service, and other volunteer work.

Step 2   For each experience, paid or not, develop a complete list of responsibilities.

Step 3   For each *area* of responsibility, develop a complete list of job tasks.

Step 4   Describe these job tasks in the P-A-R format; that is, the *problems* you were attempting to solve, the *actions* you took, and the *results* you achieved.

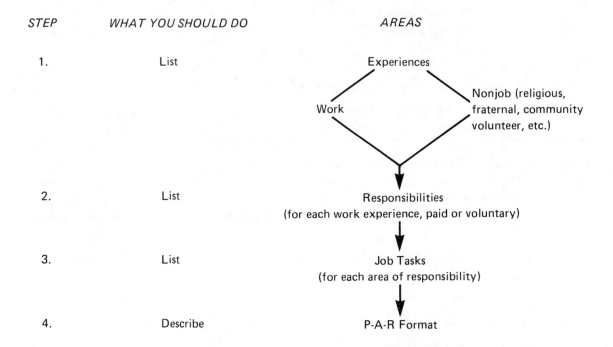

STEP	WHAT YOU SHOULD DO	AREAS
1.	List	Experiences — Work / Nonjob (religious, fraternal, community volunteer, etc.)
2.	List	Responsibilities (for each work experience, paid or voluntary)
3.	List	Job Tasks (for each area of responsibility)
4.	Describe	P-A-R Format

Make No Mistake: Career Changing Is Hard Work

Two issues need to be addressed here. First of all, is career changing worth the effort? And second, are the time and effort required more than you would normally spend using your former methods of job hunting?

Regarding the issue of whether an extensive job effort is worth the effort, consider the following points.

1.   Most of you will live twenty or thirty years beyond your fiftieth birthdays. Will you have the financial means to enjoy your ten, fifteen, or more years of retirement? You will if you plan your career properly. Part of that planning is making the correct career switch(es).

2.   In 1970 executives used the yardstick for success of $1,000 earned for each year of age he or she had attained. That is, if you are currently thirty-seven years old, you should be earning $37,000 per year! In the 1980s, because of inflation, the figure is $1,300 for each year of age (and this *may* be a conservative estimate). Based upon

this yardstick, *how well are you doing?* How can you expect to improve your earning capability without working hard on your job campaign?

A rule of thumb that job seekers have found is to expect to spend, for every thousand dollars of anticipated income, one week looking for work. In other words, if you want to obtain a new job paying $32,000, you must expect to be looking for a period of approximately 32 weeks. Even with professional help, if you are unemployed and looking, the time required to get a new job is quite substantial. Outplacement companies, those that employ people who specialize in helping fired employees, reported in *Forbes*, January 19, 1981, that white-collar workers

- who had been earning over $40,000 and who were forty years of age took 4 to 6 months to find another job,
- who had been earning between $20,000 and $39,000 and who were under forty took 2 to 4 months.

3. Recent studies on the quality of work in America indicate that fully 85 percent of the workers in this country are not satisfied with their jobs and the *psychic* benefits. Are you one of these people? Do you want to find a more fulfilling job? Without working hard at doing so? If you weren't "lucky" in the past, why do you think the future will be any different?

Business Week reported in the February 5, 1981, issue that "according to a study by the National Commission on Working Women, the average woman worker is a lonely person in a dead-end job, seething with frustration over her lot." The number of women at work is expected to have risen from 48.4 percent in 1977 to 60 percent by 1989. Yet this study, which is based on the results of over 150,000 questionnaires, found that "40% felt that their jobs were boring and did not utilize their skills," and 60 percent named lack of advancement opportunity as their major obstacle on the job. Although the statistics for men would be different, these points affect them too.

The second point of consideration in "job hunting is hard work" is whether the time and effort required to apply the strategies of *Career Changing* are more than you would normally spend using traditional methods.

Although the effort involved is probably the same as in the usual ones, the methods discussed in this book may require a greater degree of *concentrated* effort. However, we believe that the time you spend to obtain a successful switch will be appreciably less. There are a number of reasons for this. First, the frustrations usually associated with a job search have been eliminated or reduced to a minimum. Next, the "Insiders' Tips" that are provided throughout this book give you a clearer understanding of how the job market really functions.

Knowing these things will permit strict control of energy, effort, time, and money on your part. Third, the skills you will develop and the strategies you will employ, along with the experience you will gain from their application, will (a) have practical application for your next job, (b) provide you a level of psychic security few people have experienced before, and (c) will reduce sharply the amount of time, effort, and money required to effect all of your future switches successfully.

The P-A-R Process in Action

So much for theory. Let us look at the process by which a Problem-Action-Result (P-A-R) paragraph is developed.

We are in the home of Steve Walters in Saddle Brook, New Jersey. Steve is a thirty-eight-year-old regional sales manager for a small (625-employee) New Jersey–based business equipment service company. He has had sixteen years of sales experience with three companies and has a B.S. in marketing from New York University. Steve now finds his career advancement blocked and plans to switch to a larger company in order to increase the scope of his job responsibilities, raise his income, and move along in his career. To help him develop a résumé or letter, he has enlisted the aid of a friend who also works as a sales executive.

> ☞ *Insiders' Tip:*   To develop your own Problem-Action-Result (P-A-R) paragraphs, obtain the help of a friend or business associate who works in the *same field* or job area as you if you are staying in the same or similar work. If you're making a major switch (of job, title, or industry), find someone who can help you reorient your materials.

Below (written in the format of a script for a play) is an example of a conversation between Steve Walters and his friend. It helps to show a P-A-R paragraph evolving out of the give-and-take of their dialogue. Although you'll see some sales jargon, concentrate on the *process* of developing the P-A-R paragraph rather than its *content*.

Constructing the P-A-R Paragraph: Two Examples

Let's produce the body of a P-A-R paragraph in the job of greatest interest to Steve, that of sales manager. He identified this category by doing a want-ad analysis on sales manager ads. This method is quite easy. It consists of one person's (a friend's) asking questions of another person (Steve Walters, the person looking to switch jobs). During this process, the friend takes notes, which are later expanded and refined into a P-A-R paragraph. We recommend that you use a cassette tape recorder, which will help preserve the give-and-take of the questioning technique and will prevent the possible loss of any important thoughts or concepts.

The most important activity identified from the ten want ads Steve collected for his want-ad analysis was *"to maintain and strengthen existing business accounts."* Following our P-A-R format, the first part that needs to be defined is the *problem* that Steve was attempting to solve. In doing this kind of exercise, don't think in terms of how *you* see the problem, but rather what a hiring *organization* sees as the problem.

This is the conversation between Steve Walters and his friend.

FRIEND: In your company, what is the major problem you hoped to overcome as it related to maintaining existing business accounts?

STEVE: Let me think. I'd say it's reducing, if not totally eliminating, those bureaucratic errors which create customer dissatisfaction. I've always found it more difficult to get new business than to hold on to existing customers. So if bureaucratic mistakes could be reduced, my company's ability to retain its existing business base would be maintained.

FRIEND: How would you start your P-A-R paragraph?

STEVE: "In order to maintain our ..." I'm stuck! What is the common terminology we've seen in the want ads? Do they use *maintain accounts* or *prevent loss of accounts* more often?

FRIEND: In your want-ad analysis, the phrase *maintain accounts* is definitely used more often than *prevent loss of accounts.*

STEVE: Yeah, but I've always used *prevent loss of accounts.*

FRIEND: Well, maybe—but unless you start using the jargon we identified from your want-ad analysis, anyone who reads your letter or résumé will see you as an outsider. Don't forget, Steve, you've been employed by the same company for nine years. Terminology has changed somewhat over the past few years.

STEVE: OK. I understand what you're saying.

FRIEND: Then you can begin your P-A-R paragraph as follows: "To maintain existing business accounts ..." What types of things did you do to prevent these losses?

STEVE: (Pause) I did a number of things. I interviewed customers by phone, in person, and by written questionnaires to determine what problems they were having. I questioned the drivers of our delivery trucks and I reviewed our customer service records to see if I could spot problem areas. I had another source of data too, the weekly field reports submitted by my sales reps.

FRIEND: (After finishing jotting down brief notes) A thought came to me while I was taking notes. What are you specifically trying to accomplish when you say you want to maintain business accounts?

STEVE: To maintain the highest possible level of equipment rental!

FRIEND: That's better. Here's what I've written down so far. (Reading from his notes, as he starts to write the P-A-R paragraph) To maintain the highest level of equipment rental, I ...

☞ *Insiders' Tip:* Whenever possible, express your experience in *positive* instead of negative terms. Example: "To maintain the highest level of equipment rental" reads more positively than "to prevent the *loss* of business accounts."

STEVE: It sounds pretty good so far.

FRIEND: Let's now add the *action* part. "To maintain the highest level of equipment rental, I ... (pause, reviews his notes) interviewed customers, questioned our delivery truck drivers, and reviewed accounts receivable records as the basis for improvement in service." How does that sound?

STEVE: OK, but it only *describes* the fact-finding phase. What about the ways I *improved* service?

FRIEND: Let me try and add what you just said to your P-A-R paragraph. "To maintain the highest level of equipment rental, I interviewed customers and delivery drivers and reviewed customer service records to determine a basis for service improvement. I established feedback mechanisms through monthly questionnaires, weekly driver reports, and daily review of customer service incident reports." Steve, how successful were these information feedback mechanisms?

STEVE: I have the lowest customer attrition rate in the company.

FRIEND: How many sales regions are there in your company?

STEVE: We have twelve regions.

FRIEND: When you say "lowest" attrition rate, can you quantify that for me?

STEVE: I think so. (Steve enters some figures on his calculator.) I was consistently under one percent attrition each month.

FRIEND: OK. How is this for your *result?* "This resulted in the lowest customer attrition rate throughout the company's twelve sales regions: consistently under one percent per month."

STEVE: Sounds good to me.

Their discussion having ended, Steve's friend then put all three parts of the P-A-R paragraph together for their mutual review. Below is their completed paragraph.

To maintain the highest level of equipment rental, I interviewed customers and delivery drivers and reviewed customer service records as the basis for service improvement. I established feedback mechanisms through monthly customer questionnaires, weekly driver reports, and daily review of customer service incident reports. This resulted in the lowest customer attrition rate throughout the company's twelve (12) sales regions: consistently under 1% per month.

PROBLEM: To maintain the highest level of equipment rental.

ACTION: I *interviewed* customers and delivery drivers and *reviewed* customer service records as the basis for service improvement. I *established* feedback mechanisms through monthly customer questionnaires, weekly driver reports, and daily *review* of customer service incident reports.

RESULT: This resulted in the lowest customer attrition rate throughout the company's twelve (12) sales regions: consistently under 1% per month.

This conversation between Steve Walters and his friend was a simple re-creation of the process used to develop any P-A-R paragraph. To increase your understanding of this process further, so that you can use it to develop your own P-A-R paragraphs, we will show you another, more elaborate conversation. Only slightly altered, it represents the recorded conversation of a job hunter and his friend. Certain concepts that appeared in our first P-A-R script are deliberately repeated in the second conversation for the purpose of emphasis. In addition, more Insiders' Tips are provided.

We are in the home of Ellen Jacobs in Stamford, Connecticut. Ellen is a thirty-seven-year-old union negotiator for a Washington-based professional transportation association. She has sixteen years of labor relations and union negotiations experience and two degrees, a B.S. from the School of Industrial and Labor Relations at Cornell University and an M.B.A. from Georgetown University. Ellen finds herself at a dead end with her employer of fourteen years. To revive her career, she hopes to switch from a "public sector" career to one in private industry. Ellen has enlisted the help of a friend who works in a major manufacturing company as a labor-relations specialist. This illustrates how a P-A-R paragraph results from their discussion. Although, as before, there is a lot of industry jargon, notice the *process* of digging out the P-A-R format rather than the *content* of the dialogue. Once you understand this process, you will be able to repeat it, assisted by a friend or business associate, and develop your own P-A-R paragraphs.

As above, one person (the friend) asks questions of the other (Ellen Jacobs). As before, the friend takes notes, which the pair expand and refine into a P-A-R paragraph. A cassette tape recorder, as we've suggested, will help the participants remember any significant ideas.

From her want-ad analysis, Ellen decided that "administering the union contract" was her chief concern. The first P-A-R part needing definition is Ellen's *problem*. Remember, think in terms of what the *organization* sees as the problem, rather than *your* problem.

FRIEND: As far as your organization is concerned, what is the major problem you address in administering a union's contract?

ELLEN: Well, from my experience I'd say it's whether management can interpret a rule to mean something particular. . . whether they are allowed to require that work be performed in a particular manner as they view the contract.

FRIEND: How could we start your P-A-R paragraph?

ELLEN "In order to interpret . . ." What is the usual terminology that we have seen used in the want ads? Do they use the term *contract* or *collective bargaining unit* more often?

FRIEND: In your want-ad analysis ads, the term *contract* is definitely used more often than *collective bargaining unit*. In fact, it's used in eight out of ten ads.

ELLEN: But I've always called it a *collective bargaining unit*.

FRIEND: That's all well and good, but unless you use the jargon that currently appears in ads, a company will view you as an outsider to the field. Don't forget, terminology has changed since you began working fourteen years ago. The terminology used by corporations is different from what you've learned.

ELLEN: I see what you mean. I guess the term *contract* could also refer to a side letter of agreement as well as to the basic contract.

FRIEND: OK. So far we have "In order to interpret the contract. . ." Now, do you just want to concentrate on your side of the negotiating table, or do you think it's better to present both sides?

ELLEN: Since I'm trying to switch from the union side to the management side, I think it's better to expand it to encompass both. In reality, I act like a consultant to both sides, anyway. After all, if a contract is too one-sided toward the union, and management can't make any profit, then the company would go out of business and our union members would be unemployed. So I have to be fair to management too.

FRIEND: I'll jot that down. So far we have "In order to interpret the contract . . ." Should it read: "to the company's advantage" or "the organization's advantage"?

ELLEN: Well, the interpretation has been made by the company to *their* advantage. Obviously it is to their advantage, otherwise they wouldn't have done it. Now, I try to figure out what the correct approach is concerning the contract so I can advise the union people who want to file grievances. I have further discussions about it to determine if I should take a firm or not-so-firm position. Or maybe I just ignore the issue.

FRIEND: Then what are you trying to achieve in terms of the interpretation of the contract?

ELLEN: The *intent* of the agreement at the time the contract is signed.

FRIEND: Then can we say: "In order to interpret the contract to achieve the full intent of the agreement"?

ELLEN: Yes, but I would like to get the concept of my impartiality somewhere in this sentence. Maybe I could add to the sentence that I was an advocate of my organization?

FRIEND: I understand what you're saying, but don't we achieve more by leaving the advocate issue out of the sentence? After all, none of the ads asks for an advocate, but rather an administrator of the contract!

ELLEN: OK. I'll agree with that. Leave "advocate" out.

FRIEND: Then our description of "P" (*Problem*) from the P-A-R format is finished. Let me read what we have so far: "In order to interpret a contract to achieve the full intent of the agreement . . ."
Good. But don't we assume that the agreement has already been read? It's a question of rereading the agreement, isn't it?

ELLEN: Yes, true. Also, I review similar circumstances to determine a consistency of application. (In other words, what led to the problem?)

FRIEND: Let's see if this answers the "A" part of our P-A-R format.

- Discuss the facts and circumstances of the point at issue.
- Research the negotiating history with its accompanying documentation.
- Review earlier discussions with interested personnel.
- Reread the agreement.
- Review similar circumstances to determine a consistency of application. (That is, what led to the problem?)

Do we gain anything by presenting these actions in a particular order?

ELLEN: I'm not sure, but there is a logical and normal progression to these steps. "Discussion with the people" would come first while "research the negotiating history" would be last, since it involved getting into deep research.

FRIEND: Do we "reread the agreement" first, or do we "review similar circumstances"?

ELLEN: We reread the agreement.

FRIEND: OK, fine; so we have the proper order. Let me read you the first two parts ("P" and "A") of the paragraph. "In interpreting the contract to achieve the full intent of the agreement, I discuss with interested personnel the facts and circumstances of the points at issue; I reread the agreement; I review similar circumstances to determine a consistency of application (that is, what led to the problem?), and then I research the negotiating history with its accompanying documentation."

ELLEN: Not bad! But we'll have to tighten it later. That brings us to the "R" part of the P-A-R format. This is the part I have trouble with.

FRIEND: How do you document to the reader's satisfaction how successful you were?

☞ *Insiders' Tip:* The value of what Ellen just did is the hardest to assess. To overcome the hurdle of documentation, be specific and quantify your results.

☞ *Insiders' Tip:* It is perfectly all right to report a *negative* result in your work history. Very often, negative data are useful to an organization as they provide information for decision-making. Examples: Surplus inventories to be reduced, eliminating a communications bottleneck. *Typical example:* After spending six months reviewing a possible company acquisition, a manager of corporate planning decided it would not be in his company's best interests to buy this particular company (even though the president wanted it). *Reasons:* The *price-earnings ratios* were not good, *the debt to equity ratios* were terrible, people were quitting left and right, etc. It was an unpopular decision, but he reported the negatives. On the basis of his report, his corporation did not buy the little company. Later, another firm did buy it and they consistently lost money on it, eventually selling it off. The company *was* in terrible shape, as had already been determined.

ELLEN: I was successful in resolving almost all grievances without having to go to arbitration. Probably ninety-five percent successful, to quantify it.

FRIEND: Were you able to do this within a specific time limit?

ELLEN: No. Some issues take months or even years to resolve. When you deal with small, financially unstable companies who have small labor-relations staffs, it's difficult for them to block out large chunks of time, aside from contract negotiations.

FRIEND: What do you mean by small? A hundred-million-dollar company versus a two-billion-dollar company?

ELLEN: In terms of my industry, transportation, I mean a regional carrier or lines above the commuter level as opposed to the big trunk lines.

☞ *Insiders' Tip:*   The jargon Ellen uses is indigenous to only the transportation industry. The reader of her job-hunting letter might (1) not know this jargon or (2) not be able to tell what industry she's in as a labor negotiator. But if you *are* too specific as to which industry you're in, you may not get the initial interview. A reader of Ellen's letter might conclude that because she works in transportation, she might not be well suited to the reader's industry, which might be consumer packaged goods or manufacturing. This type of prejudice (the reader jumps to conclusions based only on the information contained in the letter) is quite common and must be avoided. Your marketing materials should include *only* that information which will help you to get interviews. Leave out any specific facts which the reader can use against you (that is, *not* bring you in for the interview). The time to cover sensitive information is during the interview itself, when you can adequately explain any extenuating circumstances.

ELLEN: By "small companies" I mean ones that have fewer than five hundred employees.

FRIEND: That's a better way of defining "small." Can we say, "Five hundred employees in the bargaining unit"?

☞ *Insiders' Tip:*   The ability to choose when to be specific and when to be general will make you an experienced and successful job hunter. With your examples, try to be specific so the reader doesn't jump to erroneous conclusions. Give the reader facts instead of making him/her draw inferences. Your letter or résumé should *answer* questions for the reader, not raise them.

For example, the term *small companies* is open to a wide range of interpretation. *Small* is viewed differently by a personnel vice president in a $4 billion giant from the way an executive of a $15 million company views it. Therefore, *500 employees in the bargaining unit* is preferable to the word *small*.

FRIEND: OK. Let's see what we have in your section on results. "Resolved ninety-five percent of the grievances without a need to go to arbitration."

ELLEN: Maybe we should characterize the types of case I was dealing with.

FRIEND: That's a good idea. It's specific rather than general. It also allows us to get some jargon into your paragraph.

ELLEN: My cases involved issues of contract terms, seniority questions, pension issues, work rules, and compensation.

> ☞ *Insiders' Tip:*   The use of jargon in this case works in the candidate's (Ellen's) favor. Jargon tells the reader the person is experienced in a particular job category: she is an insider. Proper use of jargon allows the job applicant to speak the language of the prospective reader/employer.

FRIEND: I think we can finish the paragraph. "Resolved ninety-four-point one percent of the grievances related to union/management questions on work rules, compensation, pension, and seniority without a need to go to arbitration, in companies with five hundred or fewer employees constituting the collective bargaining unit."

> ☞ *Insiders' Tip:*   When developing your written marketing materials, avoid using numbers that end in 5 or 0, unless they are *real* figures. They look contrived or estimated. Instead, use decimal numbers and percentages such as 94.1 percent rather than 95 percent. These will be assumed to reflect an actual figure from your work experience. Example: "Increased new profits 23 percent" (not 25 percent); "decreased department personnel 37.5 percent" (not "16 people to 10 people"); "increased sales $37,484 in the first quarter," not "$40,000."

Here is a rough draft of the completed P-A-R paragraph that Ellen Jacobs developed with the help of her friend.

> As contract administrator for a large professional organization, I am responsible for interpreting the contract to achieve the full intent of the agreement. To accomplish this, I discuss with interested parties the facts and circumstances of the point(s) at issue, evaluate the applicable portions of the agreement, review similar circumstances to determine a consistency of application (i.e., what led to the problem?), and research the negotiating history with its accompanying documentation. This has resulted in a resolution of 94.1 percent of the grievances related to questions of work rules, compensation, pension, and seniority without a need to go to arbitration.

After reviewing this draft, Ellen was able to tighten up the paragraph by eliminating nonessential phrases and simplifying the language. The results of Ellen's efforts are reflected in the next paragraph.

> As an industrial relations manager for a large professional organization, I am responsible for interpreting contracts. To accomplish this I discuss with interested parties the facts and circumstances at issue, evaluate the applicable portions of the agreement, review similar circumstances to determine past practice, and research the negotiating history. This has resulted in a resolution of 97.8 percent of contractual grievances without arbitration.

Before summarizing the P-A-R technique, let us analyze the discussion between Ellen Jacobs and her friend. Ellen and her friend encountered the greatest difficulty when they attempted to define the *problem.* As you read this section, you may have found it somewhat confusing. This confusion was mainly due to Ellen's vagueness and lack of direction. When Ellen's friend asked her to define the *problem* ("As far as *your* organization is concerned, what is the major problem you hoped to overcome?"), Ellen's response was general, almost tangential. The reason for this obliqueness is simple: the discussion between Ellen and her friend is a real conversation. If you followed the discussion closely you saw that the clarification resulted from the question-and-answer method of the counseling session. This process is very typical of the P-A-R approach. The counseling session begins with groping for information.

As the question-and-answer session continues, the friend further helps Ellen to clarify her thoughts, sorting the information into a well-defined problem. Later this same process is applied toward defining the *action* and the *result*.

The vagueness, the generality of the thoughts and statements, is typical. Do not allow it to frustrate you. Recognize that it is natural and necessary to the P-A-R process. The specifics develop from the general dialogue—once the direction is provided by the good listener.

Summary

To achieve a strong, concise P-A-R paragraph that accurately describes your experiences in the best possible way, simply follow the questioning procedure outlined above and try to include most of these key points:

- Use the same jargon that appeared in your want-ad analysis.
- Present your experience as a means of solving a specific problem.
- Include only data that work to your advantage.
- Present your "Problem" in general terms, but the "Action" and "Results" in specific terms.
- Present your "Action" data in a logical sequence using action words (see examples in chapter 4.)
- Quantify your "Results" using real figures (for example, 94.1 percent rather than 95 percent).
- Don't be wordy; wordiness shows you don't think clearly. Keep each sentence to a maximum of ten to twelve words. Keep each paragraph to a maximum of three to four sentences.

When describing your work history in the P-A-R format, remember to select experiences that were real and major accomplishments. For example: has your analysis of the functioning of your department ever resulted in major improvements? Have you ever worked on a project that expanded the nature of your company's business? Have the people you recruited and trained been promoted to more responsible positions?

A Portfolio of Sample P-A-R Paragraphs

For reference we have included additional examples of P-A-R paragraphs from various job categories. The action verbs used are italicized.

Training

To increase the effectiveness of employee communications throughout the organization, I *negotiated* the purchase and adoption of the American Airlines customer treatment program. I *selected* and *trained* 20 discussion leaders, then *supervised* the implementation of the 14-week program for 5,108 employees. Evaluation included questionnaires, interviews, and (random) analysis of employee job performance, which resulted in an average improvement of 22 percent above initial performance levels.

Problem: To increase the effectiveness of employee communications throughout the organization.

Action: I *negotiated* the purchase and adoption of the American Airlines customer treatment program. I *selected* and *trained* 20 discussion leaders, then *supervised* the implementation of the 14-week program for 5,108 employees.

Results: Evaluation included questionnaires, interviews, and (random) analysis of employee job performance, which resulted in an average improvement of 22 percent above initial performance levels.

Personnel

To improve the reporting of status changes in personnel, I interviewed department heads and administrators in order to produce an instruction manual with flowcharts. It explained the steps required in each of 34 methods to revise an employee's status. I conducted seminars on the personnel action form and manual for managers. I reduced errors from an average of 31 per day to 6.

Problem: To improve the reporting of personnel status changes.

Action: I *interviewed* department heads and administrators in order to *produce* an instruction manual with flowcharts. It explained the steps required in each of 34 methods to revise an employee's status.
I *conducted* seminars on the personnel action form and manual for managers.

Results: I *reduced* errors from an average of 31 per day to 6.

Hospital Administration

To centralize administrative functions, I interviewed key staff members, assessed the types of work required and the methods to accomplish them. I developed job descriptions and instituted clerical procedures to replace arbitrary use of staff by physicians. I created lists of job tasks and trained staff in their functions to permit rotational assignments. These changes had organizationwide effects and resulted in improved morale, cooperation, and initiative, and allowed closer supervision of clerical staff.

Problem: To centralize administrative functions.

Action: I *interviewed* key staff members, *assessed* the types of work required and the methods to accomplish them. I *developed* job descriptions and *instituted* clerical procedures to replace arbitrary use of staff by physicians. I *created* lists of job tasks and *trained* staff in their functions to permit rotational assignments.

Results: These changes had organizationwide effects and resulted in improved morale, cooperation, and initiative, and allowed closer supervision of clerical staff.

NOTE: In this example the hospital administrator was *not* able to quantify her *results*. Though the P-A-R paragraph is not as strong as if the results had been quantified, this format is perfectly permissible.

Stock and Securities Sales Assistance

I screened and handled all customer inquiries, including instructions for buying and selling securities and changes in the status of accounts. By being a good listener and using my ability to placate irate customers, I was able to overcome hostility and then satisfy their business needs. This resulted in the stockbrokers' having more time to call clients and sell securities.

Problem: To placate irate customers.

Action: I *screened* and *handled* all customer inquiries, including instructions for buying and selling securities and changes in the status of accounts. By being a good listener and using my ability to placate irate customers, I was able to *overcome* hostility and then *satisfy* their business needs.

Results: This resulted in the stockbrokers' having more time to call clients and sell securities.

Retail Buying

To improve relationships with vendors, I initiated continuous verbal and written communications. Consequently, I planned advertising and inventory levels with vendors and documented advertising agreements. I then negotiated return privileges or markdown money with 72.7 percent of my manufacturers.

Problem: To improve relationships with vendors.

Action: I *initiated* continuous verbal and written communications. Consequently, I *planned* advertising and inventory levels with vendors and *documented* advertising agreements.

Results: I then *negotiated* return privileges or markdown money with 72.7 percent of my manufacturers.

Being a Travel Agent

To satisfy the overseas travel needs of a large midwestern Shriners' organization, I determined the requirements and limitations of my client. Within that framework, I arranged for transportation, accommodations, meals, transfers, sightseeing trips, excursions, and banquets for a group of 335 people. I also coordinated the work of support staff in four countries. This resulted in a 17.4 percent increase in bookings the first year and a 27.8 percent increase in repeat business the second year.

Problem: To satisfy the overseas travel needs of a large midwestern Shriners' organization.

Action: I *determined* the requirements and limitations of my client. Within that framework, I *arranged* for transportation, accommodations, meals, transfers, sightseeing trips, excursions, and banquets for a group of 335 people. I also *coordinated* the work of support staff in four countries.

Results: This resulted in a 17.4 percent increase in bookings the first year and a 27.8 percent increase in repeat business the second year.

Marketing Magazines

To increase sales, I developed and implemented a new concept called split logo, which enabled supermarket chains to sell two different monthly magazines, having an on-sale date 15 days apart, out of the same checkout pocket. This gave the chains 26 turns instead of 12. When the concept was implemented, a major publisher gained 73,210 new checkout locations for its magazines and increased sales of its leading women's fashion magazine from 779,826 copies per month to 1,274,533 in only 2 years, an increase of 63.4 percent. I achieved this at 60 percent of the normal cost for checkout pockets.

Problem: To increase sales.

Action: I *developed* and *implemented* a new concept called split logo which enabled supermarket chains to sell two different monthly magazines having an on-sale date 15 days apart, out of the same checkout pocket.

Results: This gave the chains 26 turns instead of 12. When the concept was implemented, a major publisher gained 73,210 new checkout locations for its magazines and increased sales of its leading women's fashion magazine from 779,826 copies per month to 1,274,533 in only 2 years, an increase of 63.4 percent. I *achieved* this at 60 percent of the normal cost for checkout pockets.

4. Résumés: Oh, No—Not Again!

> "We do not really see ourselves. All mirrors are in fact quite useless except the living, human mirrors who reflect us: they do not lie."
>
> —François Mauriac

The issue of the résumé—how it should be constructed, the various forms it can take, and the ways in which it is used—has, in recent years, generated a vast library of material. We will be approaching this issue in a non-traditional fashion. From our discussion there will emerge a specific philosophy contrary to much of today's conventional wisdom about résumés. Though we do not expect to convert everyone to our point of view, we believe that a careful review of this chapter will provide you with some new insights. These can greatly improve the effectiveness of your switching strategies.

The Ten-Second Story, or How Personnel Departments View Your Résumé

When you mail your résumé in response to an advertisement what actually happens to it? With only minor variations, there is one pattern followed. To illustrate, let's follow a typical candidate's response to this ad for a product manager.

Product Manager
Entrepreneurial Specialist

Growth-oriented consumer package goods manufacturer headquartered in suburban northern New Jersey seeks a seasoned marketing specialist to assume a key decision-making position. We seek a "hands-on" strategist, capable of assuming total responsibility for marketing, promotion strategy, packaging, budgeting, copy, media, forecasting, as well as new product development. The individual we are seeking will be capable of combining creative strength with organizational ability. This is a highly visible opportunity for an innovative, implementation-oriented specialist with 3–5 years related experience. We offer a generous salary and competitive benefits package. Forward résumé including salary history in confidence to Y9274.

Since this is a "blind" ad, that is, the organization has chosen not to identify itself, the candidate must forward his response to the box number, "Y9274," to the mailing address of the newspaper, magazine, or journal in which it appeared. Even if he responds the day he sees the ad, it will take several days to reach the publication. It will then take two to six business days for the publication to forward his response to the person in the company who placed the ad.

☞ *Insiders' Tip:* Responses to *blind* ads take about seven to ten days longer to reach the organization that advertised than do *open* ads, which identify themselves by company name and address.

Ads are usually placed by personnel ("human resources") people. If the advertisement is fairly large and appears in the financial or business section of a major newspaper, it can generate more than eight hundred responses. To appreciate how one résumé is treated in this kind of avalanche, let's continue.

The résumés and letters are opened as received by a secretary or personnel assistant, stamped with the department's name and the date received, then placed on the desk of the person screening the responses. Depending on his or her schedule, this pile of papers may be reviewed right away or left untouched for a week. Receiving *your* response to an ad, particularly an ad that generated upward of three hundred to five hundred résumés and letters, is not the most important event in the workday of a typical personnel person. Responding to telephone requests by senior managers, handling a sticky employee termination, meeting with union delegates, and directing subordinates all take precedence over a day's mail. That's why it always seems an inordinately long time between your answering an ad and getting a response, be it positive or negative. Companies run blind ads so they do *not* have to respond to your résumé. Sending out five hundred or more "Thank you, but no thank you" letters becomes an extremely expensive and time-consuming task.

Pretend you are the personnel representative for this job at Company X and have decided to review the first two days' mail. Almost all of the responses consist of a résumé with an accompanying cover letter or just the résumé.

Fewer than 8 percent are "action" letters. This is the first time you are reviewing responses to this ad, so you read the cover letter and the résumé in their entirety. You soon realize that you will tire of being so thorough. It will take you too long to do it this way. In 2 hours you have read only 36 résumés and you still have 108 to go! You now learn to do what all personnel recruiters do: *skim.* But, when skimming, what do you look for? Most personnel professionals use what we call *the ten-second story,* a method used to match résumés against specific criteria.

1. Are you a "job hopper"?	If you have spent two years or less in each job held (particularly your most recent two or three positions), you are considered a job hopper. Holding seven or eight full-time jobs in fifteen years is *not* acceptable, no matter what the reasons.
2. Is there a progression in your job responsibilities and titles?	If your résumé fails to show a progression in job titles and responsibility, you will not be considered. Though experienced in one given area, you will be viewed as not being very aggressive or promotable.
3. Is there a progression in salary throughout your career?	The most meaningful form of recognition in private industry is financial reward. Salary (in dollars) should not be mentioned, if upward title changes are shown. From this the reader knows that your salary was increased. Some companies reward performance with perquisites other than salary or bonus but if "rewards" are not reflected in steady increases, your real value to any organization is marginal.

It takes a personnel professional only ten or fifteen seconds to review a résumé for these three indicators. If your résumé is found wanting, it ends up in the "circular file."

To accomplish a successful switch, you must pass the ten-second story with good grades. This may be difficult if you have deficiencies in some or all of the above criteria. However, you can overcome these weaknesses by being able to answer the following questions:

1. Are your marketing materials (résumé or letter) logical and well thought out? Or do they tell the reader that you haven't spent much time or effort in developing them?
2. Does your action letter and/or résumé give evidence that you are a generalist or a specialist?
3. Does your action letter or résumé contain information that can be viewed as negative? Are you providing too much information? (A common error often made when writing résumés. This is *not* true-confessions time.)

Developing strategies to overcome any ten-second story objections will be discussed later in this chapter. At this point, let's review what a résumé is and what it is not.

The Résumé: An Introduction

A résumé is a series of carefully selected facts, deliberately arranged to create impressions and conclusions about *you*. In short, it is a marketing tool, your advertisement for yourself. *The objective of a résumé is to introduce you to an organization for the purpose of obtaining an interview and job offer.*

What a Résumé Is Not

It is *not* a short chronological list of your job titles and responsibilities.
It is *not* an essay.
It is *not* an autobiography.
It is *not* an employment application.

What a Good Résumé Is or Does

1. A sales piece that attempts to sell a product: YOU.

2. A means of packaging your *relevant* work and educational experience.

3. Should cause you to get more interviews than the competition.

4. Should be specific rather than general.

1. In any organization, you only have one chance to make a good first impression. It is vital that your résumé sells you as effectively as possible.

2. Your résumé generally precedes you before an interview is granted. Good packaging techniques should be used to maximize your chances for success in gaining that interview.

3. Your résumé should be constructed to maximize the number of interviews you can obtain.

4. Regardless of what employers say in want ads, they seldom hire generalists. All employers want to hire winners (persons who can contribute to profits), and most winners are specialists or they have distinct strengths in several areas.

5. Presents facts in a carefully selected manner.

5. Most résumés suffer from the disease of too much information. Overabundance of data will eliminate you from job interviews (more on this later).

6. Written for a specific, well-defined audience.

6. Each job in which you have an interest may require a separate and distinct résumé. Failure to customize your résumé, when necessary, will prevent interviews from being granted.

Profit: The Language of the Person Who Will Hire You

Though few people in business will directly say so, the *primary* purpose of a business organization is to perpetuate itself. To achieve this all-important objective, an organization must make a sufficient profit to meet its current obligations and to plan for the future. Everything else an organization does must take a back seat to profits. This is why "line" employees—sales, marketing, or production people—have greater risks and rewards than "staff" employees—those in personnel, administration, auditing, et cetera. The message for the person changing jobs is clear: show how your past experience can contribute to an employer's *future profits*, and the number of job interviews you get will increase dramatically. Again, remember that businesses exist to make *profits*.

The Résumé as a Marketing Tool

Two existing strategies can be adapted to help you, the serious job hunter, in your job search. One is used to market consumer products; the other is for getting writers published.

To switch jobs successfully you must remember that you are marketing a product and that the product is you. On page 69 we showed an ad for a product manager. Look at this job more closely; we'll show you how consumer companies market their products to the public.

Product managers, whether they work for giants like Procter & Gamble, General Foods, or smaller companies like Hudson Pharmaceutical Corporation, all use the same five methods to market existing consumer products.

Marketing an Existing Product—Five Steps

1. Identify the current market competition for your product.
2. See if the advertising and promotion budget allotted for your product is being well spent and how it is being spent.
3. Ask yourself: To whom is this product marketed? Do you have the right audience for this product? How well targeted is your buyer? (Too sophisticated? Not sophisticated enough?)
4. Develop incentives for the sales force to promote your product more effectively.
5. Check with manufacturing to see if the product is being competitively produced and priced. Maybe it's too costly compared to its competition. Should you repackage the product? If you keep the existing packaging, can it be less expensively produced?

Let's examine these five points and see how they apply to the search for a new job.

1. Identify Current Market Competition.   There is no accurate way to determine who will compete with you for a particular job. But one important assumption *can* be made: the job will be offered to the person who is best at *getting* that job (the person who did the best marketing, both on paper and at the interviews), not the person who necessarily has the best work qualifications for the job. Therefore, you must "out-market" your competition regardless of who they are, how many there are, or how well qualified they may be to perform the job. In the final analysis, what counts is whether or not you or someone else does the best selling job to the prospective employer.

2. Promotion Budget for Your Product.   You don't need to spend a lot of money in order to switch jobs. Don't waste your dollars on *expensive* job counseling (although some job counseling may be valuable), résumé preparation services, or professional typing or mailing services (see chapter 9). Successful job hunting is based on personal effort expended, not dollars spent.

   You must ask yourself, "How much time have I really spent promoting my product?" As mentioned in chapter 3, men typically spend four hours a week looking for work; women, three. When you use the techniques described in this book, you will not only spend time more productively promoting yourself than 99 percent of all other job hunters; you will get results. These will be more job interviews granted and more job offers received. You'll be working smarter, not harder.

3. To Whom Is the Product Marketed?   The problem of determining who should receive your résumé or action letter is not insurmountable. Our want-ad analysis technique, described in chapter 5, turns this problem into one of the strengths of your job campaign. Through systematic but simple analysis procedures, using the want-ad analysis forms, you can easily determine what kinds of jobs are being advertised and who's looking. This will greatly improve your ability to target your résumé and action letters.

4. Develop Incentives for the Sales Force to Promote Your Product.   Your "sales force" will be personnel departments and other people who read your "product" literature (résumé or letter) and who bring you in for an interview. If you're the person who can fill their job (contribute to profits), their lives are made a little easier. They can save time, effort, and money by not advertising again and not having to interview for weeks or months to select a candidate.

   These readers need to know if you (1) are credible, (2) have a good, dependable "product," and (3) can solve their problems. Later in this chapter the P-A-R format and its use in your résumé will show you how to achieve these goals.

5. Check with the Manufacturer.   Consumer products are never sold nationally until extensive test-marketing is done. This test-marketing should be done for the materials you use in your job campaign.

   Do you know how to test-market your résumé or action letter? Most people send out five to a hundred résumés, with cover letters, either in response to ads or as part of a mass effort to "cold-canvass" various employers. They receive negative responses or, worse, none at all. Conclusion? "It's a bad job market." It's *not* the job market but the résumés or letters they use that are not making the sale.

   Or the résumé is often sent to the wrong person at an organization.

> ☞ *Insiders' Tip:*   If you're not certain to whom to send your résumé (when cold-canvassing), send it to two or three different people within the same company who hold significant positions in areas that you wish to work in.
>
> Most job hunters fail to be persistent enough. This relates directly to the second major strategy that can aid you in overcoming other ten-second story deficiencies.

> ☞ *Insiders' Tip:*   Before doing a mass mailing of your résumé or action letter, ask friends and business associates whose opinions you respect (particularly if they hold higher-level positions than you do) to criticize your materials. Have them pretend to be the employer to whom you've sent your résumé.

Benefits from a Writer's Experience

All professional writers, including free-lancers, follow five rules to get published. After you examine these rules, you will be able to apply them to switching jobs, in general, and in overcoming any of the deficiencies of the ten-second story in particular.

Five Rules for Success in Writing

1. You must write.
2. You must finish what you write.
3. You must refrain from rewriting (until it's been field-tested).
4. You must place what you write on the market.
5. You must keep what you write on the market until you sell it.

That's it! It is a guaranteed way for getting anything published unless you are hopelessly untalented at writing! At closer scrutiny you will see that this is an excellent method of getting a new and better job.

Apply these rules to the job hunt and see how they work. The size of the work force, both reported by the federal government and those who work off the books, is approximately 100,000,000 people. At any one time, about 40 percent of this population is looking for new jobs: 40,000,000 people.

Nine out of ten people who *say* they are serious about looking for a new job never really get around to doing a viable job campaign. Most are trying to elicit sympathy from friends and business associates. That leaves 4,000,000 people.

Only about one in ten of this 4,000,000 who begin to write their résumés and cover letters ever completely finish them. (By "completely," we mean in the proper format, typewritten and printed without error, on one side of a piece of paper, and one or two pages in length.) That leaves 400,000 people who are serious.

Of those people who do finish their résumés, 90 percent won't leave well enough alone. They will discuss their prospective job hunt with anyone within earshot and constantly redo their résumés and letters. They rewrite and polish...and, most important, they will lose interest in sending them out. This brings the number to 40,000 serious job hunters at any one time: people who actually send their marketing pieces out in search of a new position in a consistent fashion.

So, off goes the résumé in response to an ad or to cold-canvass a specific company. Forty to 60 percent of these 40,000 people will get the usual reply: "Thanks, but no thanks!" A flow of rejections is hard to tolerate, particularly on a continuing basis. Sometimes a job hunter feels relieved when there is *no response* to the résumé or letter. At least it wasn't a rejection notice (very painful to the ego).

The average job hunter stops sending out résumés after one or two months of rejections or after having several unproductive interviews. Many become so discouraged that they put away their résumés and letters and become resigned to making the best of their current position; doing so is commonly known as settling.

Experience shows that only a small handful of determined job seekers (and of these "determined" people many are unemployed and must find work) will continue to send out their letters and résumés (usually in response to ads). But ads represent only about 15 percent of available job openings. Our persistent job hunter is overlooking 85 percent of the positions really available. Yet this small handful will keep sending out their materials, as many times as necessary, until one "sells" (gets the interview).

For you will get some interviews. If your work history has any merit at all (almost everyone's does), and you keep trying, eventually someone will request to see you face-to-face. To get these interviews, it is necessary to be stubborn, to continue to keep your résumés on the market. Lack of perseverance alone has probably eliminated 90 percent of the remaining job hunters.

These remaining survivors are spread over a wide range of job titles and levels. In actuality, the number of people who can compete and *qualify* for one particular job opening is probably less than four to five hundred nationwide. Geography is important too. Five hundred may qualify but only seventy-two of them may want to live in the part of the country where the job is located.

These figures are substantially accurate. In late 1980, Lloyd Feinstein was asked to recruit a senior level marketing and sales executive for one of Cadence's operating companies. The original ad is shown below.

PLANNING AND BUSINESS DEVELOPMENT EXECUTIVE

Fortune 1000, NYSE conglomerate seeks a top executive to develop corporate wide marketing and sales objectives, policies and pro-grams. Play a key role in our continued growth by developing long- and short-range marketing and sales strategies which maxi-mize impact on the "bottom line." Recommend new products and sources of distribution through development or acquisition. Reporting to the CEO, this highly visible position requires an aggressive, highly energetic degreed individual with extensive marketing, sales and P&L experience.
If your objectives include the opportunity to directly impact on an organization's growth and a competitive compensation package, send your résumé including complete salary history to: Box M

It appeared in a Tuesday edition of a major business journal in December and drew 297 responses.

A second ad, substantially rewritten, but looking for the same type of person, appeared in the business section of a Sunday newspaper in January.

SEASONED MARKETING/SALES PROFESSIONAL

Fortune 1000, NYSE corporation seeks an experienced "pro" with
entrepreneurial flair to develop marketing and sales (short- and
long-range) in a consumer package goods environment. Reporting
to the CEO, this position will play an active & key role in our
continued growth. Expertise in selling to various distribution
channels required (independent retail, wholesaler, and mass merchandisers). Knowledge of new product introduction via acquisition or development a must. If your background includes a strong
mix of sales, marketing and P&L, forward résumé and salary
history in confidence to:

B. H. BOX 1234
1179 Avenue of the Americas
New York, N.Y. 10022

This ad pulled 275 responses. What is fascinating is that 9 percent of the same
candidates responded to both ads, but not one of them modified his résumé or letter at all.

Résumé Formats

In choosing a résumé style, keep one important thought in mind. Regardless of your
title or length of total employment, you must be able to demonstrate tangible results to the
reader. To accomplish this, we suggest you use the P-A-R format described in chapter 3.

How many types of business résumés are there, and what are their strengths and
weaknesses?

If you have reviewed any of the vast literature on this subject, you have discovered
there are really only three basic résumé formats. They are the chronological résumé, the
functional résumé, and a type that is a combination of chronological and functional.

Characteristics of Each Type of Résumé

Chronological	Functional	Combination
• Details work experience from most recent to beginning.	• Organized according to the functions of jobs held rather than by where they were held or for how long.	• Same as functional except that employers and titles are also listed in reverse chronological order.
• Includes total work history and education.	• Data relate only to the job you are aiming for. If it is constructed correctly, this format omits items irrelevant to your job hunt.	
• Easiest to prepare and the one most favored by organizations.	• Harder to prepare—favors those who can express themselves well.	
Positive: Best to use if your work history shows an upward path.		
Negative: If there are time gaps in your work history or if your jobs do not demonstrate increased responsibility and titles, it will be used against you.	*Negative*: Organizations presume you're "hiding" information if you don't list all employers, dates, and your titles.	

Format for Résumés

1. Your *name and address* should appear centered at the top or in the upper right-hand corner.

2. Your *telephone number* (under the address) should include the area code. Give your home number and, if possible, an office number, or a number where messages can be left for you. (Candidates have lost interviews because they could not be reached.) Leave off your work number if you work in an open area.

3. *Career objectives* are not necessary; give them in your cover letter. When answering an ad, *paraphrase the job description* given in the ad in your cover letter and list the job title you're applying for.

4. The *educational institutions* you attended should be listed in reverse chronological order. List your dates of graduation. State your degree and major. Your grade point average is optional. Do *not* mention it if it is less than 3.0 to 4.0. Do not put your education first if you are forty or over; put it near the end. Interest the reader in your business successes. Even though it's illegal to discriminate on the basis of age, employers still do it, particularly to women.

5. List *extracurricular activities* and offices held in college, if *significant*.

6. If you have *financed your education* through part-time, summer, or full-time jobs, you should make note of it. Other financing such as scholarships, graduate assistantships, or savings should also be mentioned. *Note:* This is more important for those with limited business experience. For example, "Financed 75% of educational expenses through part-time jobs and scholarships."

7. *Honors and awards* received in college and graduate school should be listed.

8. Under a section entitled *Business Experience*, the positions you have held should be listed in reverse chronological order. Military service can be stated here or in a separate section. For each job, list the dates of employment, the company, the location (city and state are sufficient), position title, and results. For summer positions, a title of "intern" is fine.

9. *Additional information:* personal data such as height, weight, date of birth, marital status, or health are no longer necessary. If your name and where you were educated might cause some confusion as to your visa status, indicate your country of citizenship. If you are willing to relocate, say so at the conclusion of your résumé. If you have a security clearance, list it.

10. *Languages* in which you are fluent can be listed under *personal data* or within a separate section, especially if you know several. Indicate your level of expertise such as "fluency" or "working knowledge." Languages are important if you are seeking a position in international business or banking.

11. *Special skills or courses* such as computer languages and business courses are important additions to your résumé. If you were a liberal arts major, do not list your courses unless you took statistics, other math, or business courses. No one at Bank of America will care that you turned two of Henry James's novels into iambic pentameter.

12. *Relevant certifications* such as C.P.A. or C.F.A. should be included and highlighted (if they are appropriate to the position for which you are applying).

13. *Publications/papers* you have published can be listed on your résumé under a separate section, but doing this is recommended only if the material is related to the business opportunity you seek. Or make an addendum sheet for them and use it judiciously.

14.   Listing *special interests* is optional, but it does provide information for discussion on a common, nonwork meeting ground and it serves as an ice-breaker for an interview. If you have room, list a few, but no more than four. You don't want to convey the impression that you prefer playing to working.

15.   Do not list *references* on your résumé. A statement such as "References will be furnished upon request" is sufficient.

A Résumé Is Much More than a Fact Sheet

Your résumé is a significant statement about how you view yourself. The entire résumé presentation describes you to the reader and it should clearly state:

- I'm a good organizer (or well organized).
- I'm a clear and logical thinker.
- I'm efficient.
- I've had significant accomplishments at my jobs and in volunteer organizations (ask a business associate if you have doubts).
- I'd be perfect for the job at your organization, and I WANT IT!

Your résumé is *not* a summary of your total experience. Instead, it should focus on your qualifications for a specific career opportunity. If you have very few objections or none to overcome in your background and work experience, the preferred résumé format is *chronological*. If you need to overcome any important negatives, such as being out of the work force for several years, then the functional or combined résumé is the format of choice. More on this later.

A RÉSUMÉ IS A SELLING DOCUMENT.   It is your first contact with the prospective employer and must indicate what you can do for his/her firm. What you will do in the future is reflected in what you have *achieved and accomplished in the past*. The discipline required to collect, analyze, and prepare the data for the résumé is not only useful for seeking employment, but gives you the opportunity for self-evaluation. As a result of thoughtful preparation of your résumé, you will be able to interview more effectively by having this information at your fingertips.

EFFECTIVE RÉSUMÉS ARE WRITTEN BY PEOPLE WHO KNOW THEIR MARKET.   A good résumé should tell just enough about you to make the employer think that your skills, experience, and potential make you an excellent candidate for a position within their firm. It should be concise, organized, and readable, an outline of your past experiences. Use the want-ad analysis to find out what skills are important to the industry or area of employment in which you are interested and slant your résumé accordingly. Company representatives are looking for potential demonstrated through your *excellence, leadership, competitiveness,* and *initiative*. They also look for evidence of basic skills such as *problem solving, oral and written communication,* and *management experience.*

YOU CAN OVERCOME LIMITED BUSINESS EXPERIENCE.   If you have a limited amount of business experience that is related to the job you are seeking, emphasize your educational background. In addition to the information concerning the colleges you attended, dates of graduation, and majors, include in the appropriate areas of your résumé academic achievements, offices held in student government or organizations, internships, part-time jobs, volunteer work, and community activities. The focus of your résumé should be on what *you initiated, were responsible for, and achieved.*

THE IMPORTANCE OF EMPHASIZING RELATED BUSINESS EXPERIENCE.   If you have related work experience, college activities will be less important. Gear the job description toward the position sought. For instance, if you were the manager of an art gallery and are now interested in a financial analyst position, emphasize the financial responsibilities involved in that position. *Always* discuss the *managerial* or *supervisory* functions in your past positions and give the *number* of people who reported to you.

THE WORDING OF YOUR RÉSUMÉ IS IMPORTANT.   Use clear, concise, simple language. Company representatives do not have time to read thoroughly the large number of résumés they receive. Write and rewrite your résumé, trimming your wording until it projects, in as few words as possible, a clear positive image of you. Pertinent facts and skills should be highlighted and not buried in wordy narrative statements. The pronoun *I* is implicit and therefore not necessary. Focus on action words rather than job descriptions (see pages 82–83).

DON'T CROWD YOUR RÉSUMÉ WITH TOO MUCH INFORMATION.   Your résumé must follow certain standards to be successful. It must be neat and typed in an easy-to-read typeface (no script typefaces, please). There must be enough white space at the margins and between topics so that it doesn't look like a tremendous amount to read. It's better to have two pages with enough white space than one that's cramped. However, never do more than a two-page résumé. Avoid long, rambling paragraphs. Make them relatively short and to the point. Résumés are supposed to whet the interest of the employers, not satiate it.

Your approach should be accurate and professional. Most important, your résumé must demonstrate your accomplishments, *not* just give a job description. A job description states only *what* you were hired to do; it doesn't say anything about *how* you performed.

THE RÉSUMÉ IS A REFLECTION OF YOU.   The average résumé has about 10 to 15 seconds to make an impression, either positive or negative, on the employer. It is, therefore, important that your résumé is neat. It should be typed on a clean, new typewriter.

Proofread your résumé carefully and have another person proofread it as well. Check for misspelled words, grammatical and typographical errors. Your résumé should be offset on good-quality bond paper. Be sure that your résumé is 100 percent accurate *before* you leave the copy center. *You are paying for perfection, so demand it.*

If you are well known in your local community or have won awards for meritorious service, list them (but make the list short—it shouldn't dilute your work accomplishments).

If you belong to professional associations connected with your work, list them. And list any *significant* offices held in them.

(If you went through school on scholarship, say so. If you financed 60 percent or all of your own schooling, say so. Companies look for a "constellation of characteristics," not only work experience, in employees.)

Don't list all your part-time and summer jobs. No employer really cares if you were the best waiter at the Hyatt-Regency or a governess on Cape Cod. Just say, "Financed 47 percent of own education through part-time and summer employment...."

If you are now enrolled in a part-time M.B.A. or other relevant graduate program, list several courses that are related to the job you seek. If you are an M.B.A. or have other graduate degrees, list three or four courses that would be of specific interest to a new employer.

What Not to Do

1. Do *not* list your marketing courses if you are applying for an accounting position.

2. Do *not* give reasons for leaving past positions on your résumé; they will be interpreted as defensive. Mention leaving only if you were employed at a place for a year or less and the firm has since folded.

3. *Never* mention salary in your résumé or in your cover letter. When ads in newspapers state "Only résumés with complete salary history will be considered," write back in your cover letter, "My salary is competitive." If the ad doesn't tell *you* their salary, don't tell *them* yours. If your résumé intrigues the company, believe us, they'll contact you! Have dignity. Many firms put ads in the paper without stating the salary, knowing full well that most women earn less than men and that they can hire men or women who are equally qualified but get a woman for less money. So, no salary discussion.

4. *Never* name your references on your résumé. You don't want your references contacted by people who may have no intention of hiring you anyway. Save references for when it counts. And make certain that all your references have agreed in advance to help you and will give you excellent reviews when called. Don't have someone surprised by a reference call when you haven't talked to them in four years.

5. Do *not* name your superiors. You *can* say, "Report to the corporate controller or the VP of Marketing" (but never name him or her).

6. If there is a gap of several months on your résumé, do not list your jobs by months. Use years instead (1976–1979, 1982 to present; not October 1976 to September 1979, February 1982 to present).

7. Never have any statements on your résumé that an interviewer may interpret as negative. See inclusive list later on in this chapter.

CONFLICTING PHILOSOPHIES
To Use or Not Use the Résumé in Your Job Search

There are several schools of thought regarding résumés. The conventional wisdom, reinforced daily by the want ads, says, "Only candidates submitting a detailed résumé and salary history will be considered." In other words, in order to get their job, you must use a résumé. It is implied that a résumé, usually written in chronological format, must be used for *all* of your job search: to answer ads, to send out inquiries directly to employers, and during the interview process.

This is probably the most widespread and popular theory.

The Résumé as the Basis of Your Job Search: The Traditional Approach

1. With an accompanying cover letter, your résumé is
    (a) sent directly to employers (cold canvass),
    (b) sent in response to help-wanted advertisements.

2. Your résumé reflects your past work history.

3. Your résumé reflects your responsibilities and results.

4. Your résumé reflects your progression (or lack of progress) in salary via job titles (or lack of them).

A second philosophy forgoes the use of the résumé entirely. Instead, this non-résumé approach relies solely on the use of an *action letter* (see chapter 7 for further details). Here the résumé is relegated to the position of being a reference tool. This reference résumé is *not* used to answer ads or contact employers, or during the interview process. The letter approach has been gaining a larger audience in recent years on the strength of the advancing technology of office equipment, particularly automated typewriters that can type individual "original" letters quickly.

The Résumé as a Reference Source: A Non-Traditional Approach

This is the *non-résumé* approach to job hunting.

1. Never send out a résumé nor bring one to an interview.
2. Use one to construct action letters.
3. Use one to analyze your work experience.
4. Use one as preparation for the job interview.
5. This approach results in an improved self-image and greater self-esteem.

A third philosophy, the basis of this book's switching technique, is to use the best elements of both the résumé and the action letter. It consists of two steps: (1) use an action letter to get the interview; (2) use your résumé to help get the job. The process would look something like this:

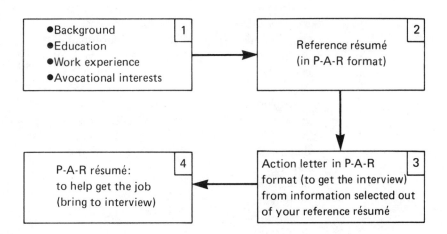

A Middle Ground: A Combination Three-Step Method—The Winning Job Strategy

1. Develop your reference résumé in the P-A-R format.
2. Strategy 1: Using carefully selected pieces from your reference résumé, develop an action letter in P-A-R format.
3. Strategy 2: Develop specialized résumés for the jobs you get interviews for.

This combination approach to the job search allows the strength of the conventional résumé to be used effectively with the nonrésumé action-letter method. Here is how it works.

ference Résumé, with Examples

key component in this combination job-search method is to create a reference résumé that encompasses every aspect of your past vocational and avocational experience, including education, work experience (paid and unpaid), community work, and interests.

This all-inclusive résumé, done in P-A-R format, then becomes your reference source from which specialized action letters and résumés can be developed. Under no circumstances is this reference résumé ever sent to a prospective employer. Instead, pertinent sections of it are used to create your marketing tools (action letter and each new résumé). These newly created materials are sent to prospective employers. In this way, you are assured that your selected marketing approach addresses the employer's specific needs (you *did* do your want-ad analysis, didn't you? See chapter 5). This method presents you as a specialist ready to solve a particular employer's problems. It also eliminates extraneous information, which employers often use as the reason for not granting interviews.

When creating your reference résumé in P-A-R format, you should use action words to describe the "action" portion of your P-A-R experience. Each sentence should begin with an action verb, if possible. To assist you in this step, consult the list of action words below. There are many others, but this will give you a head start.

Action Words

accelerated	conducted	examined
accomplished	consolidated	executed
achieved	constricted	expanded
administered	constructed	extended
allocated	contracted	forecast
amended	contributed	formulated
amplified	contrived	fortified
analyzed	controlled	founded
appointed	convinced	gathered
approved	coordinated	governed
arbitrated	created	guided
arranged	cut	harmonized
assisted	delegated	headed
attained	delivered	hired
audited	demonstrated	implemented
augmented	designed	improved
awarded	determined	increased
broadened	developed	initiated
built	devised	installed
calculated	devoted	instituted
catalogued	directed	insured
chose	distributed	interpreted
collected	documented	interviewed
commented	drafted	introduced
communicated	edited	invented
compiled	elected	investigated
completed	eliminated	issued
computed	enlarged	launched
conceived	ensured	led
conceptualized	established	liaised
condensed	evaluated	listed

maintained	proposed	strengthened
managed	promoted	studied
marketed	published	suggested
moderated	purchased	summarized
modified	reacted	superseded
monitored	recorded	supervised
negotiated	recruited	systematized
offered	rectified	terminated
opened	reduced	traced
organized	regulated	trained
originated	reinforced	transferred
overhauled	researched	translated
performed	restored	traveled
planned	resulted	timed
prepared	revamped	unified
presented	reviewed	utilized
preserved	revised	widened
presided	scheduled	won
processed	selected	wrote
produced	served	uncovered
programmed	serviced	unraveled

The Reference Resource

To understand fully the important role played by the reference résumé, we will look at the experience of Lloyd Feinstein, one of the authors of this book.

Like many people who wanted to make a job change, Lloyd had a varied work history, including both profit and nonprofit employment, and lacking a specific, fast-track career pattern. His background, however, had a central theme: industrial training leading to a career as a well-rounded personnel generalist.

In early 1977, Lloyd decided to look for a new position. He was then the director of training and assistant director of personnel for Bellevue Hospital Center in New York City. His actions were precipitated by New York City's financial crisis and his wanting to work for a profit-making corporation. Lloyd first reviewed his entire work experience since obtaining his M.A. in 1966.

Listed below under each job are his major accomplishments. In addition, there is a separate list of accomplishments achieved outside his normal workday. These included teaching, consulting, and writing. For presenting this very rough reference résumé we have grouped the activities to represent the chronological sequence of events from 1965 to 1977.

LLOYD FEINSTEIN
1000 Third Avenue
New York, New York 10022

Education

M.A. History; Adult Education, Rutgers University, New Brunswick, New Jersey, 1966. Additionally received 24 credits beyond Master's in Modern European Social History.

B.A. Communications, Newark State College, Union, New Jersey, 1964.

Bellevue Hospital Center
New York, NY
September 1973-March 1978

Director of Training

•Employing extensive needs-assessment techniques, I developed and conducted a two-part management development/supervisory training program: interpersonal skills training and management skills training. The first covered team building, group problem solving, communication, leadership participation, feedback laboratory, and confrontation styles. The second part included planning and organizing, analysis, delegation and control, job instruction, and performance analysis.

•Developed and conducted Out-Patient Department clerk training in interpersonal skills. Result: A 38% decline in patient complaints.

•Developed training programs to effect a smooth transition to the new 1,900 bed hospital building. These included:

1. Vendor training by objectives. Training sessions were videotaped: i.e., HVAC. This enabled the 30-person engineering staff to maintain and operate the 110 critical building systems for the 1.6-million-square-foot structure. Since opening in June 1975, there has been zero mechanical breakdown time.

2. Scripted and produced a 30-minute orientation film on the new hospital. Showed the film to 4,200 employees (3 shifts).

3. Conducted a new-equipment and procedural techniques training for Nursing and Medical/Surgical Support departments. Training sessions were video-taped for future in-service use.

4. Produced a 21-minute simulated inpatient move videotape. The program was given to all hospital services directly involved in the movement of patients to the new building.

•Coordinated an audiovisual department, providing both conventional (20%) and CCTV (80%) services in addition to the initiation of regular programing via the master antenna.

•Developed and scripted 4 role-play scenes for a Transport Service courtesy train-ing videotape.

•Reactivated an employee service award program, which identified 1,600 eligible employees having 15 or more years service. Awarded pins and certificates and generated the most effective morale boost in 20 years.

•Developed a performance improvement program for the 110-person Medical Records Department. I originated daily and weekly feedback mechanisms from on-line analysis. Instructed supervisors in methods of praising performers and correct-ing problems. This increased productivity 26% and saved $33,105 over 12 months.

<u>Assistant Director of Personnel</u>

•As Assistant Personnel Director interviewed administrators and department heads
to improve the reporting of status changes in personnel. Produced an instructional
manual with flowcharts that explained the steps in each of the 34 methods of revising an employee's status. Conducted seminars on the Personnel Action Form (PAF)
and manual for managers that reduced daily errors from 41 to 6.

•Supervised Benefits Administration Department (6 employees), servicing health
insurance, pension, workmen's compensation, blood credit, new employee orientation,
and benefit needs of physicians on rotation.

•To reduce costs related to extended sick-leave benefits, researched evaluation
criteria and established standards, resulting in a savings of $204,086 for 1977.

•To produce an accurate monthly vacancy report covering 5,692 budgeted positions,
I compared wage and salary files against a printout of budgeted positions and the
existing organization chart. Corrected a job number, job title, and distribution
code. This manually compiled report was organized by department and job title
within each division, showing budgeted positions, number filled, number vacant,
percentages of each, and the vacancies compared to previous reports.

•To revise 234 distribution codes for reimbursement purposes, the corrected
organization chart used in the preparation of the vacancy report was further
amended to identify the job number, name of employee, title, status (FT/PT),
job condition (active/inactive), and salary for all 5,692 budgeted positions.
The report was manually compiled by section, department, and division.

Montclair State College
Department of Adult Continuing Education
Upper Montclair, NJ 07043
January 1972-September 1973

Director: <u>National Multimedia Center for Adult Basic Education--Material</u>
            <u>Acquisition Unit</u>

•Developed, tested, and administered a nationwide system for the continuous
search for and retrieval of selected continuing adult education instructional
and curriculum materials (multimedia) developed through special projects, teacher
training institutes, state programs, colleges and universities, industry, commercial publishers, and federal agencies.

•Conducted and chaired semiannual national advisory council meetings.

Director: <u>National Multimedia Center for Basic Education--Marketing Sales Unit</u>

•Developed and implemented a nationwide advertising campaign for dissemination
of subscription literature to:

    National, state, regional, and local conferences in adult education, via
    conference packets.

    America's education press (newsletters, journals, magazines, etc.), via press
    releases.

    Individual adult educators/trainers, via direct mail campaigns. Coordinated
    the writing, graphic design, and printing of the direct mail brochure.

•Generated sales sufficient to make the project self-supporting.

Director: <u>Adult Education Clearinghouse (AEC)</u>

•Conceived, explored relationships, and integrated selected theories and techniques
from outside the adult education arena. Developed, produced, and marketed a monthly
newsletter to professional adult educators and trainers.

Bell Telephone Laboratories
Murray Hill, NJ 07974
June 1970–October 1971

Training Consultant/Project Manager

•As Project Manager I developed and administered a multiphased Affirmative Action training program for minority high-school graduates with nonacademic diplomas.

•63% completed the 18-month program successfully. 94% were reclassified into higher salary categories.

•Conducted interpersonal skills training at three sites for supervisors involved in the Affirmative Action training program. Results: 42% reduction in employee turnover.

•Coauthored a preparatory engineering curriculum (7 courses) for program use.

•Coauthored a 200-page evaluation of this 3 1/2-year training program. Program history, both administrative and educational, statistics, conclusions, and recommendations for future programs were covered.

In June 1970 EPSI went out of business. I was one of seven EPSI employees hired directly as a consultant to Bell Telephone Labs in order to complete their commitment to this AAP. Went from Assistant Project Manager to Project Manager. Work at Bell Labs was the same as EPSI.

Education Performance Systems, Inc.
501 Madison Ave.
New York, NY
June 1968–June 1970

Assistant Project Manager

•Directed the National Alliance of Businessmen's (N.A.B.) jobs programs for Bell Telephone Laboratories' three New Jersey locations.

Federal Electric Corporation
Kilmer Job Corps Center
Edison, NJ
June 1965–June 1968

Administrator, Curriculum Development

•Established a videotape feedback program to aid corpsmen in dealing with critical, real-life situations.

•Introduced the "Edex" Mediamaster response-oriented teaching system for administrative personnel.

•Directed weekly in-service training for 30 professional educators.

•Interviewed and evaluated job applicants for the teaching staff.

•Participated in the writing of two federally funded training proposals. One awarded for $550,000.

•Stimulated and supported research toward development and evaluation of new techniques and materials.

•Compiled and edited 6 instructional units, which were accepted by the company and Job Corps (Washington, D.C.) as the center-wide social education curriculum.

Outside Activities

In addition, Lloyd developed separate sheets that summarized his experience in two areas of concentration: writing and leadership. This list is seen below.

Curriculum Development and Writing:

•Authored the training curriculum for the Affirmative Action Department of Bell Telephone Laboratories (N.J.).

•Authored a semiprogrammed text entitled "Organizing a Speech."

•Coauthored a two-volume consumer education work text entitled "It's Your Money," published summer 1973 by Steck-Vaughn Company, Austin, Texas.

•As a consultant to General Learning Corporation, authored an administrators' manual for GLC's General Education Curriculum.

•As a consultant to the United States Armed Forces Institute, authored an evaluation report of the instructional program in general mathematics for adults.

•Conducted an extensive task analysis as the basis for revision of the Bell Labs' Affirmative Action program.

•Authored the evaluation of the Bell Labs' 38-month Affirmative Action training program.

•Authored article "Motivating Adult Students," published in BTSD Review, the journal of the Department of Manpower, Ottawa, Canada.

•Authored research proposal for National Institute of Education's mini-grant program.

Information Dissemination:

•Assembled and edited the monthly Adult Education Clearinghouse Newsletter.

•Director, National Multimedia Center of Montclair State College.

Conference Leadership

•Workshop Leader--Educational Technology Conference, March 19-23, 1973, sponsored by EDUCATION TECHNOLOGY magazine.

•Organized and conducted advisory committee meetings for the National Multimedia Center.

•Organized and conducted seminars for Bell Labs' technical and administrative supervisors.

•Presentation at the Annual Institute for Adult and Continuing Education, Rutgers University, New Brunswick, N.J.

•Adjunct faculty member of Newark State College, Union, N.J.

•Workshop Leader at Majority Money, New York City.

Once this all-inclusive "reference résumé" was compiled, Lloyd rearranged it according to specific job functions. In so doing he came up with eight separate job areas. Also during this process, some of the descriptions were revised, amplified, or condensed.

1. Organization development
2. Project management, educational
3. Curriculum development/writing experience
4. Audiovisual
5. Affirmative action
6. Personnel
7. Training
8. Employee relations

His list by each job area appears below. Some items could be classified into more than one job area and were so done in Lloyd's reorganized "reference résumé."

Organization Development

1. To develop a performance improvement program for the 110-man Medical Records Department, I originated daily and weekly feedback mechanisms from on-line analysis. Instructed supervisors in methods of praising performers and correcting problems. This increased productivity 26% and saved $33,105 over twelve months.
2. To improve the reporting of status changes in personnel, I interviewed personnel administrators and selected department heads. Originated an instructional manual that explained the steps in each of the 34 methods of revising an employee's status. Conducted training for managers that reduced average daily errors from 41 to 6.

Project Management, Educational

1. Developed, tested, and administered a nationwide system for the continuous search for and retrieval of selected continuing adult education instructional and curriculum materials (multimedia) developed through special projects, teacher training institutes, state programs, colleges and universities, industry, commercial publishers, and federal agencies.
2. *Sector:* National Multimedia Center for Adult Education Marketing Sales Unit.
   (a) Developed and implemented a nationwide advertising campaign for dissemination of subscription literature to
   national, state, regional and local conferences in adult education via conference packets,
   America's education press (newsletters, journals, magazines, etc.) via press releases,
   individual adult educators/trainers via a direct mail campaign. Coordinated the writing, graphic design, and printing of the direct mail brochure.
   (b) Generated sales sufficient to make the project self-supporting.
3. Directed the National Multimedia Center for Adult Education and the Adult Education Clearinghouse—Montclair State College.
   (a) Administrator of Audiovisual Services and Curriculum Development for the Kilmer Job Corps Center in Edison, New Jersey.
   (b) Established a videotape feedback program to aid Job Corpsmen in dealing with critical real-life situations.
   (c) Introduced the "Edex" Media-Master response-oriented teaching system for administrative personnel.
   (d) Directed weekly in-service training for 30 professional educators.

(e) Interviewed and evaluated job applicants for the teaching staff.

(f) Participated in the writing of two federally funded training proposals. One awarded for $550,000.

(g) Stimulated and supported research toward development and evaluation of new techniques and materials.

(h) Compiled and edited 6 instructional units, which were accepted by the company and Job Corps (Washington, D.C.) as the centerwide social education curriculum.

Responsibilities (July 1968–January 1972)—Training Consultant

(i) As Project Manager I developed and administered a multiphased Affirmative Action training program for minority high-school graduates with nonacademic degrees. 63% completed an 18-month program successfully. 94% were reclassified into higher salary categories.

(j) Conducted interpersonal skills training at 3 sites for Bell Labs supervisors involved in the Affirmative Action training program. Results: a 42% reduction in worker turnover.

(k) Authored the training curriculum for the Affirmative Action Department of the Bell Telephone Laboratories (N.J.).

(l) Authored a 200-page evaluation of this 3½-year Affirmative Action training program. Program history, both administrative and educational statistics, conclusions, and recommendations for future programs were covered.

4. Federal Electric Corporation
   Kilmer Job Corps Center
   Edison, New Jersey

   Responsibilities (June 1965–June 1968)—Administrator, Curriculum Development and Audiovisual Services for the Kilmer Job Corps Center in Edison, New Jersey.

   (a) Coauthored a preparatory engineering curriculum (7 courses) for program use.

5. Curriculum Development

   (a) Authored the training curriculum for the Affirmative Action Department of the Bell Telephone Laboratories (N.J.).

   (b) Authored a self-instructional work text, "Organizing a Speech."

   (c) Coauthored a two-volume consumer education work text, "It's Your Money," published summer 1973 by Steck-Vaughn Company, Austin, Texas.

   (d) As a consultant to General Learning Corporation, authored an administrators' manual for GLC's General Education Curriculum.

   (e) As a consultant to the United States Armed Forces Institute, authored an evaluation report of the instructional program in general mathematics for adults.

6. Conceptual Writing

   (a) Wrote scenario for 30-minute videotape orientation film of the New Bellevue.

   (b) Conducted an extensive task analysis as the basis for revision of the Bell Labs' Affirmative Action program.

   (c) Authored the evaluation of the Bell Labs' 38-month Affirmative Action training program.

   (d) Authored article, "Motivating Adult Students," published in *BTSD Review*, the journal of the Department of Manpower, Ottawa, Canada.

   (e) Authored research proposal for National Institute of Education's minigrant program.

(f) Wrote a proposal for a demonstration project following U.S. government guidelines. Awarded funding of $110,000 for one year.

7. Formal Presentations

(a) Workshop Leader—Educational Technology Conference, March 19–23, 1973, in New York City.

(b) Annual Institute for Adult and Continuing Education, Rutgers University, New Brunswick, New Jersey.

(c) Adult Education Division, USOE, Department of HEW, Washington, D.C., November 1972.

(d) National Adult Education Conference, Minneapolis, Minnesota, November 1972.

(e) Workshop Leader—Majority Money, 1977–1978. Topic: "So You Want to Work for a Fortune 500 Company."

(f) Adjunct faculty member, Newark State College, Union, New Jersey, 1966–1972.

Curriculum/Writing Experience

1. Authored the training curriculum for the Affirmative Action Department of the Bell Telephone Laboratories (N.J.).

2. Authored a 200-page evaluation of the 3½-year training program. Program history, both administrative and educational, statistics, conclusions, and recommendations for future programs were covered.

3. Authored a self-instructional work text, "Organizing a Speech."

4. Coauthored a two-volume consumer education work text, "It's Your Money," published 1973 by Steck-Vaughn Company of Austin, Texas.

5. As a consultant to General Learning Corporation, authored an administrators' manual for GLC's General Education Curriculum.

6. As a consultant to the United States Armed Forces Institute, authored an evaluation report of the instructional program in general mathematics for adults.

Audiovisual

1. Conducted new-equipment and procedural-techniques training for Nursing and Medical/Surgical Support departments. Training sessions were videotape-recorded for future in-service use. The VTR library consists of over 125 films.

2. Scripted and produced a half-hour videotape orientation film on the new hospital. Coordinated showing the orientation film on all three shifts to 4,200 employees.

3. To prepare the new hospital building, set up vendor training by objectives for the 87 critical building systems. This instruction, aided by VTR, enabled the engineering staff to operate and maintain the 1.6-million-square-foot structure. Since opening in June 1975, there has been zero mechanical breakdown time.

4. Coordinated an Audiovisual Department providing both conventional (20%) and CCTV (80%) services in addition to the initiation of regular programming via the master antenna.

5. Seminar Leader—United Hospital Fund workshop, "Open Up Training with Closed Circuit TV," April 1976.

6. Seminar Leader—New Jersey Nursing Home Officials, October 1975; sponsored by Montclair State College.

7. Workshop Leader—Use of Audiovisual Media in Pre-Retirement Education Programs, July 1975, sponsored by Montclair State College and Glassboro State College.

8. Workshop Leader—Educational Technology Conference, March 19–23, 1973, which was sponsored by *Educational Technology Magazine.*

9. Developed and scripted 4 role-play scenes for Transport Service courtesy training videotape.

Affirmative Action

1. As Project Manager, developed and administered a multiphased Affirmative Action training program. 63% completed an 18-month program successfully. 94% were reclassified into higher salary categories.

2. As Project Manager of an Affirmative Action program for the Bell Telephone Laboratories, developed and administered a multiphased training and job enrichment project, using a systems approach.

3. Conducted on-site Affirmative Action training for Bell Telephone Laboratories.

Personnel (Nontraining)

1. As Assistant Personnel Director of a large health-care facility, interviewed administrators and department heads in order to improve the reporting of status changes in personnel. Produced an instructional manual with flowcharts that explained the steps in each of the 34 methods of revising an employee's status. Conducted seminars on the Personnel Action Form (PAF) and manual for managers that reduced daily errors from 41 to 6.

2. To reduce costs related to extended sick-leave benefits, researched evaluation criteria, then established standards that have resulted in a savings of $204,086 for FY 1977.

3. To produce an accurate monthly vacancy report covering 5,692 budgeted positions, compared wage and salary files against both a printout of budgeted positions and the existing table of organization (draft). Corrections were made regarding job number, job title, and distribution code. This manually compiled report was organized by department and job title within each division, showing budgeted positions, number filled, number vacant, percentages of each, and vacancies compared to previous reports.

4. To revise the 234 distribution codes for reimbursement purposes, the corrected table of organization used in the preparation of the vacancy report was further amended to identify the job number, name of employee, title, status (FT/PT), job condition (active/inactive), and salary for all 5,692 budgeted positions. The report was manually compiled by section, department, and division. Salary expenditures were summarized by department and division.

5. Supervised Benefits Administration Department with 6 employees servicing health insurance, pension, workmen's compensation, blood credit, new-employee orientation, and benefit needs of physicians on rotation.

6. Administered Affirmative Action policies and wrote compliance reviews.

Training

1. As Training Director for Bellevue Hospital, employed extensive needs-assessment techniques to develop a supervisory training program in two phases: interpersonal skills training and management skills training. The first phase covered team building, leadership participation, feedback laboratory, confrontation styles, and group problem-solving. Some second-phase topics included communication, record keeping, motivation, job instruction, labor relations and discipline (handling), delegation and cooperation, and performance evaluation.

2. Developed and conducted Out-Patient Department clerk training, covering basic interpersonal skills. Program resulted in a 38% decline in patient complaints.

3. Conducted new-equipment and procedural-techniques training for Nursing and Medical/Surgical Support Departments. Training sessions were videotape-recorded for future in-service use. The VTR library consists of over 125 films.

4. Conducted interpersonal skills training at three Bell Labs sites for supervisors involved in the Affirmative Action training program. Results: a 42% reduction in worker turnover.

5. Adjunct faculty member of Newark State College, Union, N.J., from 1966 to 1973.

6. Developed training programs to effect a smooth transition to the new 1,900-bed hospital building. These included:

    (a) vendor training by objectives. Training sessions were videotape-recorded, HVAC, thus enabling the 30-man engineering staff to maintain and operate the 110 critical building systems for the 1.6-million-square-foot structure. Since opening in June 1975, there has been zero mechanical breakdown time.

    (b) Scripted and produced a half-hour videotape orientation film on the new hospital. Coordinated showing the orientation film on all three shifts to 4,200 employees.

    (c) Coordinated and produced a 21-minute simulated in-patient move videotape. The program was given to all hospital services directly involved in the movement of patients to the new building.

Employee Relations

1. Developed and coordinated the reactivation of an employees' service award program, which identified 1,600 eligible employees in a total work force of 6,000. The all-day presentation for 15 years or more of service awarded pins and certificates and generated the most effective boost in morale in the last 20 years.

2. To improve employee courtesy, negotiated the purchase and adaptation of a commercially produced customer-treatment program. Selected and trained 20 discussion leaders, then supervised the implementation of the 14-week program for 5,100 employees. Evaluation included questionnaires, interviews, and random analysis of employee job performance, which resulted in an average improvement of 22% above baseline data.

Once Lloyd had reorganized the reference résumé into separate job areas, he was able to review critically his experiences and identify those that would assist him in achieving his career objective: a switch to a profit-making corporation.

Because the bulk of work was in two areas, training and general personnel, he chose to concentrate his job efforts in these two fields. Shown below are the top five items from Lloyd's want-ad analysis for a training/organization development specialist and personnel generalist, which he compiled during December 1977 and January 1978.

But which of the eight job areas had the highest potential for effecting a switch to industry? To answer this question, and to assist in the evaluation of his work experience, Lloyd developed the want-ad analysis technique.

Want-Ad Analysis—Training/Organization Development Specialist

1. Conduct management training programs.
2. Utilize organization development methods.
3. B.A. degree and advanced degree (or experience) in related areas.
4. Determine management needs.
5. Five years or more experience.

Want-Ad Analysis—Personnel Generalist

1. Recruit at various levels (interviewing and selection)
2. Develop and implement training programs
3. B.A. degree
4. 3-5 years experience
5. Organization and manpower planning

Lloyd compared the items from each want-ad analysis against the job categories selected from his reference résumé. He was then able to identify the most relevant experience from his work history. The next step was for him to use this data to create an action letter for each ad answered (see chapter 7).

Below is the blind ad that Lloyd answered from a Sunday newspaper's business section.

```
TRAINING MANAGER: Specialist with Personnel Generalist Instincts

Tired of the specialist straitjacket? Here is the opportunity to
increase your exposure and develop your skills in the fast-paced
Personnel Department of a Fortune 1000, NYSE diversified corpora-
tion in northern New Jersey. Initial responsibilities include
analyzing training needs, recommending then developing training
and development programs in cooperation with top management. In
addition, you'll get involved in Employment, Salary Administra-
tion, and Employee Relations. At least 4 years corporate T & D
experience required for this fast-track opportunity. Strong com-
municative abilities are a must. Salary commensurate with ex-
perience, excellent benefits package. Send résumé with complete
salary history in strict confidence to: Box Z
```

Lloyd answered this ad even though it was likely that the salary was only up to $30,000. He was already earning more than that at Bellevue Hospital but, if necessary and if the job was right, he was willing to "pay his dues" and take a pay cut finally to enter a profit-making company.

By sending out his action letter and stating, "My salary is competitive," he didn't scare off the hiring company. Had he told them his salary, they might never have interviewed him. As it turned out, Cadence Industries Corporation hired him at more than $30,000—in fact, his starting salary was somewhat higher than what he'd been earning at Bellevue!

Now you can see why we've cautioned you not to reveal your salary if the organization that is advertising doesn't reveal salary or lists one slightly less than what you're earning.

Here is a copy of the action letter Lloyd used that got him his first interview appointment at Cadence, and the résumé he was requested to bring to the interview. He developed the résumé based upon the ad's description of the job and his brief conversation with the secretary who called him to arrange his first interview.

☞ *Insiders' Tip:*   Never waste a phone call. Always turn it to your advantage by interviewing the secretary or assistant for useful information (i.e., salary range, data on previous incumbent, whom the position reports to, etc.).

1000 Third Avenue
New York, New York 10022

November 17, 1977

Box Z
New York, New York 10036

Dear Sir:

As Training Director and Assistant Director of Personnel for Bellevue Hospital, I employed extensive needs analysis techniques to develop a Supervisory Training Program in two phases: Interpersonal Skills Training and Management Skills Training. The first phase covered team building, leadership participation, feedback laboratory, confrontation styles, and group problem-solving. Some second-phase topics included Communication, Record-keeping, Motivation, Job Instruction, Delegation and Cooperation, Goal Analysis, and Performance Analysis.

I am writing because of your ad for a Training Manager that appeared in the New York News of November 13th. You may find my following accomplishments of interest.

To develop a Performance Improvement Program for the 110-person Medical Records Department, I originated daily and weekly feedback mechanisms for on-line analysis. Instructed supervisors in methods of praising performers and correcting problems. This increased productivity 26% and saved $33,105 over twelve months.

To improve the reporting of status changes in personnel, I interviewed personnel administrators and selected department heads. Originated an instructional manual that explained the steps in each of the 34 methods of revising an employee's status. Conducted training for managers that reduced daily errors from 41 to 6.

To prepare the new hospital building, I set up Vendor Training by Objectives for the 110 critical building systems. This instruction, aided by VTR, enabled the engineering staff to operate and maintain the 1.6-million-square-foot structure. Since opening in June 1975, there has been zero mechanical breakdown time.

I graduated from Rutgers University, M.A., in 1966 and Newark State College, B.A., in 1964. My salary requirements are competitive. I would be glad to discuss my experience further in a personal interview.

Sincerely yours,

Lloyd L. Feinstein

(212) 355-1234

LLOYD L. FEINSTEIN
1000 Third Avenue
New York, New York 10022
(212)355-1234

EDUCATION:

M.A. History/Adult Education, Rutgers University, New Brunswick, New Jersey, 1966.
Additionally received 24 credits beyond Master's in Modern European Social History.

B.A. Communications, Newark State College, Union, New Jersey, 1964.

BUSINESS EXPERIENCE:

1973 to
present

BELLEVUE HOSPITAL CENTER, New York, New York, as <u>Assistant Director</u>
<u>of Personnel</u> and <u>Director of Training</u>.

- Interviewed administrators and department heads to improve the
reporting of status changes in personnel.
--Produced an instructional manual with flowcharts explaining the
steps in each of the 34 methods of revising an employee's status.
--Conducted seminars on the Personnel Action Form (PAF) and Manual
for Managers that reduced daily errors from 41 to 6.

- Supervised a Benefits Administration Department of six, servicing
health insurance, pension, workmen's compensation, blood credit,
new-employee orientation, and benefit needs of physicians on
rotation.

- Employing extensive needs-assessment techniques, developed and
conducted a two-part Management Development/Supervisory Training
Program: Interpersonal Skills Training and Management Skills
Training.
--The first covered team building, group problem-solving, communication, leadership participation, feedback laboratory, and
confrontation styles.
--The second included planning and organizing, analysis, delegation
and control, job instruction, and performance analysis.

- Developed training programs to effect a smooth transition to the
new 1,900-bed hospital building, including Vendor Training by
Objectives.
--Training sessions were videotaped: i.e., HVAC.
--This enabled the 30-person engineering staff to maintain and
operate the 110 critical building systems for the 1.6-million-
square-foot structure.
--Since opening in June 1975, there has been zero mechanical breakdown time.

- Scripted and produced a 30-minute orientation film on the new
hospital. Showed the film to 4,200 employees (3 shifts).

1972-1973

MONTCLAIR STATE COLLEGE, Upper Montclair, N.J., as <u>Director of</u>
<u>Adult Education Projects, Department of Adult Continuing Education</u>.

- Managed the National Multimedia Center.

- Prepared nationwide advertising campaign.

- Designed and produced a monthly newsletter.

*Accomplishment:

Generated sales sufficient to make the project self-supporting.

1968-1972   BELL TELEPHONE LABORATORIES, Murray Hill, N.J., as Project Manager/
Training Consultant for in-house Affirmative Action Training
Program.

- Developed and administered a multiphased Affirmative Action training program for minority high-school graduates with nonacademic
diplomas.

- 63% completed the 18-month program successfully. 94% were reclassified into higher salary categories.

- Conducted Interpersonal Skills Training at three sites for supervisors involved in the Affirmative Action Training Program.
Results: 42% reduction in employee turnover.

*Accomplishment: This program has formed the basis of the Labs'
Affirmative Action Programs since.

1965-1968   FEDERAL ELECTRIC CORPORATION, Kilmer Job Corps Center, Edison, N.J.,
as Administrator of Curriculum Development.

- Designed six instructional units which were accepted by the Company
and the Job Corps (Washington, D.C.), as the centerwide social
education curriculum.

- Directed weekly in-service training for 30 professional educators.

- Participated in the writing of two federal training proposals. One
awarded for $550,000.

INTERESTS:

Sports cars; gardening; reading.

REFERENCES:

Available upon request.

CHRONOLOGY: Lloyd answered the ad of November 13, 1977, on November 17, 1977. It was stamped "Received" by Cadence's personnel department on November 23, 1977. He was called about a week later, and his first interview was arranged for December 6, 1977. He saw the director of personnel and the employment manager.

Because of the Christmas holidays and the fact that the personnel director was taking two weeks of vacation, Lloyd's second interview wasn't held until January 10, 1978, five weeks after his first. He was then asked back for a third and final round of interviews on January 19, 1978.

Then he sent thank-you letters to everyone he'd seen. He called and was told that no final decision had been made but that he was "in the running." Then he waited some more. Finally, on February 6, 1978, he was called and offered the job. Lloyd accepted, gave one month's notice to Bellevue Hospital, and started at Cadence as corporate training manager on March 6, 1978, exactly three months after his first interview.

How the Combination Approach Works

Once you complete your reference résumé, the next step is to create two key marketing tools: the action letter and a specific résumé. Both should be for only *one* job and written in

P-A-R format. The selection of items to be contained in each should be based upon your want-ad analysis summation of the particular job for which you are applying. In this way you are assured that your experience matches the employer's needs and that your experience is presented in the strongest time-tested format possible: the action letter.

Using an action letter (if it is well written) will increase the number of interviews you are granted. Once you are assured of the job interview, your accompanying P-A-R résumé comes into play. You don't have to prepare a résumé unless your action letter gets you the interview.

☞ *Insiders' Tip:*   With the exception of recruiters in personnel departments, most managers, no matter how high-level they are, interview job candidates infrequently. Many are poor interviewers and find the task unsettling, even unpleasant. To reduce their own anxiety about having to interview, most managers will request a résumé from the person being interviewed and proceed to conduct the interview only from what the résumé states. By having your résumé in the P-A-R format and by answering questions in P-A-R format, *you* can direct the interview's course, be viewed as a specialist in one or more job areas, and increase the comfort level of both yourself and the interviewing manager. These factors will improve your interviewing ability and will increase the number of job offers you receive.

Why Hire You?

What do employers want in the applicants they eventually hire and how can you assist employers in this area?

If you are at all familiar with employment advertisements and have followed them for any time, you're probably aware that employers advertise for the "perfect" or superperfect candidate. However, perfection rarely exists, and employers settle for less than what they say they want. Nevertheless, the closer you appear to fit an employer's job description, the better prospects you have of being granted an interview.

When employers place an ad, they attempt to accomplish specific objectives. They want to hire the best possible person at the lowest starting salary they can get away with, compatible with their internal wage and salary structure. Why? The longer it takes to recruit for and fill a position, the more expensive it becomes for any organization. These costs include reduced productivity, lost sales, morale loss in the department, a growing backlog of work in the affected area, lost growth opportunities because the position has been vacant a long time, etc. In a nutshell: LOST PROFITS. Therefore, if the response you mail to an advertisement even partially convinces an employer that your experience and background could help restore their balance, you will be requested to interview. To do this effectively and consistently you must show tangible *results* in your work background.

Answering the Question "What Have You Accomplished?"

Employers are interested first and foremost in how you can make a contribution to the organization's bottom line: its profits. This can be done in many ways. You don't have to make a contribution to profits in the way a sales representative would make them. You could do it through a reduction in costs, an improved public relations program, a new product or service idea, creative use of existing resources, better control of personnel costs, reduced inventory, improvement in employee morale or employee turnover. The list is almost endless.

The important point here is that, whether you are in a line or a staff job, you should and do contribute to an organization's bottom line in some way. Your ability to demonstrate these contributions to the bottom line must be evident in your marketing tools. You must show *results*, not just a job description of what you were hired to do.

What are considered tangible results? They vary greatly from job to job and organization to organization. Generally, however, they are a contribution to the bottom line expressed in a carefully quantified format. The various contributions listed above, when quantified, are tangible results.

For example:

Developed a key account program after only 7 months' effort, yielding $241,700 in 1980 revenue (first year). 1981 revenues project to exceed $650,000.

Changed customer mix and increased base volume of business. Achieved $107,212 savings in distribution costs.

Instant Credibility: P-A-R

Relying solely on tangible results is not enough. If you briefly review the P-A-R format discussed in chapter 3, you will see that the "Action" and "Result" parts have their limitations. Though to the reader these two parts demonstrate tangible results clearly, they share one major weakness. They could be fabrications. The hiring employer has no way of verifying your claims to greatness, particularly at your present job. After all, a prospective employer probably doesn't know you personally. Why should you be believed? This creates a major hurdle for all job seekers. How do you make yourself credible?

Happily, the solution to the credibility issue is strict adherence to the "Problem" section of the P-A-R format. By defining the specific problems you were hired to solve (the "P" part of the format), you create *instant credibility*. This allows prospective employers to compare the problems in their organization with the problems you handled in your work. If the description of your work experience is well written, an employer will see the similarity of their own problems to the problems you solved. You may be the person for their current vacancy. To make certain, you will be asked in to interview.

The credibility gained through discussion of problems you solved also overcomes a common myth associated with job hunting: "Only a detailed résumé with complete salary history will be considered" (to get the job interview). Logic and extensive experience in the area of obtaining jobs for people have convinced us to the contrary. Employers will ask to interview an applicant who submitted an action letter because the applicant's discussion of the problems solved created credibility. This will happen regardless of the fact that the applicant did not submit a résumé and that the salary history was omitted. *Note:* Some employers will ask you to submit a résumé or bring one with you to the interview. Since both a résumé and salary information can be obtained before or during the job interview, no credible candidate will be overlooked.

Premium Products Command Higher Prices

Has anyone ever offered you an expensive item such as a watch, camera, piece of electronic equipment, car or mink coat at a ridiculously low price? If so, wasn't your gut response to ask "What is wrong with it?" After all, if an item that should be expensive is cheap, there must be something wrong with it. Right? Well, this type of reaction occurs when you, a highly qualified candidate, put too low a value (price) on your experience.

Remember that you have spent a great deal of time and effort to develop your P-A-R paragraphs, which were then incorporated into your marketing materials (résumé and action letter). These marketing materials will insure that you get more interviews and job offers because: they give you instant credibility; you can go into any interview as an equal, not hoping for charity and looking for a handout; they present you as a premium product.

How you handle the salary issue is critical to your successful job search. So as not to cheapen the quality of the product you are attempting to market, *avoid mentioning salary.* Let the reader of your letter conclude your worth to their organization. Just to show that you didn't forget to address this important aspect, however, always use the phrase (in writing) "My salary requirements are competitive." The time to discuss salary is after you have made a "sale" with the organization. If necessary delay the salary discussion by stating, "It's more important to establish a possible fit on both sides, including a detailed discussion of job responsibilities and career growth, than to cover the issue of salary right now." However, if you suspect the salary is less than what you are earning, you can question the *salary range* when you are called for an interview. Our experience has shown that hiring organizations often place a higher value on your experience than you do (sound familiar? You're better than you think you are!). Convinced of this strategy, of not divulging salary, an assistant office manager was counseled to let the prospective employer make the initial dollar offer. It turned out to be $2,500 higher than what the candidate had targeted! If, however, you are pushed into a discussion of salary, always state the range in which you are looking. *Example:* "I've been interviewing for positions that pay between twenty-two and twenty-eight thousand." This tells the interviewer very clearly that you're earning $17,000 to $20,000, won't accept less than $22,000, and probably want more and that you'll negotiate.

☞ *Insiders' Tip:*   If an organization wants you for a particular position, they will sometimes go beyond the established salary range and offer what it takes (within reason) to make the "sale" (and hire you).

In summary, the point should be clear. *You* are a quality product, so charge what the traffic will bear. Use your want-ad analysis to establish the salary range for any job in which you're interested, or supplement this data by speaking with colleagues who may know the going rates. Also contact local employment agencies or search firms in your area.

Overcoming Weaknesses in Your Background

Successful salespeople will tell you that their career growth has been directly influenced by their ability to overcome objections raised by customers. This is also true of the job search: to be successful, you must present (market) yourself to overcome the objections of the reader of your résumé (the employer). To aid in overcoming objections, we have listed a description of the problems many people confront when attempting to switch jobs. Alongside each are suggested ways in which these objections (usually the employer's) can be successfully overcome.

☞ *Insiders' Tip:*   Psychologically, and practically, speaking, it is important that any negatives in your work experience be addressed openly in your résumé and action letter and during the interview. Removing the skeletons of age, lack of college degree, being fired, et cetera, from the closet of your work experience will remove stress from your interviews and your new job. You can't be found out because you have already disclosed all. Often the negative appears larger in your mind than in the minds of others. Overcome it by confronting it and talking about it until it's comfortable for you to discuss it with any potential employer.

Strategies

Weakness	Résumé	Action Letter
Fired from most recent job	Show actual dates, but use only year: e.g., 1976–1981, not March 1976–November 1981.	Not applicable
Currently unemployed (less than 3 months)	Don't send out résumés showing you're unemployed. Use 1979 to present, not March 1979 to November 1981, if it's already February 1982.	Not applicable
Currently unemployed (longer than 3 months)	If appropriate, identify yourself as a self-employed consultant, either part-time or full-time. However, you may be asked for a client list, so don't do this unless you can produce a client or two. Or say you were starting your own business and changed your mind.	Not applicable
Lack of a degree or "inappropriate" educational background: e.g., have an M.A. degree, but not M.B.A. degree	List in-house courses or ones taken on your own at places like the American Management Association, university courses, etc., which are appropriate to the job (such as business courses).	Illustrate how on-the-job education progressed from small profit or sales base to large profit or sales figures.
Too much education, very light work experience	Include your most appropriate undergraduate degree. Avoid giving the impression of being a perpetual student. Also avoid date of graduation if it makes your degree obsolete or doesn't pertain to the work you seek. Omit your Ph.D. if you were employed while you got it, particularly if you're switching out of your field. Some types of company are very chary of Ph.D.'s. (This is unfair, but it is a fact of life.)	Same as above

Strategies

Weakness	*Résumé*	*Action Letter*
Too young; lack necessary experience: i.e., no experience in "our" industry	Expand your relevant experience by (1) taking credit for a team effort, (2) report part-time and voluntary work experience, (3) expand your military experience, (4) quantify your experience, (5) use a functional or combination résumé. For a full discussion, see chapter 1.	Same, but action letter is especially suited to overcome this weakness.
Too old; too much or inappropriate experience. (Being refused for being "too old"—over 40—is illegal, but companies discriminate all the same.)	Several approaches should be considered, including (1) putting dates of your education at end of résumé, (2) describing only your work experience of the last few years, and (3) using functional instead of chronological résumé or making a combination résumé and putting chronological on page 2 of your résumé.	Omit date of birth and avoid dates of educational experience.
Salary questions: Are you too high-priced? Are you too low-priced?	Avoid tipping your hand. Instead, simply state that your salary requirements are competitive or some wording to that effect. Don't state salary if answering an ad where the salary is not given, even if the ad requests it. (They don't tell you; you don't tell them.)	Same, use wording like "my salary requirements are competitive." This shows you have addressed the issue even if you haven't told them what you're earning.
Lack of progression in job titles	Use a functional or combination résumé and try to show a clear progression in job responsibility, authority, and budgeting control. Quantify whatever you can.	Action letters can easily overcome this type of objection.
Job hopping: e.g., 3 jobs within past 5 years	Use functional or combination résumé. Omit dates when listing your work record.	Action letters are particularly good when dealing with this problem.
Large gap in your work history: e.g., from a long unemployment, reentering the job market	(1) Use a functional or combination résumé. (2) Omit dates when listing your work record.	Again, one of the major advantages of the action-letter approach is its ability to cover gaps in anyone's work history.

As you can see from the above chart, the need to overcome your weaknesses is paramount if you use a résumé, but the need to overcome weaknesses can be entirely avoided by using an action letter. This is the single most important reason for utilizing the action-letter approach to switching jobs. It allows you to present your strengths without having to reveal your weaknesses (real or imagined).

☞ *Insiders' Tip:*   One of the key strategies presented in this chapter is to use the action letter to get the interview and then in the interview to use a P-A-R résumé to get the job. Since the people hiring you, if they are not in Personnel, probably do not interview on a regular basis, it is essential you provide them with a résumé from which they can conduct the interview. Managers and supervisors always feel more secure with a piece of paper in front of them. They prefer to conduct the interview via your résumé rather than an action letter.

Strategies for Using the Résumé in Your Career Campaign

The Preferred Strategy

```
┌─────────────────────────┐1       ┌─────────────────────────┐2
│ Create a reference       │        │ Develop specialized action│
│ résumé for your entire   │───────▶│ letter to match each job  │
│ work history.            │        │ in which you're interested.│
│                          │        │ See chapter 7.            │
└─────────────────────────┘        └─────────────────────────┘
                    ┌─────────────────────────┐3
                    │ Use action letter to get │
                    │ the interview, résumé to  │◀──────
                    │ get the job.              │
                    └─────────────────────────┘
```

Advantages

1. Reference résumé summarizes your work history in P-A-R format.

2. Reference résumé can be updated quickly to reflect new accomplishments.

3. A reference résumé helps lay the foundation to create actions: letters and new résumés for any specific job.

4. Provides maximum flexibility.

5. Forces you, the job hunter, to be completely familiar with all of your work background.

6. Allows you to be able to discuss any and all aspects of your work history in P-A-R format in an interview.

Limitations (Personal)

1. Your unwillingness to spend the time and effort required to develop the reference résumé in the P-A-R format.

2. Overcoming personal insecurities that favor allowing others (friends, family, employment agencies, et cetera) to take charge of the job search for you.

An Alternative Strategy

Example:

Create a reference résumé of work experience for *only one* specific job area, such as marketing, while leaving out your experience in sales and advertising.

Create a specialized action letter (see chapter 7).

> Use action letters to get your interviews, résumés to help get the job.

Advantages	*Limitations (Personal)*
1. A reference résumé for one job area—marketing, for instance—can easily be used to create an action letter.	1. Your unwillingness to spend the time and effort required to develop the reference résumé for a specific job area
2. Provides you with maximum flexibility but only within one specific job area of your entire employment history.	2. Overcoming your personal insecurities that favor allowing others to take charge of your job search
3. Forces you to be completely familiar with one specific job area in your work history.	
4. Allows you to discuss one specific job area in an interview in the P-A-R format.	
5. Compared to creating the total reference résumé, creating a *limited* reference résumé for one specific job area substantially reduces the amount of time and effort required for preparation.	

A Half-Fast Strategy

(A shortcut strategy)

Create a reference résumé that matches three or four requirements identified in your want-ad analysis.

Create a specialized action letter (see chapter 7).

Use an action letter to get interviews, résumé to get the job.

Advantages	*Limitations*
1. A reference résumé that matches the top requirements identified in any want-ad analysis can be used to create an action letter (see chapter 7).	1. Provides minimum flexibility. Would have little value in developing a new action letter.
2. Minimum of time and effort required. Particularly useful approach to deal with an immediate employment opportunity.	2. Your familiarity with one specific job area is limited to only the points identified in the want-ad analysis.

Carefully assess your own particular circumstances in order to determine which approach, the résumé or the action letter, is the most appropriate. The time restraints imposed upon you by an employer or your willingness to put forth the necessary effort are usually the major factors limiting a decision. Remember, regardless of which approach you select, it is important that you be as accurate and thorough as possible and you use the P-A-R format for your paragraphs in the selected strategy.

To help you make this decision and to provide models that you could easily adapt, examples are provided below of the three major résumé variations: chronological, functional, and combination.

Chronological Résumé

WALTER B. STEVENSON
57 East 68th Street
New York, New York   10021
(212) 462-1174

EDUCATION:

M.B.A. Finance, University of Rochester, Rochester, New York, 1977. Worked as an Institutional Research Analyst at U. Rochester, maintaining an on-line management information system. Provided interface between university administrators and computerized systems; identified and performed special analytical projects in support of short- and long-range planning. Financed 100% of education.

B.A. Computer Science; Minor; Mathematics, magna cum laude, University of Connecticut, Storrs, Connecticut, June 1970. Member, Economics and Data Processing honor societies; Varsity Volleyball Team; Intramural Track Team.

BUSINESS EXPERIENCE:

1979 to
present

VENTURE RESOURCES, LTD., White Plains, New York, a subsidiary company of a major financial institution, as Business Manager, Profit Center.

Responsible for the development of a new business venture to provide turnkey computer processing systems to the Securities Processing industry. This includes market identification, product positioning, economic feasibility analysis, business planning, initial product sales, installation, and customer retention.

- Successfully negotiated a joint venture with a minicomputer manufacturer, providing for funding (development money), marketing and sales programs, hardware and operating system software upgrades and enhancements.

- Developed a key account after only 5 months of sales effort, yielding $400,000 in 1980 first-year revenues. 1981 revenues projected to exceed $1 million.

- Directly manage one professional, one system consultant, and a secretary on a day-to-day basis. Manage 4 professionals on a matrix basis: one product manager, one assistant product manager, a customer engineer, and a systems support manager.

- Additionally manage the efforts of 3 sales representatives, one in New York City, the others in San Francisco and Boston.

- This includes sales and product training.

Major Accomplishments:

- Developed a new Securities Processing System Business while working as Venture Manager.

- Broke even in only 1 year of business operations; this business will make a significant profit in 1981.

1978-1979   AMERICAN PATENT, INC., Wilton, Connecticut, as <u>Senior Financial Planner</u>, Corporate Financial Planning & Analysis Department.

- Prepared new business plans.

- Evaluated acquisition candidates.

- Determined pricing strategies for domestic and international ventures.

- Responded to special requests from the CFO, CEO and Chairman of the Board.

<u>Accomplishment</u>:

*Responsible for the financial analysis resulting in the Company's successful acquisition of Turnkey Systems, Inc.

1977-1978   DICTAPHONE CORPORATION, Norwalk, Connecticut, as <u>Senior Operations Research Analyst</u>.

- Designed and implemented a market distribution model used to prepare market forecasts for communications transmissions between geographic centers. This model was highlighted in a successful bid for a NASA research grant for satellite communications potential.

<u>Accomplishment</u>:

*This market distribution model is still used today to generate forecasts for communications services.

1970-1975   HARTFORD PUBLIC SCHOOLS, Hartford, Connecticut, as <u>Teacher, Secondary Mathematics</u>.

- Designed and developed a multilevel Mathematics program for students taking Algebra I, II, and Plane Geometry.

- Designed a special remedial program for students who had failed Algebra I and Plane Geometry.

<u>PROFESSIONAL AFFILIATIONS</u>:

*Asked to be Guest Speaker, Eastern Region Data Processing Management Association, May 1981. Subject: "Decentralized Processing in the Stock Transfer Industry."

<u>PERSONAL DATA</u>:

Age 34; Married, 2 children; Height: 5'11"; Weight: 168 lbs. Will travel to 35%.

<u>INTERESTS</u>: Tennis, squash, bridge, collect antique war medals, travel.

<u>REFERENCES</u>: Available upon request.

Functional Résumé

JOAN A. GRITZ
6913 Bergen Line Avenue
Guttenberg, New Jersey 07024
(201) 242-8268

SUMMARY

Experienced marketing professional with profit and loss responsibility for $35,000,000 business. Stanford M.B.A. 1976 with particular expertise in Industrial Marketing; B.A. University of Pennsylvania, magna cum laude.

MAJOR ACCOMPLISHMENTS

Marketing

*Currently manage $35,000,000 food ingredients business. Consistently meet volume and profit objectives in highly competitive, price-volatile market (Fortune 500 company).

*Coordinated ingredient conversion programs for major customers, employing resources of engineering, technical services, sales, and quality control departments.

*Developed and implemented advertising campaign for major products.

*Consolidated distribution system to achieve $142,000 savings annually in inventory costs.

*Changed customer mix. Increased base volume of business. Achieved $100,000 savings in distribution costs.

*Analyzed food ingredients line, recommended product additions and deletions, new market directions.

*Made presentations to trade organizations and sales groups.

Planning and Control

*Directed operations analysis staff of 17 persons in developing personnel and equipment budgets for $23,000,000 federally funded multisite job training/placement program.

*Measured cost-effectiveness of $37,000,000 citywide job placement program, to recommend and oversee substantial operational improvements.

*Administered international materials aid and economic development programs valued at $1,400,000 annually.

Organizational Development

*Supervised and trained staff of 6 employees in computerizing process documentation system for baking operations.

*Managed research and program design staff which restructured jobs and conducted training programs for unskilled and technical-level employees of $600,000,000 company.

*Developed and implemented training program for international aid representatives of U.S.-funded private-sector agency.

LANGUAGES:

Facility in German and Spanish.

REFERENCES:

References are available upon request.

Combination Résumé

JOAN A. GRITZ
6913 BergenLine Avenue
Guttenberg, New Jersey   07024
(201) 242-8268

SUMMARY

Experienced marketing professional with profit and loss responsibility for
$35,000,000 business. Stanford M.B.A. with particular expertise in industrial
marketing.

MAJOR ACCOMPLISHMENTS

Marketing

• Currently manage $35,000,000 food ingredients business. Consistently meet volume
  and profit objectives in highly competitive, price-volatile market.

• Coordinated ingredient conversion programs for major customers, employing resources
  of engineering, technical services, sales, and quality control departments.

• Developed and implemented advertising campaign for major products.

• Consolidated distribution system to achieve $140,000 savings annually in inventory
  costs.

• Changed customer mix. Increased base volume of business. Achieved $100,000
  savings in distribution costs.

• Analyzed food ingredients line, recommended product additions and deletions, new
  market directions.

• Made presentations to trade organizations and sales groups.

Planning and Control

• Directed operations analysis staff of 17 persons in developing personnel and equipment budgets for $23,000,000 federally funded multisite job training/placement
  program.

• Measured cost-effectiveness of $37,000,000 citywide job placement program, to
  recommend and oversee substantial operational improvements.

• Administered international materials aid and economic development programs valued
  at $1,400,000 annually.

Organizational Development

• Supervised and trained staff of 6 employees in computerizing process documentation
  system for banking operations.

• Managed research and program design staff which restructured jobs and conducted
  training programs for unskilled and technical-level employees of $600,000,000
  company.

• Developed and implemented training program for international aid representatives of
  U.S.-funded private-sector agency.

WORK HISTORY

AMSTAR CORPORATION, New York, New York, 1978 to present

Product Manager, Sweetener Ingredients

P & L responsibility for industrial food ingredient product line. Market analysis and development; product and profit planning. Prepare and implement pricing policy in accordance with functional values of product, competitive environment and new product opportunities. Analyze commodity trends. Evaluate new businesses.

NESTLÉ CORPORATION, White Plains, New York, 1976-1978

Account Manager

Marketed industrial coffee and tea line to an $8,000,000 territory. Directed and conducted market analyses. Recommended investment opportunities and changes in product line strategies.

BANK OF AMERICA, San Francisco, California, 1975

Summer Intern, Operations Division

Translated program requirements into computerized document preparation and editing standards. Trained and supervised 6 employees. Made presentations to officers of the bank.

GOVERNMENT AND PRIVATE SECTOR ORGANIZATIONS   1970-1974

Supervisory and Management Positions

Worked with city government, university, and other nonprofit entities in program analysis, budgeting, and human resources functions.

EDUCATION

M.B.A., Stanford University Graduate School of Business Administration, Palo Alto, California, 1976.
    Second-year emphasis in Agribusiness Marketing. Member, Marketing Society and
    Finance Club; Corporate Issues Forum; scholarship student.
B.A. University of Pennsylvania, Philadelphia, Pennsylvania, Economics Major:
Minor: European History magna cum laude, 1970

PERSONAL

Single; Language facility: German, Spanish; Interests: Racquetball, skiing, travel.

Chronological Résumé (before revisions)

SUSAN E. JONES, 400 East Main Street, New York, New York 10010
(212) 491-6314 (home); (212) 842-9196 (work)

Education:

B.A. degree, State University of New York at Albany, May 1968.
Concentration in Psychology.

Experience:

1977-present   XYZ Company, 1700 Taylor Street, Brooklyn, N.Y., as Administrative
                  Assistant. Responsible for all administrative functions of a small
                  office. Also work on special projects as assigned by manager.
                  Handle payroll and accounts receivable. Purchase office supplies.

1970-1976   ABN Corp., 1252 South Street, Long Island City, New York, as
                  Executive Secretary. Work for officer of company handling adminis-
                  trative and clerical functions. Additionally responsible for
                  organizing meetings and trips.

1968-1970   State University of New York at Albany, Albany, New York, as
                  Administrative Assistant to the Dean of Women. Responsible for
                  all administrative functions of the dean's office.

Personal: Age 33; married, one daughter age 8; height: 5'4"; weight: 126 lb.
                  good health.

Skills: Type 85 w.p.m.; shorthand 115 w.p.m.

References: Will be furnished upon request.

Chronological Résumé (improved)

SUSAN E. JONES
400 East Main Street
New York, New York 10010
(212) 491-6314

EDUCATION:

B.A. Psychology; Minor: Economics, cum laude, STATE UNIVERSITY OF NEW YORK AT ALBANY, Albany, New York, May 1968. Activities: Dean's List; Residence Counselor, 2 years; Treasurer, Psychology Club; Varsity Swimming Team; New York State Regents Scholarship.

ADDITIONAL EDUCATION: In-house training (IBM) on COBOL and FORTRAN on IBM 370-155.

BUSINESS EXPERIENCE:

1977 to present — XYZ COMPANY, Brooklyn, New York--XYZ is a major retailing chain specializing in moderate to expensive (designer) clothes and home furnishings. Currently Executive Assistant to the Corporate Controller.

•Oversee smooth running of an office staff of 12 (4 professionals, 6 clericals).

•Hire, train and supervise all nonexempt personnel.

•Disperse biweekly payroll and manage the Accounts Receivable Department (4 people).

•Purchase all equipment and supplies.

Accomplishments:

*Reduced staff from 18 people to 12, maintaining efficiency and reducing costs by over $100,000 annually.

*Instituted a system that reduced Accounts Receivable collections from an average of 54 days to 29 days.

*Selected as liaison for EDP Department during conversion of manual to computer system, ensuring a smooth transition.

Result: Our department was officially praised by the president for being the group to make this transition most easily. (Used IBM 370-155.) Saved over $12,300.

1970-1976 — ABN Corporation, Long Island City, New York, as Administrative Assistant to the President. ABN is a medium-sized chemical company specializing in industrial and laboratory chemicals.

•Handled all business functions of the president's office including arranging meetings, booking hotels and conferences, and airline arrangements.

•Dispensed memos to other executives and managers, handled own correspondence, and screened calls and visitors.

•Directly supervised one secretary.

Accomplishments:

*Instituted a formal technical library including hiring and supervision of 2 part-time librarians.

*Redesigned 3 reporting forms, cutting back on paperwork processing by 23% in three departments with an estimated annual savings in printing and labor of over $65,000.

*Developed and dispersed an in-house monthly employee newsletter.

1968-1970   STATE UNIVERSITY OF NEW YORK AT ALBANY, Albany, New York, as Administrative Assistant to the Dean of Women.

•Supervised all women's activities, coordinating with the dean.

•Wrote copy and dispersed memos and notices to the dormitories and off-campus residences.

•Purchased supplies.

•Supervised the office staff of 3.

Accomplishments:

*Instituted a freshman get-together with upper-class students to act as "buddies" during Orientation Week.

This was so successful it has become an annual university event.

*Changed 2 supply vendors, saving the university over $3,500 a year.

INTERESTS: Tennis, swimming, collecting 19th-century oak furniture.

REFERENCES: Available upon request.

Functional Résumé

SUSAN E. JONES
400 East Main Street
New York, New York 10010
(212) 491-6314

BUSINESS EXPERIENCE:

Management
- Managed/supervised professional and clerical staff.
- Trained staff in office procedures and in various work functions including accounting and administrative.
- Oversaw the running of an Accounts Receivable department, a technical library, office of a corporation president and of the dean of women at a major university.

Finance
- Dispersed payroll and managed an Accounts Receivable department.
- Selected supply vendors based upon cost and efficiency.
- Purchased equipment and supplies in excess of $80,000 a year.

Administrative
- Successfully ran small to large offices for senior management personnel, including booking all flights, hotels, and meetings as well as handling all day-to-day functions.
- Handled own correspondence.
- Liaison with other departments and top management.

EDP
- Liaison on a major manual on computer conversion with EDP department. Knowledge of FORTRAN and COBOL on IBM 370-155.

Accomplishments:

*Reduced staff by 33% without affecting efficiency and eliminated annual costs by over $100,000.

*Designed system to reduce A/R collections from 54 to 29 days.

*Set up and staffed a technical library.

*Redesigned reporting forms, eliminating paperwork processing by 23% and man-hours by $65,000 worth annually.

*Changed vendors, saving a university office $3,500 a year.

EDUCATION:

B.A. Psychology/Economics, State University of New York at Albany, Albany, New York, May 1968. G.P.A.: 3.40; Dean's List; Varsity Swim Team; Residence Counselor; Scholarship, 4 years.

INTERESTS: Tennis, swimming, travel, antiques.

REFERENCES: Available upon request.

Functional/Chronological Résumé

SUSAN E. JONES
400 East Main Street
New York, New York 10010
(212) 491-6314

BUSINESS EXPERIENCE:

Management
- Managed/supervised professional and clerical staff.
- Trained staff in office procedures and in various work functions, including accounting and administrative.
- Oversaw the running of an Accounts Receivable department, a technical library, office of a corporation president and of the dean of women at a major university.

Finance
- Dispersed payroll and managed an Accounts Receivable department.
- Selected supply vendors based upon cost and efficiency.
- Purchased equipment and supplies in excess of $80,000 a year.

Administrative
- Successfully ran small to large offices for senior management personnel including booking all flights, hotels and meetings as well as handling all day-to-day functions.
- Handled own correspondence.
- Liaison with other departments and top management.

EDP
- Liaison on a major manual to computer conversion with EDP Department. Knowledge of FORTRAN & COBOL on IBM 370-155.

Accomplishments:
- Reduced staff by 33% without affecting efficiency and eliminated annual costs by over $100,000.
- Designed system to reduce A/R collections from 54 to 29 days.
- Set up and staffed a technical library.
- Redesigned reporting forms, eliminating paperwork processing by 23% and man-hours by $65,000 worth annually.
- Changed vendors, saving a university office $3,500 a year.

EDUCATION:

B.A. Psychology/Economics, State University of New York at Albany, Albany, New York, May 1968. G.P.A.: 3.40; Dean's List; Varsity Swim Team; Residence Counselor; Scholarship, 4 years.

EMPLOYERS:

- 1977-present   XYZ COMPANY, Brooklyn, New York, as Executive Assistant to the Corporate Controller.
- 1970-1976   ABN CORPORATION, Long Island City, New York, as Administrative Assistant to the President.
- 1968-1970   STATE UNIVERSITY OF NEW YORK AT ALBANY, Albany, New York, as Administrative Assistant to the Dean of Women.

INTERESTS: Tennis, swimming, travel, antiques.

REFERENCES: Available upon request.

Summary

Many of us have had either good or bad experiences in the past with résumés. Although we will show how to conduct a successful job search using a nonrésumé approach, the résumé still has an important role to play in the job search process. The fact remains that most personnel recruiters and line managers expect to review an applicant's background and work experience in a format that they are comfortable with. This format is still the traditional résumé. Therefore, it is in your own interest that you become knowledgeable in its varieties and development so you can put your best foot forward.

Like many of the concepts presented in this book, they build upon each other in order to create a system of job hunting that is stronger than the sum of its parts. Therefore, always be sure to use the P-A-R format in constructing your résumé. In our next chapter, "The Want-Ad Analysis Technique," we will continue this building process by showing you how to choose those parts of your background and work experience that will maximize your chances for getting interviews and subsequent job offers.

5. The Want-Ad Analysis Technique: The Rudder That Steers the Ship

"He who hesitates is last."

—Mae West, The Wit and Wisdom of Mae West

A Fable

Once upon a time a Sea Horse gathered up his seven pieces of eight and cantered out to find his fortune. Before he had traveled very far he met an Eel, who said,

"Psst. Hey, bud. Where 'ya goin'?"

"I'm going out to find my fortune," replied the Sea Horse, proudly.

"You're in luck," said the Eel. "For four pieces of eight you can have this speedy flipper, and then you'll be able to get there a lot faster."

"Gee, that's swell," said the Sea Horse, and paid the money and put on the flipper and slithered off at twice the speed. Soon he came upon a Sponge, who said,

"Psst. Hey, bud. Where 'ya goin'?"

"I'm going out to find my fortune," replied the Sea Horse.

"You're in luck," said the Sponge. "For a small fee I will let you have this jet-propelled scooter so that you will be able to travel a lot faster."

So the Sea Horse bought the scooter with his remaining money and went zooming through the sea five times as fast. Soon he came upon a Shark, who said,

"Psst. Hey, bud. Where 'ya goin'?"

"I'm going to find my fortune," replied the Sea Horse.

"You're in luck. If you'll take this short cut," said the Shark, pointing to his open mouth, "you'll save yourself a lot of time."

"Gee, thanks," said the Sea Horse, and zoomed off into the interior of the Shark, and was never heard from again.

The moral of this fable is that if you're not sure where you're going, you're liable to end up someplace else.

(From *Preparing Instructional Objectives*, by Robert F. Mager, Pitman Learning, Inc., 1975.)

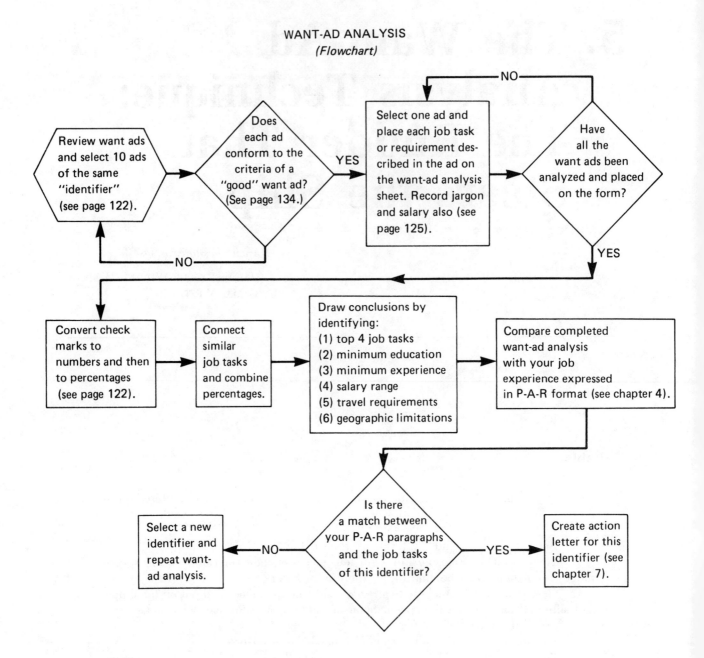

WANT-AD ANALYSIS
(Flowchart)

The Want-Ad Analysis Flowchart

According to *Webster's New Collegiate Dictionary*, 1980 (1973) edition, a *flowchart* is "a diagram...that shows...progression through a...procedure or system." It is a communication tool that has been developed in the writing of computer programs; it is used in this chapter as a visual aid. Specifically, it summarizes the key steps you have to take to complete successfully the want-ad analysis. If you look at the chart you will see each distinct step, the proper sequence of the steps, and the important questions you have to ask yourself to ensure that you have covered all points in the techniques of the want-ad analysis.

Throughout the chapter on the want-ad analysis, reference to this flowchart will be made, and it will be referred to at the end of each section where application of any piece of the flowchart is important. At each one of these points, refer back to the flowchart, to make sure you understand the sequences.

As mentioned previously but worth repeating, there are two main issues in marketing your job talents. The first part is to determine your own capabilities and then to express them in a format that will help your marketing efforts. Having just finished chapter 4, you now have a self-assessment profile of your entire work experience expressed in a highly salable format: Problem-Action-Result (P-A-R).

You hope you know yourself and your capabilities better than at any previous time in your life. But the second part of marketing your job talents still needs to be addressed. Specifically, "Where can this enlightened view of myself be used best? I know I'm terrific, but who needs me and how can I convince them I am *best?*"

Interestingly enough, employers answer both of these questions while at the same time pursuing their own self-interest. This is done through the hundreds of job advertisements or want ads that appear almost daily. Our premise is that by using the techniques described here you will be able to compare your skills with the requirements of any particular job in order to determine *realistically* if you could fill that job. A visual overview of these techniques can be seen by reviewing the Want-Ad Analysis Flowchart, which will be explained to you as we go along.

The Truth about Newspaper Help-Wanted Ads

Let's look more closely at the issue of want ads. Although this chapter deals with want ads, most jobs are never advertised. And this happens despite the fact that most people use want ads when switching. A study has shown that only 15 percent of all jobs available are ever advertised at any one time. The following appeared in the *Wall Street Journal* on November 20, 1974.

> DO WANT ADS fully reflect a city's job situation: A study says no.
>
> An examination of five years of help-wanted ads in newspapers in San Francisco and Salt Lake City shows their total volume does correlate with the cities' unemployment rate. But Olympus Research Corp. finds they provide a poor reflection of the local job market. For instance, sales jobs are overrepresented in the ads, while government and blue-collar work is undercovered.
>
> In 88% of job ads placed by employment agencies, the study finds the employer's business wasn't identified. Agency ads also were repetitive, reflecting multiple listings of the same job offer. Only 25% of employer ads disclosed wages offered, and 61% of ads in San Francisco gave no clue to job location. Many ads were merely come-ons for risky business ventures.
>
> The researchers said that 35% of San Francisco employers and 76% of Salt Lake City employers they surveyed in 1972 hired no workers through want ads.

If only 15 percent of all jobs are advertised, then 85 percent of all jobs are never advertised. This is the "hidden" job market; 70 percent of these jobs are filled through the buddy system. The remaining 15 percent are listed through employment agencies and executive search firms.

What you have observed is only 15 percent of the available jobs each week during a six-week period.... So, how does the want-ad analysis help you find the major part of the job market, that 85 percent known as the "hidden" job market? Very simply. Once you have determined the position for which you qualify and want to pursue (by doing want-ad analyses of the newspaper ads), you have defined the qualifications necessary for *that* job, whether or not it's advertised. After creating appropriate marketing pieces, action letters, and résumés, you can send them out to the appropriate individuals in the "hidden" job market! (Details on doing this will be discussed in chapter 9.)

JUDY A. PRICE
63-10 93rd Avenue
Hollis, New York 11532
(212) 631-4918

CAREER GOAL: An entry-level position that will use my college degrees, managerial and sales experience, and strong communication skills.

EDUCATION:

1979   Katharine Gibbs School, New York, N.Y.: Entree Program for College Graduates. Intensive training in Management Procedures, Typing, Stenoscript and Business Correspondence.

1980   New York University Graduate School of Business, Evening Division, Candidate for M.B.A. Completed 3 courses to date: Economics, Accounting, General Management I.

St. John's University, Jamaica, NY
M.S. in Education, 1972.

Rutgers University, Douglass College, New Brunswick, New Jersey
B.S. in Education and Psychology, 1970.
Dean's List (four years), cum laude graduate, National Honor Society member, staff reporter on the newspaper.

EXPERIENCE

1978-
present   New York City Board of Education
Welfare Education Program: National Education Act.

Instructor in Adult Basic Education: Math and Reading Skills, Instructor in English as a Second Language.

1972-present   New York City Board of Education
Teacher of High School English Composition.

1970-1972   Abraham & Straus Department Store, Brooklyn, New York
Retail Assistant Buyer in Fashion Accessories Division.
Supervisor of all sales, receiving, and stock personnel within the Small Leather Goods Department.

ABILITIES: Knowledge of retail business operations, familiarity with economics and accounting procedures, organizational and planning ability, effective selling techniques, problem-solving analysis, and reading and writing ability in Spanish.

INTERESTS: Ballet and jazz dance, theatre group member, squash player, community block association member, fund-raiser for social and church groups.

REFERENCES: Available upon request.

The Want-Ad Analysis Technique Is Used to Define Pertinent Job Content and Other Critical Parameters for Any Job Title

Example: You have always wanted to work at Colgate-Palmolive in consumer-package-goods marketing. After determining your qualifications through doing several want-ad analyses for, say, product manager, and revising your résumé and/or action letter to fit better the qualifications needed to do product management in a consumer-package-goods marketing firm, you send out your marketing piece to the vice president of marketing at Colgate-Palmolive, or to any other firm in package goods, and state that you will call within a week to arrange an appointment. This is called cold-canvassing and it is how many people find new positions. If you have friends, relatives, and business associates working in organizations that interest you, ask them for the names of the appropriate people to whom you should submit your résumé or action letter and follow up in the same way.

For those of you who are contemplating leaving industry to start your own business, the want-ad analysis gives you an excellent tool for assessing the character and personality traits as well as the content necessary to become an entrepreneur in any chosen field.

If you're like most people, you don't really know what the important components are in most jobs outside your own areas of specialty. However, using the techniques of the want-ad analysis, you can learn to use your particular talents and skills when switching career fields. Let's see exactly how this is done.

Judy Price recently completed her ninth year as a high-school English teacher. Judy realizes that in the 1980s the secondary-education field will continue to shrink, which means continuous budget cutbacks, larger classes, staff reductions, growing disciplinary problems, et cetera. Long-range prospects for continuing as a high-school English teacher, either in a large city or a suburban school system, offer very limited growth and income. *Her hurdle:* how can she get the information necessary to evaluate her skills and where can these skills, once identified, be best applied outside education? As most of us did, Judy Price updated her résumé as the first step in her desire to *switch*. The result of her first efforts is on page 118.

Conclusions from Judy Price's Original Résumé:

1. She used jargon of the education field and will be viewed by readers of her résumé as "only a teacher," a *nonbusiness* person (even though she mentions two years in retail sales).

2. She can take dictation and she can type (see Katharine Gibbs experience at top of résumé). Company people who read her résumé *may* bring her in for an interview but will most likely talk about her being an *administrative assistant* (a euphemistic title for a secretary with a college degree). This often translates to "We can get someone smart who will work hard and whom we don't have to pay too much money and needn't promote too quickly."

☞ *Insiders' Tip:* Remember: companies have as much trouble in getting good secretarial help as they have in hiring top executives. To attract administrative assistants (secretaries), they often promise promotions they can't or won't deliver. If you were a harried, overworked boss lucky enough to get a degreed, bright assistant, would *you* want him/her to be promoted? And to leave you with the very real possibility of not being able to find as competent a person to replace him/her? Probably not, not if you are really honest with yourself. So take heed!

However, after applying the techniques of past chapters to develop her self-assessment, Judy Price's résumé has been reconstructed to emphasize her strengths, not her weaknesses.

Below are the results of her efforts, most of which came from reading in various newspaper ads the qualifications for the job she sought. She turned her teaching jargon into corporate training jargon. This transition came about through two separate avenues of investigation: reviewing want ads and speaking to friends and neighbors employed in industry. From these sources she concluded that she could translate her education experience to Training and Development, a subtype of Personnel within industry.

JUDY A. PRICE
63-10 93rd Avenue, Apt. 14M
Hollis, New York 11532
(212) 631-4918

SUMMARY OF QUALIFICATIONS:

Background and expertise in accounting procedures and economics, effective selling techniques, analytical problem solving, and organization and planning.

EDUCATION:

M.B.A. candidate, New York University Graduate School of Business, New York, New York, 1980 to present. Courses of Interest: Accounting; Economics; General Management.

M.S., St. John's University, Jamaica, New York, 1972. Major: Education. B.S. Psychology & Education, cum laude, Rutgers University, New Brunswick, New Jersey, 1970. Activities: Dean's List, 4 years; National Honor Society; University Scholarship, 4 years; staff reporter, college newspaper; worked part-time and summers financing 100% of own education.

BUSINESS EXPERIENCE:

1972 to present

NEW YORK CITY BOARD OF EDUCATION, New York, New York, as Instructor, English Composition (secondary level).

• Develop, design, and instruct curricula.

• Test and evaluate curriculum design and instructional methods, making changes when necessary.

• Develop and disseminate workbooks and tests.

• Conduct special seminars for students having difficulty with course content.

• Research previously used curricula and methodologies.

• Write up summary reports for superiors and parents.

• Supervise over 170 students per day.

1978-present
part-time

- As part of Adult Basic Education, Welfare Education Program, instruct "English as a Second Language" (per diem).

- Selected from 50 instructors to be the after-school instructor for teachers, to help them improve their instructional skills.

- Instruct up to 25 teachers per day, one day a week (paid).

SUMMERS
1973-1977

TIME-LIFE BOOKS, New York, New York, as Telephone Sales Representative (commission).

- Worked double four-hour daily shifts and outperformed all other representatives.

- Maintained excellent relationships with current clients.

- Identified and sold to new customers.

- Kept current on new products by checking competition.

- Participated in marketing strategy meetings.

Result: Was asked to take on a permanent position.

1970-1972

ABRAHAM & STRAUS DEPARTMENT STORE, Brooklyn, New York, as Assistant Buyer, Fashion Accessories ($900,000 annual sales).

- Supervised 12 sales, receiving, and stock personnel.

- Reduced overstocks in slow-moving merchandise by weekly branch-store visits.

- Increased promotional leather line by 25%.

- Planned advertising space and placed ads.

INTERESTS:

Squash, tennis, stock market, community block association member, fund-raiser for church and social groups, dance theatre group member.

LANGUAGE:

Spanish

REFERENCES:

References are available upon request.

By following our analysis, you will see that Judy has a core group of skills. Her problem now is to identify where these skills can be applied *outside* teaching. How does she do it?

Until now, one way to determine where a person could successfully apply his or her skills and aptitudes was through professional career counselors. Except for colleges, these career services, which often use extensive psychological testing, can run into hundreds or thousands of dollars and yet often fail to effect a successful career change.

Using the Want-Ad Analysis Technique

But there is a simpler, much less expensive, and, we feel, more effective technique for determining where a person's skills and experience can best be employed: the want-ad analysis technique. This is a systematic method of analyzing want ads in order to achieve the following:

a. Define the job tasks.
b. Determine which job tasks are most frequently requested.
c. Define educational requirements.
d. Define the jargon of the job.
e. Define the geographic location.
f. Define the amount of travel required.
g. Define the salary range.

Within the context of Judy Price's desire to switch, let's take a closer look at the want-ad analysis technique to see how it is applied.

The want-ad analysis form shown on the next two pages is the basic tool that Judy Price will use to determine if her skills and experience can be applied outside her current field of teaching.

Below is an explanation of what the want-ad analysis is and how you go about using it.

A. List the job titles ("identifiers") in the ten ads you're analyzing (they should all be the same or very similar).

B. List the sources of your ads (newspaper's name, what trade journal you took an ad from, et cetera).

C. List the kinds of organizations advertising—you may discover your job title crosses all industry lines or that it is pertinent only to one industry.

D. From *each* of the ten ads you have selected, list the job requirements, educational level, geographic locations, salary ranges, and skills needed to perform the job. Some will be identical or very similar; do *not* write these a second or third time (see "E").

NOTE: If all ten ads require an M.B.A. in Finance and you have a B.A. in French, your chances, unless your work experience is exactly on target, are slim for getting an interview. Pick another "identifier." If one of the ads states that the position is in Seattle, Washington, it doesn't make sense to use the ad as one of your ten if you are not willing to relocate.

E. When you list something under "D" put a check mark ($\sqrt{}$) or a vertical line beside "Frequency in Ads" ("E"). If the same requirement comes up a second, third time or more, *don't* rewrite it; just add a mark in the "Frequency" column next to the first requirement you wrote down.

F. After all ten ads have been put on your want-ad analysis worksheet, add up the check marks under "E" ("Frequency in Ads") and convert these to a number. *Example:* If salary has consistently shown up as $25,000–$30,000 in six ads out of ten, write "6" in the "F" column.

G. Convert your numbers to a percentage. *Example:* Salary has been $25,000–$30,000 for six ads. This is 60 percent (now you see why we use ten ads as a good sample size!). Place "60%" under "G" next to the $25,000–$30,000 line.

WANT AD ANALYSIS WORKSHEET

Ad Title(s) 1. (A)		5.		Sources of Ads: (B)		
2.		6.		1.		
3.		7.		2.		
4.		Industries Represented (C)				
Number of Ads	1.		4.		7.	
Dates of Ads	2.		5.		8.	
Salary Range	3. (E)		6. (F) (G)		9. (H)	

Job Requirements/Skills Education/Location, etc. (D)	Frequency in Ads	Number of Ads	%	Jargon
1.				
2.				
3.				
4.				
5.				
6.				
7.				
8.				
9.				
10.				
11.				
12.				
13.				
14.				
15.				
16.				
17.				
18.				

Job Requirements/Skills Education/Location, etc.	Frequency in Ads	Number of Ads	%	Jargon
19.				
20.				
21.				
22.				
23.				
24.				
25.				
26.				
27.				
28.				
29.				
30.				

Conclusions

Top Four Job Tasks or Skills

Ⓘ

1. _____

2. _____

3. _____

4. _____

Minimum Education Required_____Salary Range_____

Minimum Experience Required_____Travel Requirements (%)_____

Geographic Limitations_____

Other_____

H. Every time you read an ad in which a term appears that you don't know, put it in the jargon column under "H." Look at our glossary in the back of this book. If the term isn't there, it may be so esoteric as not to be very meaningful (particularly if it only showed up in one ad). If, however, it's in several ads, and it's not in our glossary, check further. Knowing jargon allows you to "speak" the language of that job, both in your marketing materials and at interviews.

I. *Conclusions—Page 2 of the Want-Ad Analysis Worksheet.* Look over your completed worksheet and put the four highest percentages obtained for job tasks and skills under "Conclusions." If you have at least three of the four in your background *and* you have the minimum education level, experience level, and so on, as well, you can realistically apply for these positions. If you don't have at least 75 percent of the top skills or performance requirements and your education and experience levels are either too low, too high, or just not appropriate, you should probably discount this job title and try another title. It will not be realistic for you to attempt a switch.

How would Judy Price use the want-ad analysis worksheet? By speaking to her friends and neighbors who worked in various industries, Judy discovered that "educator" types in industry are called training specialists. Their job is usually an entry-level position, but a likely place to start in the business world. Judy proceeded to start collecting as many ads with the "training specialist" title as possible. She collected ten training-specialist ads for her analysis. (Ten ads statistically represent about one month's worth of ads from various sources and will be a realistic sample size with which to work. It is possible to collect ten ads if you are reading two major papers per week, including a Sunday edition.)

Here are the ten ads that Judy Price clipped out during four weeks of reading the newspapers.

Ad 1: CORPORATE TRAINING SPECIALIST

Now that you're ready to make that important next move, it's time to consider our billion dollar company headquartered in northern N.J. The candidate we seek must possess at least 3-5 years' experience conducting Management Skills Training. Experience within a retail organization is desired but not necessary. A B.S. in Communications or a related field is a must. You will be responsible for conducting classes in management skills, leadership, group dynamics, motivation, and communication, as well as possessing good platform skills. If you think we have something to talk about send résumé along with salary history to:

Ad 2: TRAINING SPECIALIST

Expanding division of major NYC financial institution seeks a Training Specialist to assume new position with impact and responsibility for design, development, and implementation of a technical and skills development training program; conducting the classroom training for all levels of management. The Training Specialist we seek will innovate. You'll start from ground zero, develop and implement the training program for a newly formed division of a prestigious financial institution. The focus will be on sales, customer service, and supervisory instruction for all levels of management. To qualify, you must have bachelor's degree level skills, and at least 3-5 years' training experience, preferably in a banking or securities environment. We are prepared to offer an attractive starting salary plus excellent benefits. For consideration, please send résumé in confidence to:

Ad 3: TRAINING SPECIALIST

For human resources development department of prominent communications corporation in NYC. An extremely fine career opportunity is now available for a dynamic training professional with a degree in Business, Psychology, Education, or related discipline, coupled with a minimum of 18 months' experience in conducting training programs within a corporate environment. To be considered for this key spot, applicants must possess a solid working knowledge of behavioral sciences, learning theory, motivation, etc., as well as the ability to conceive, write, implement, and conduct effective training programs. Salary in the high teens range plus comprehensive company benefits. Please send detailed résumé including salary history and requirements, in confidence to:

Ad 4: TRAINING SPECIALIST

Multi-branch Savings Bank headquartered in Brooklyn is looking for a degreed individual with a minimum of 2 years' corporate personnel training background. Successful candidate will be responsible for the development and implementation of new programs. Excellent writing skills essential. Please submit résumé, establishing qualifications, along with current and desired income, in full confidence to:

Ad 5: TRAINING SPECIALIST

Major banking corporation is seeking applicant with college degree plus 2 to 3 years of training experience, preferably in industry or banking. Design and instruct training program. Heavy interface with line management. Ability to conceptualize, plan, research, and write. Salary to $17,000. Send résumé, in confidence to:

Ad 6: TRAINING SPECIALIST

We have an excellent opportunity at our Corporate Headquarters for a professional trainer with experience in the automobile field. You will conduct sales and management training seminars for dealer personnel and, equally important, you will have input regarding the seminar's content. Our consistently favorable sales give this position outstanding career potential with several possibilities available after a reasonable period of service. If qualified, please send your résumé to the address indicated below.

Ad 7: TRAINING SPECIALIST

This challenging position offers immediate visibility and opportunity to survey requirements, develop and implement significant programs for a major investment banking firm. Results-oriented track record concurrent with ability to innovate is essential. Experience should also include accessing departmental requirements, devising and directing programs to include supervisory and management development, and departmental skills training. Knowledge of multi-media methods a must; brokerage experience preferred. In addition to a career opportunity, we offer salary commensurate with experience and excellent firm-paid benefits. Please reply in confidence to:

Ad 8: TRAINING SPECIALIST

General Corporation is a rapidly expanding international leader
in the development, manufacture, and sale of medical equipment.
Continued growth has created a challenging opportunity for a
Training Specialist at the Corporate Office in Atlanta. Reporting to our Manager of Human Resources Department, you will be
involved in the design and implementation of management development programs for our All-Salaried Operations in Georgia and
California. Emphasis will be on team development, project
management, and skills assessment in the context of a matrix
organization. If you have 2-4 years' training experience in a
manufacturing environment, a B.S. degree, and are currently
earning a salary in the high teens, please send résumé and salary
history to:

Ad 9: TRAINING & DEVELOPMENT SPECIALIST

To $18,000. Unique firm has a challenging position for a skilled
trainer who possesses excellent group dynamic skills as well as
the ability to design, market, and implement training programs.
Must be able to develop and write case studies, group exercises,
lecturettes in the areas of affirmative action management and
career development. 30% travel. Please send résumé including
salary history to:

Ad 10: CORPORATE TRAINING SPECIALIST

Now that you're ready to make that important next move, it's
time to consider our billion-dollar company headquartered in
northern N.J. The candidate we seek must possess at least 2-4
years' experience in conducting Non-Management Skills Training.
Experience within a retail organization is desired but not
necessary. A B.S. in Communications or a related field is a
must. You will be responsible for knowledge, skills, and attitude training; organizing and conducting nonmanagement seminars;
assisting in developing manuals and workbooks; testing and
evaluating training programs. If you think we have something to
talk about, send résumé along with salary history to:

To illustrate how Judy analyzed these ads, we will take a blank want-ad analysis worksheet form. (We have provided a copy for you on pages 158–159 at the end of this chapter. Have it photocopied or offset so that you have a good supply of them on hand.)

Applying the information contained in Ad 1, Judy's worksheet begins to develop (page 128).

Once one ad was completely analyzed and put on the want-ad analysis worksheet, Judy repeated the process adding ads 2 and 3. Each time a new item was placed in the Job Requirements column, Judy remembered to place a mark in column "E," "Frequency in Ads." Each time the item was repeated it was only necessary to place another mark in the "Frequency in Ads" column opposite the appropriate item.

Adding the data contained in want ads 2 and 3, Judy's worksheet continues to expand (page 129). It's still too early to draw conclusions even if you see patterns beginning to develop.

WANT AD ANALYSIS WORKSHEET

Ad Title(s) 1. Corporate Training Specialist (1) 5.		Sources of Ads:
2.	6.	1. New York Herald
3.	7.	2.
4.	Industries Represented	

Number of Ads	1	1. Retail	4.	7.
Dates of Ads	1/23	2.	5.	8.
Salary range		3.	6.	9.

Job Requirements/Skills Education/Location, etc.	Frequency in Ads	Number of Ads	%	Jargon
1. 3–5 years experience	1			Group dynamics
2. Retail experience	1			Platform skills
3. B.S. in communications	1			
4. Conduct classes in management skills	1			
5. Conduct classes in leadership	1			
6. Conduct classes in group dynamics	1			
7. Conduct classes in motivation	1			
8. Conduct classes in communications	1			
9. Good platform skills	1			

Conclusions

Top Four Job Tasks or Skills

1.

2.

3.

4.

Minimum Education Required_____ Salary Range_____

Minimum Experience Required_____ Travel Requirements (%)_____

Geographic Limitations_____

Other

WANT AD ANALYSIS WORKSHEET

Ad Title(s) 1. Corporate Training Specialist (1)	5.	Sources of Ads:	
2. Training Specialist (2)	6.	1. New York Herald	
3.	7.	2.	
4.	Industries Represented		
Number of Ads — 3	1. Retail	4.	7.
Dates of Ads — 1/23	2. Banking	5.	8.
Salary Range — High teens	3. Communications	6.	9.

Job Requirements/Skills Education/Location, etc.	Frequency in Ads	Number of Ads	%	Jargon
1. 3-5 years experience	11			Group Dynamics
2. Retail experience	1			Platform skills
3. B.S. in communications	11			Ground zero
4. Conduct classes in management skills	1			
5. Conduct classes in leadership	1			
6. Conduct classes in group dynamics	1			
7. Conduct classes in motivation	1			
8. Conduct classes in communications	1			
9. Good platform skills	1			
10. Design and instruct programs	11			
11. Conduct and organize seminars	11			
12. Focus on sales	1			
13. Focus on customer service	1			
14. Focus on supervisory training	1			
15. Banking or securities experience	1			
16. Degree in Business, Psychology, Education	1			
17. Eighteen months experience in Corporation	1			
18. Knowledge of behavioral sciences	1			

Repeating this process with ads 4 through 10, Judy's completed want-ad analysis looks like the chart below.

WANT AD ANALYSIS WORKSHEET

Ad Title(s)		Sources of Ads:	
1. Corporate Training Specialist (2)	5.		
2. Training Specialist (4)	6.	1. New York Herald	
3. Training & Develop. Specialist (1)	7.	2. City Journal-Ledger	
4.		Industries Represented	

Number of Ads	10	1. Retail	4. Financial	7.
Dates of Ads	1/23, 1/30, 2/6, 2/13	2. Banking	5. Automotive	8.
Salary Range	High teens	3. Communications	6. Medical Equipment	9.

Job Requirements/Skills Education/Location, etc.	Frequency in Ads	Number of Ads	%	Jargon
1. 3-5 years experience	11	2	20	Group dynamics
2. Retail experience	11	2	20	Platform skills
3. B.S. in communications	11	2	20	Ground zero
4. Conduct classes in management skills	11	2	20	Multimedia methods
5. Conduct classes in leadership	1	1	10	Skills assessment
6. Conduct classes in group dynamics	1	1	10	Project management
7. Conduct classes in motivation	1	1	10	Matrix organization
8. Conduct classes in communications	1	1	10	Affirmative action
9. Good platform skills	1	1	10	
10. Design and instruct programs	1111111	7	70	
11. Conduct and organize seminars	111	3	30	
12. Focus on sales	11	2	20	
13. Focus on customer service	1	1	10	
14. Focus on supervisory training	1	1	10	
15. Banking or securities experience	11	2	20	
16. Degree in Business, Psychology, Education	11111	5	50	
17. Eighteen months experience in corporation	1	1	10	
18. Knowledge of behavioral sciences	1	1	10	

Job Requirements/Skills Education/Location, etc.	Frequency in Ads	Number of Ads	%	Jargon
19. 2-4 years experience in training	111111	6	60	
20. Accessing departmental requirements	1	1	10	
21. Knowledge of multimedia	1	1	10	
22. Focus on team development	1	1	10	
23. Focus on project management	1	1	10	
24. Focus on skill assessment	1	1	10	
25. Group dynamic skills	1	1	10	
26. Develop and write case studies	1	1	10	
27. Develop and write group exercises	1	1	10	
28. Develop and write lecturettes in Affirmative action	1	1	10	
29. Develop and write lecturettes in career development	1	1	10	
30. 30% travel	1	1	10	
31. Nonmanagement skill, training	1	1	10	
32. Attitude training	1	1	10	
33. Testing and evaluating training programs	1	1	10	
34. Develop manuals and workbooks	1	1	10	

Conclusions

Top Four Job Tasks or Skills

1. Design and instruct programs

2. Conduct classes in management skills (Items 5, 6, 8, 9, 15, 23)

3. Conduct and organize seminars

4. Conduct classes in management skills, group dynamics, nonmanagement skills training

Minimum Education Required Degree (Bachelor's) in Education, Psychology, Bus. Admin.   Salary Range Consistently in high teens

Minimum Experience Required 2-5 years with the upper limit at 5 years   Travel Requirements (%) Mentioned in 10% of advertisements & listed as 30% travel.

Geographic Limitations Wide ranging—primarily in New York area with 10% in California and Florida area

Other

In doing her analysis, Judy Price realized that there were exceptions she had to watch out for:

(1)   Very rarely will two organizations call the same task or requirement by exactly the same name.

(2)   Sometimes similar jobs have different titles.

Example: A large company's title might be Trainer, a medium-sized company might call the job Training Manager, and a small one Training Director. Smaller companies usually have more-important-sounding titles than big ones.

Having completed the analysis of ten want ads, Judy Price is ready to draw her conclusions. To do this, she converts the marks of each task to a number (placing the number in the column marked "Number of Ads") and then makes the number into a percentage (of ten ads). Her analysis revealed the following conclusions:

(a)   The top four job tasks (by percentage) as exhibited in the ten advertisements for "Training Specialist" were:
(1)   Designing and instructing programs (70)
(2)   Developing manuals and workbooks (60)
(3)   Conducting and organizing seminars (50)
(4)   Conducting classes in management skills, group dynamics, and nonmanagement skills (50).

(b)   The minimum education required is a bachelor's degree. Fields asked for are Education, Psychology, Business Administration, and Communications.

(c)   The minimum experience required is two years, with the upper limit at five years.

(d)   The salary range was consistently in the high teens.

(e)   The travel requirements for such a position were mentioned in 10 percent of the ads (one ad) and listed as 30 percent travel.

(f)   The geographic opportunities were mostly in the New York metropolitan area (80 percent); 20 percent were outside the New York area (one in California, one in Florida).

In "fine tuning" her want-ad analysis, Judy collected and analyzed ads for *only* one specific title, *Training Specialist.*

Often, various ads define the amount of travel as either "light" or "extensive" (over 50%), or they don't mention it at all, which usually means no, or almost no, travel.

Jargon for a job is frequently used in an ad but never defined, for people in the field know that terminology. As an aid to save time, our *glossary* will define the jargon for you for the positions we discuss in detail throughout the book.

NOTE: As you probably noticed, Training Ad 1 and Training Ad 10 are similar. These two ads appeared one month apart, one in the Classified and one in the Business section of a Sunday New York paper. What does this say to you? (1) The company never filled the position (for any number of reasons) or (2) the person hired didn't work out.

Either way, if you interview for a position that has been advertised this way, *you must determine what happened.* This is a key to your success on the job. Now you can see the value of keeping accurate records as to when an ad appeared. Always date the ads you clip out.

Technically, Judy's want-ad analysis is skewed, as it actually represents only nine different jobs. However, we felt it important to leave it just like this because it was a real situation and one that could happen very easily to you. After all, a company can advertise in two (or more) papers at the same time. If you had both of the papers, particularly if one or more ads were "blind" (box number) ads, you might think they were distinctly different jobs. With the exception of the box number, the wording of these two ads is nearly identical. With a time spread of one month between the two ads, it would be easy to overlook their similarity.

Having completed her want-ad analysis for ten Training Specialist ads, Judy Price can now realistically compare her own expertise and skills as defined in previous chapters (expressed in the Problem-Action-Result format) against the employer's needs as defined by the want-ad analysis. For a visual summary of the process, see the flowchart at the beginning of this chapter.

BOTTOM LINE: Judy can now answer the most critical questions related to switching:

(1)   Do I have the right work experience and education to do this job?
(2)   On the basis of salary, travel requirements, and location of this organization, do I want this job?
(3)   Should I send in my action letter or résumé to get an interview?

On the basis of Judy Price's experience and the subsequent development of her reference résumé in the recommended P-A-R format, Judy concluded that there were two basic areas where her skills, experience, and interests could be applied. One was in personnel work. The specific job titles she identified were Training Specialist, Benefits Coordinator, Trainer, Training Coordinator, and Training Administrator. The other area was Sales Representation.

Since Judy decided to build upon her extensive teaching experience, she selected the job title of Training Specialist to investigate, using the want-ad analysis worksheet as a means of determining whether her skills matched industry's requirements closely enough to apply for a job with this title.

Now that we have followed Judy Price through her want-ad analysis, let's discuss the steps you would follow when doing your own.

Remember that employing this technique is a quick, inexpensive, and practical method of determining if you qualify for a particular job. Try not to overlook this step in your job hunt. The time you spend will be worth the rewards, to say nothing of the time saved and the disappointment and aggravation you can avoid. Believe us! It's well worth the effort.

Before preparing to do your own analysis, it's necessary first to discuss the sources of want ads and your ability to distinguish between "good" and "bad" ads.

"All Want Ads Are Not Created Equal!"

In recent years, the sources of want ads have grown beyond the normal newspaper ad sections. But, as expected, newspapers will still be your single most important printed resource for job leads. Besides culling your local papers on a daily basis, you should, as we've said, also search through at least one major Sunday edition of national importance. Depending upon where you want to work you should be reading the Sunday editions of the *New York Times, Washington Post, Boston Globe, Chicago Tribune, Denver Post, Los Angeles Times, Miami Tribune, Atlanta Constitution,* and so on. The *Wall Street Journal's* big ad day is Tuesday; some ads also appear on Wednesday.

It's important to note that for purposes of your want-ad analysis, old copies of your Sunday newspaper, whether two to four weeks or four to six months old, are just as useful as the current Sunday edition. (Therefore, when beginning to prepare for your own want-ad analysis, ask your friends or relatives if they have any old papers lying around.) This allows you to begin your job campaign in earnest, saving you precious time, which translates into saving you money.

Expect to spend approximately one week job hunting for each $1,000 of income (for example, a $25,000 job equals 25 weeks of job hunting).

Other important sources of want ads include trade journals and specialty magazines (the ads are usually found in the backs of these publications), newsletters published by professional associations, and listings with your college or graduate-school alumni placement office. Some graduate business schools print a monthly alumni bulletin of jobs listed by employers, agencies, and search firms. These additional sources will help you to gather quickly the minimum of ten want ads in order to complete your want-ad analysis.

Good Ads/Bad Ads

To maximize the value of your want-ad analysis it's important that you maintain the highest possible quality in the ads you select. You can do this by adhering to a few simple guidelines.

Guidelines for Selecting a "Good Ad"

1. The ad has a well-defined job title.
2. It is fairly lengthy and gives specific information about the job requirements and responsibilities.
3. It defines the industry or type of organization in which the job is offered.
4. It tells how much experience is needed and what education level the employer seeks.
5. It defines to whom you report or what levels of people you interact with.
6. Often (not always) it lists a salary *range*.

"Blind" ads are an important category of good ads. These ads do *not* identify the hiring organization by name. Instead, a box number is provided. Organizations use "blind" ads for several reasons:

1. The hiring company doesn't want to answer each inquiry sent in (it is very time-consuming and expensive to do so) and doesn't want you calling up asking, "Did you get my résumé?"
2. The organization doesn't want its competition to know it has a particular position available.
3. An employee is still in the position and may not yet have been told he/she is being replaced (promoted, fired, whatever).
4. The position may have been given to an executive search firm specifically to help screen and identify qualified candidates for the employer. If this is the case (and it often is), even if you're *not* selected to be interviewed for the particular job advertised, your action letter or résumé will probably be retained by the search firm in case they conduct a search more closely related to your expertise. If they do file your résumé, you may get a call from them six months or even a year later for another job, perhaps a better one than in the ad you first answered.

As a result, blind ads are very likely to represent real jobs, so make a regular practice of answering these ads. Doing this will increase your chances of getting the job you want. Here are two "good" ads for you to look at; one identifies the hiring company, two are blind.

Good Ads

TRAINING MANAGER

One of the world's largest financial institutions (NYC) seeks a professional Training Manager to manage a professional staff of 5, oversee all course development and program design, handle quality control, training of trainers, and scheduling of programs (clerical through senior management). Selected individual for this expansion position will have immediate contact with top management and be in position to progress rapidly within the organization. Must have excellent communications and leadership skills and have had a minimum of 5 years' expertise as a Corporate Trainer/Manager. A graduate degree is desirable; prefer experience to be from a major consumer or financial corporation. Salary to $40,000. Send résumé to:

SENIOR PUBLIC RELATIONS WRITER

In 15 short years, our company has grown into a $350 million, multinational corporation with one of the largest customer bases in the industry. We have an exciting and rewarding career opportunity for a professional writer to join our Corporate Communications Department. The successful candidate will have a B.A. in English, Journalism, or other related fields with direct work experience in DP industry and at least 5 years' experience in press-related activities--preparation of news releases, case histories, arranging press conferences, and maintaining editorial relationships. 3-4 weeks' travel per year. In addition to excellent compensation and fringe benefit programs, we offer the opportunity to grow with us. Aren't we the company you've been looking for? Please send résumé, including present salary, in confidence to:

☞ *Insiders' Tip:* When a want ad says, "This is a newly created position...," it is safe to assume the following:

1. It's a job in the organization that management wants to fill to address specific problems and to find solutions. It may be in a department that is expanding rapidly and that needs talent.
2. It may also represent problems needing to be addressed "yesterday."
3. No one in the organization has enough expertise in this area to tackle it.
4. Since this job has had no previous incumbent, you know that you won't be compared to "good old anybody." (This can be good or bad, but is probably positive.)

NOTE: If you are offered and decide to accept a "newly created" job, make certain you get the company's commitment of sufficient time to get this new area functioning smoothly.

Many, but not all, "bad" ads are written and placed by employment agencies as a means of attracting résumés and people for their files, for "future" possibilities. Their listings may or may not be "true" ads. Some agencies, particularly large ones, advertise weekly because they have yearly contracts with their local papers (for favorable rates). The agencies are billed whether or not they advertise, so many are committed to at least one ad a week. There are many laws governing "phony" job listing, but prosecution is minimal, so the practice is somewhat widespread. Nevertheless, many employment agencies are reputable and do a very effective job at placing people. This is especially true of agencies that specialize in particular job areas. Large agencies usually have one person handling each special area. If the representatives know their field they can serve you well.

"Bad" ads are usually characterized by the following:

1. They lack specifics; they are usually short and incomplete.
2. The job requires typing (usually little or no career advancement is possible despite statements to the contrary).
3. The ad has enthusiastic phrases but no real content, such as "terrific job," "fantastic work location for lunch and after-hours," "take part in world travel," "be on top of everything," "once-in-a-lifetime opportunity," "only career-minded need apply," "right hand for busy executive."
4. The ad states a specific salary, rarely a salary range.

Bad or Misleading Ads

PRESTIGE PLUS

Major Wall St. Investment banking firm has exceptional opening for a truly outstanding individual to learn all aspects of personal banking. This outstanding opportunity will afford you daily contact with prestigious clients and accounts and can lead to unlimited future growth. Excellent benefits including profit-sharing, tuition refund, company-paid lunch, etc. Good typing and some shorthand or fast longhand necessary. Write:

FOREIGN INTRIGUE

Director of Communications seeks self-motivated individual who can handle a challenging position. Deal with foreign correspondence. Assume responsibilities. Good skills required. 13K. Contact:

ADMINISTRATIVE ASSISTANT

Ground-floor opportunity. Bright college graduate with SECRETARIAL SKILLS to learn import business. Requires substantial typing (including some statistics, light steno, filing, some figure work, and other general administrative duties). Light experience OK, but above skills mandatory. Excellent benefits, good working conditions, and fine opportunity for advancement. This vacancy is due to promotion from within. Write:

SOCIAL REGISTER/$13K

A prominent name in social, civic, and business circles seeks
discreet, cultured aide for NY office. Assist with philanthropic
affairs; do contact work with cultural and educational organizations. 60 wpm typing, precise English. Write:

GAL/GUY FRIDAY

Midtown agency has entry-level growth position for recent grad
with excellent typing skills, good command of English, figure
aptitude and ability to deal with clients. You must not be
afraid to work long hours. Work for President and Senior Account
Executives. Eventually head your own department. $160-175 to
start. Write or call:

☞ *Insiders' Tip:* There are no national licensing standards for employment
agencies; however, in New York City employment agencies have to be licensed to
operate by the Department of Consumer Affairs. A similar situation may exist in your
own city. Try to determine if this is the case.

   If you feel that you have been lied to by an agency representative about a job (e.g.,
the job was "filled" when you called at 9:01 on a Monday morning when the ad
appeared on Sunday, the day before), you can call the Department of Consumer Affairs
and register a complaint. They do follow up on complaints.

   But keep in mind the following: the job *could* have been filled the Friday before.
Most newspapers close their Classified Ad sections by Thursday evening. If the job you
wanted to interview for was filled on Friday (after the closing of the paper's deadline for
putting in or removing ads), then the reason given to you is legitimate. However, you
can usually tell if you're getting the runaround. Many companies, although it is illegal to
do so, will tell the agencies they use that a particular job is for a man, or a woman, or a
minority member. If you call up and the agent knows the client wants a woman and
you're a man, he or she may tell you the position's filled. Unless *you* can prove this, if
this is what you suspect, you will waste time and effort when you should be pursuing
positive avenues for yourself. But it's good to know all this!

Define Your Interests—What Would You Like to Do?

   The first step in completing a successful career or job switch is to define your
employment interests better. Again, the want ads, if used carefully, can prove extremely
helpful. Here is how it works.

   Get the Classified and/or Business and Finance section of a major Sunday newspaper
and a pair of scissors. Next, beginning with the first page of the Classified, go through *every*
column and *every* ad on *every* page in order to cut out ads for jobs of interest to you. For this
exercise, disregard salary, job title, geographic location, and travel. *Concentrate on job
content.* Also ignore any ads placed by employment agencies. In cutting out jobs you find
interesting, remember to reach *above* your current job title. After all, *you are better than
you think you are!* (In the experience of the authors of this book, this is the *single most
important fact we have discovered* in our years of job counseling.)

By way of illustration, Judy Price was interested in Training and Development ads (a part of the Personnel Department in most companies). Yet this type of position is listed in more than one location in the Classified pages. Besides being found under Personnel, Training and Development ads may be listed under Training, Sales, Retailing, Health Care, Hospitals, or Management Training.

Therefore, to ensure that you do not overlook valuable employment opportunities it is necessary, at least the first or second time you do this exercise, to go through *every* ad in *every* column on *every* page. These "identifiers" do not usually appear in the Business or Financial pages, but they do appear in the Classified sections of newspapers. Here is a sample training ad. In the upper left-hand corner is the "identifier" for this ad. The identifier, Personnel, locates *where* in the Classified Ads this advertisement appeared.

TRAINING ADMINISTRATOR

$14-17K This is a corporate staff position located in Somerset County, N.J. The qualified individual for this situation will have a degree and a minimum of 2 years of experience in industrial training program development and administration. Must have excellent communication skills, including conducting training sessions with large groups. Will have responsibilities for conducting needs analysis; developing training programs and administering them; developing training materials; and coordination of public seminar arrangements in an industrial environment. Must be able to deal effectively with all levels of salaried personnel. Competitive salary and a comprehensive benefits package. Send résumé, including salary history, in confidence to:

After you have gone through every page and every ad of the Classified section:

(1) Sort your want ads by job title after you've cut them out.
(2) Compile a written list of "identifiers" for each job title, based upon a review of the ads in each job grouping.
(3) Once you have completed this, it becomes necessary only to review these "identifiers" for a specific job title in future editions of the newspapers. You can then look for a job title assured of seeing all the ads without having to go through the whole paper.

When you work "smarter" than everyone else who is looking, you will get what you want. For the first time around, though, remember to go through every ad, every column, every page. This holds also for the Business and Financial section of your Sunday paper. We recognize that this exercise can be a bit tedious, but it will make you a smarter job hunter, so stick with it.

The strength of want-ad analysis comes from its being a *factor analysis* of your sample want ads for a particular job title; that is, each individual fact in each ad of your sample will be recorded on the worksheet in order to establish patterns of frequency. Once established, these patterns will determine (1) if you can realistically apply for the job and, *if yes*, (2) exactly what part of your work experience should be emphasized in your action letter or résumé. It's this last point that most job hunters, even the most experienced, have trouble handling. Without doing the want-ad analysis, you have no reliable method of knowing what part of your work experience should be emphasized to a future employer. It also provides a barometer to measure the market, allowing you to "leap" into position. The more extensive your work experience and the longer your résumé, the greater the problem. It's like the old expression: you can't see the forest for the trees. Our way out of this accumulation of work experience is to match only the employer's needs with your interest and experience.

Periodically, once every three or four weeks, you should redo the want-ad analysis to reflect the increased sample size. This "fine tuning" will allow you to identify quickly any significant changes in your field such as new federal legislation. An example is ADEA, jargon in the personnel field for the Age Discrimination and Employment Act.

Trying Want-Ad Analysis Techniques

While it may seem tedious, it would be very useful to run through the want-ad analysis with another career changer. We have chosen Larry Spooner, a "financial type" who desires to switch from a nonprofit to a profit-making environment. In the 1980s this type of switch will become increasingly difficult to accomplish successfully, so this is an invaluable tool for these times.

We want you to do a want-ad analysis for Larry Spooner in three steps: (a) with one want ad, (b) with three want ads, and (c) with ten want ads (a completed want-ad analysis). To guide yourself through the analysis, follow these simple steps:

Step 1   Carefully read ad 1, and place the pertinent information in this ad on the worksheet. Then draw conclusions. Next, compare your worksheet with ours (page 158 at the end of this chapter). There should be a close similarity.

Step 2   Repeat Step 1, using ads 2 and 3. Add this information to the same worksheet. Again, compare your results with our worksheet at the end of the chapter.

Step 3   Repeat Step 1, using want ads 4 through 10. Draw your conclusions. Then compare your completed want-ad analysis worksheet with our completed form at the end of the chapter.

In this fashion, you will be able to complete a want-ad analysis in the prescribed manner, which allows you to be thorough and objective while sharpening your skills in using the analysis.

Before actually doing the want-ad analysis, let's take a look at Larry Spooner's situation. He was the assistant controller of a large division in his city's government. After six years in public service, Larry wanted out. He had a master's degree in public administration (M.P.A.) and a bachelor's in business administration (B.B.A.) in accounting. In total, he had spent over ten years in government. He was thirty-four years old and earning $28,500. He then decided to switch to industry—but exactly what job? And to what industries could he apply? Would he qualify? To answer these all-important questions, Larry did a want-ad analysis on a job title in his area of interest, one he believed he was qualified to apply for: *financial analyst.*

> ☞ *Insiders' Tip:*   If you are planning to make a significant *switch* (from nonprofit to profit, teaching to industry, et cetera), you may or may not maintain your present income level. You will probably have a lower title even if your salary is the same or higher.

LARRY SPOONER'S WANT-AD ANALYSIS: On the next three pages are the financial analyst want ads that Larry used. They are numbered from 1 to 10. Take a blank worksheet and, using ad 1, follow the procedure outlined in Step 1.

Ad 1: FINANCIAL ANALYST

Division Corporate Staff, Midtown Manhattan. We are a leading division of a Midwest-based consumer-products, Fortune 100 corporation. Reporting directly to our Divisional V.P.-Controller, you will function as the financial staff analyst for our division. To meet our expectations, you must: be a fast-track, highly motivated, and results-oriented individual; possess 1-3 years' experience; an M.B.A. in Finance/Accounting is preferred. Your duties will entail acting as liaison between subsidiaries, divisions, and parent company for financial and managerial reporting. Specific responsibilities will include coordination of periodic reporting, budgeting and long-range planning, analysis of financial statements, and review of capital projects. If successful, this challenging, highly visible position offers growth to assistant controllership responsibilities within 1-2 years. You will receive an attractive compensation package, including an excellent salary and comprehensive company-paid benefits. For confidential consideration, please send your résumé, complete with salary requirements, to:

Ad 2: FINANCIAL BUSINESS ANALYST

Immediate rewards for a strong financial background. The self-motivated individual must be capable of analyzing the information needs of all levels of financial personnel. At least 3 years of financial or accounting experience is needed with a B.B.A., finance or accounting (M.B.A. is a plus). This North Jersey-based position combines EDP with some internal consulting. The chosen individual will interface with a variety of finance, programming, and corporate staff personnel. Responsibilities will include definition of financial EDP systems, preparing specifications, schedules, and documentation and training operating personnel to use the system. If you can meet the challenge, please send résumé with salary requirements in confidence to:

Ad 3: FINANCIAL ANALYST

Participate in financial evaluation of major capital expenditures with the growing division of a Fortune 200 chemical company. This highly visible opportunity involves demanding assignments bringing frequent interface with senior management. You will exercise critical judgment of projected investments and gauge their expected financial results. You will work independently on many projects, yet must be able to work closely with associates. Position requires B.S. in Finance or Accounting (or equivalent). M.B.A. or C.P.A. highly desirable. In addition, you'll need approximately 2-3 years' related financial experience, preferably including some of the following: entity accounting, capital expenditure analysis, international operations, foreign exchange, buy vs. lease analysis, computerized systems. A high degree of creativity and strong oral and written communication skills. If you're looking for upward mobility, write in confidence, detailing experience and salary history, to:

Ad 4: FINANCIAL ANALYST

Major New York City-based industrial organization seeks an individual with a recent master's degree in finance. Additional training in economics and statistics is desirable. Should have the
ability to apply modern techniques of problem-solving and to work
independently in order to conduct various financial-economic
studies. Send résumé and salary requirements to:

Ad 5: FINANCIAL ANALYST

Entry-level position with a major U.S. record company. An immediate opening for an M.B.A./finance graduate with an impressive
record of academic achievement from a highly ranked university
. . . an individual capable of applying advanced financial management techniques to our overall finance operation. Responsibilities involve performing analyses of income statements and
balance sheets; preparing artist profitability studies; analyzing marketing and sales support plans, pricing strategies, and
cost-of-sales accounts; and conducting R.O.I. studies. If you
have good interpersonal skills and the desire to advance through
achievement, please forward your résumé and salary history to:

Ad 6: FINANCIAL ANALYST

An excellent career opportunity exists within the corporate
headquarters of the New York Daily Planet. Applicants should
have a strong background in financial analysis, modeling and
systems. The ability to write interactive computer programs is
required. An M.B.A. degree is desirable. Responsibilities include the financial analysis of acquisitions, operational and
capital budgets, as well as participating in the design and
maintenance of computerized financial systems. Attractive
benefit package. Competitive salary commensurate with experience. Send résumé and salary history to:

Ad 7: FINANCIAL ANALYST

Individual required to perform a variety of financial studies
and analysis relating to manufacturing and marketing operations.
B.S. degree and at least 1-2 years experience with some exposure
to operations analysis and systems development required. M.B.A.
a definite plus. Position offers challenging opportunity with
exposure to international and domestic markets. Salary in mid-
teens with good benefit program. Forward résumé with salary
requirements to:

Ad 8: FINANCIAL ANALYSIS AND REPORTING MANAGER

Salary to $25,000. Worldwide shipping company has a challenging assignment for an experienced individual to review and analyze cargo and terminal reports received from foreign and domestic offices. For this position we require a degree in accounting or finance and 5 years of applicable experience. Position is based in NYC and offers an excellent benefit package. Send résumé and salary history to:

Ad 9: ASSISTANT DIRECTOR OF FINANCE

The General Health Care Center in Long Island is looking for an Assistant Director of Finance. The initial assignment will encompass the development and maintenance of general ledger and subsidiary systems, including EDP accounting and billing systems along with the direct supervision of Payroll and Billing Depts. The successful candidate will have had 2-3 years' experience in the above areas and hold a bachelor's degree in Accounting. Competitive salary and liberal fringe benefits program. Send résumé to:

Ad 10: FINANCIAL RESEARCHER/ANALYST

A unique opportunity for a financially trained writer. The company is an NYSE industrial company located in Fairfield County. The position requires researching, writing, and coordinating the development financial advisory bulletins, reports and special studies for management and customer companies, and administering financial management projects. The individual is expected to understand financial and accounting concepts and have proven ability to communicate financial concepts in writing. Additional qualifications which will receive preference are an M.B.A. in Finance and experience in management consulting, financial analysis or management, auditing or administration. This highly visible position offers an exceptional opportunity to apply your talents, develop your abilities, and broaden your experience Please send detailed résumé, including salary requirements, in confidence to:

Review of Step 1

- Read ad 1 carefully.
- Place pertinent information in this ad on worksheet.
- Be sure to record all information.
- Can you draw conclusions yet? No.
- Compare your want-ad analysis with the author's want-ad analysis (page 152 at the end of this chapter).

Observations

1. Notice that we have recorded *every* useful piece of information in the ad on the worksheet. This is important to do in order to make your analysis accurate and thorough.

2. After analyzing only one ad, it is not possible to list the top four job tasks or skills or draw conclusions.

3. As your skill at reading ads becomes refined, you will be able to draw inferences even from only one ad. However, don't make the mistake of *jumping to conclusions*. One ad, or even three ads, is an insufficient sample size. Ten ads are the recommended minimum sample size.

Now complete Step 2

- Read ads 2 and 3 carefully.
- Add all pertinent information to the worksheet.
- You can't draw conclusions yet, but patterns are emerging.

Review of Step 2

- Repeat Step 1, using ads 2 and 3.
- Compare your results with the authors' want-ad analysis (pages 153 and 154 at the end of this chapter).

Observations

1. Patterns are starting to develop. Certain tasks or skills are repeated more frequently than others. However, it is still too early to see any definitive patterns. They must await the analysis of all ten ads.

Complete Step 3

- Using ads 4 to 10, repeat as before.

Review of Step 3

- Repeat Step 1, using want ads 4 to 10.
- Draw conclusions (use page 2 of the worksheet).
- Compare your complete worksheet with our completed form on pages 155 through 156.

On the basis of his completed want-ad analysis (pages 155 through 157), Larry Spooner came to these final conclusions about the financial analyst position.

(a) The minimum education level is a B.S. or B.B.A. degree in Accounting. (He has this!)

(b) Eighty percent of the ads wanted an M.B.A. (He has an M.P.A., but his ten years of experience may for an *enlightened* employer offset this deficiency.)

(c) His ten years of experience were seven more than the maximum stated in the ads. As only 30 percent of the ads asked for three years, he could be overqualified for this job. Larry might, therefore, look at higher-level financial jobs. However, these are viable positions for him to apply for, since he is radically switching industries (nonprofit to profit).

Larry can go after this title in major industries provided he keeps in mind the following limitations:

(1)   The job will carry the same or a slightly lower salary.

(2)   It is a lower job title.

(3)   There is little or no travel.

(4)   He might consider taking courses toward an M.B.A. in finance.

(5)   He might try a want-ad analysis for ten ads for a higher job title. For example, senior financial analyst.

Decision-making time: knowing that he can go after the financial-analyst-level position, does Larry want to pursue it? If not, he has to look at more senior positions, but if Larry answers, "Yes," he must then move on to the next steps:

(a)   He must collect and define *all* the jargon (see his completed want-ad analysis) for the position until he is comfortable with these terms.

(b)   Larry has to decide which type of company to apply to (service, industrial consumer, et cetera). This decision will be further limited by his own geographical restrictions and preferences in organization size (small, medium, or large).

(c)   Finally, to accomplish his switch successfully, Larry must develop hard-hitting marketing tools. In his case a résumé won't work well. As soon as most corporations see the "government," they will usually consign the paper to the wastebasket. Larry needs an excellent action letter, using action verbs like those shown to you in chapter 4. Chapter 6 will show in detail how this letter and others like it are devised.

Additional Comments on the Want-Ad Analysis

As we stated previously, in making the want-ad analysis you will notice there are many job titles that describe the same function. Very few organizations call the same job responsibilities by the same title. A senior accountant in a very large organization may be called an assistant controller in a medium-sized one, or even a controller in a small one. Senior accountant can also be listed under financial analyst. To overcome possible confusion it is necessary to read the ads carefully and group them initially by title, then *regroup* them by *job content*.

Want-ad analysis is also valuable because it can contribute to an improved self-image. You no longer have to be scared off from applying for jobs solely on the basis of their *titles*. After doing your want-ad analysis, if you find that your background and work experience closely fit an ad's task requirements, answer the ad. After all, what do you have to lose? When doing a want-ad analysis, however, you may discover that you don't have all of the top four or five skills or experience required. What should you do? As a general practice, you should *ask more of yourself.* Specifically, if you have about 75 percent of the correct experience and you've expressed your experience in P-A-R format, you should "reach" and apply for the position.

Consider these points:

1.   From the employer's standpoint his or her want ad represents all the qualifications of the perfect candidate. Since a "perfect" candidate rarely applies (and if one does, he or she is usually too high priced), the employer will almost always settle for that candidate who possesses *most* of the qualifications.

1394 Summit Lake Place
Amityville, New York 11701

Dear

As an experienced Assistant Controller in a major service organization, I am
directly responsible for monitoring performance and management of subsidiaries.
I have developed standards and procedures for evaluations, including data collection for validity and reliability. I have succeeded in establishing good working
relationships with subsidiaries, often in an adversary climate. I implemented
recommendations and monitored follow-up through effective management of 25 analysts.

I am writing because your organization may be in need of a person with my background and experience. If so, you may find the following accomplishments of
interest:

> *Uncovered $200,000 in duplicate payments at one
> organization and effected systemic changes.
> *Revamped a business marketing and business service
> organization.
> *Identified $25,000,000 savings in personnel time
> in one large group.
> *Proposed recommendations in risk management that
> will result in $15,000,000 annual savings.

Prior to this position I was a Consultant/Troubleshooter at a large service
organization. I streamlined purchasing and billing procedures, established uniform
personnel procedures, balanced budgets (yielding year-end surpluses), and interfaced
budget modifications with Accounting, producing ease in financial information
retrieval.

My formal education includes a master's degree in Public Administration from
the University of Illinois in 1971 (full scholarship) and a B.B.A. in Accounting,
magna cum laude, in 1970 from the same school. I was elected to Phi Beta Kappa,
was president of my dormitory and awarded scholarships for 4 years. My salary is
competitive.

I would be happy to discuss my experience further in a personal interview.

Sincerely,

(516) 991-1443   Larry R. Spooner

2. Employers generally judge a job candidate on two factors: qualifications and
    potential. If a candidate has both, the decision is then largely based on "personal
    chemistry."

3. Finally, throughout most organizations, meaningful learning and training are
    obtained on the job. Therefore, if you can sell a potential employer on the idea that
    you are *the* person for a particular position, you will be allowed to learn on the job.

Having established the minimum acceptable educational requirements for any specific
job category, *remember* that employers are occasionally willing to substitute applicable

experience in place of formal education. That is, your on-the-job education can be just as valid and marketable as formal education.* This is not always true—there are plenty of employers who insist that you must "have it all"—but there are enough exceptions to the rule for the above statement to be significant.

The want-ad analysis allows you to quickly see whether or not you will spin your wheels. In the final analysis, you will be prevented from punishing yourself: for example, "It's a rotten economy, the jobs are all lousy, I'm wasting my time looking, so I'll stay where I am and continue to suffer."

The Importance of Jargon

Webster's New Collegiate Dictionary defines *jargon* in one way as: "the technical terminology or characteristic idiom of a special activity or group." But why is it important to know jargon? The reason is simple but practical: your own interests are at stake. As the job seeker, you have to be knowledgeable in the vocabulary of the industry and job into which you are seeking to switch. This is true both in your marketing pieces, letters, or résumés and in person during the interview. Let us describe an actual experience that illustrates the important role jargon can play in the job hunt. Lloyd Feinstein had spent four years as director of training and assistant director of personnel at Bellevue Hospital Center in New York City. He also had had seven previous years of experience as a training consultant to the Bell Telephone Laboratories and I.T.T. When he was attempting to switch, he answered an ad in the *New York Times* for a training consultant to the medical industry. Using one of his letters, Lloyd obtained an interview at a New Jersey–based consulting firm whose clients were major medical centers across the country.

Early in the interview, the consultant threw Lloyd a piece of jargon, "CBC," which Lloyd didn't know but will never forget now (CBC is medical jargon for "complete blood count"). The interview went speedily downhill from that moment on as Lloyd had lost 85 percent of his credibility. Perhaps you're thinking that if Lloyd had been at Bellevue Hospital for four years, he should have known what "CBC" stood for. Yes, no, and maybe. A good trainer is *not* necessarily an expert in the job content of any particular field. (Teachers desiring to switch, take note!) A trainer knows how to package the information of a "content expert" so that the information is easily communicated to a diversified audience.

By using the want-ad analysis worksheet, you will be able to identify systematically the jargon for each job title in which you have an interest. Divide the jargon into terminology that you know and don't know. Take the unfamiliar words and research these terms through publications in that field, contacts who have worked in the field, and so on, to become conversant with the language of that particular profession.

To sum up, the bottom line (jargon for *conclusion*) is: *you* have to SPEAK in the terminology of the person who may be hiring you. Your knowledge (or lack of knowlege) of the jargon demonstrates whether you are "in" or "out" of that profession.

A Second Significant Switch

Let's look at another case history. Beverly Folger graduated with a B.A. in art history in 1957. A review of her résumé shows her most recent employment ending in 1977.

---

*Furthermore, you can turn this deficit into an asset. Anyone who can teach him/herself how to do a job, rather than falling back solely on a degree, shows a lot more imagination, spunk, and drive than a degreed counterpart. Your record of successful on-the-job performance is more relevant than your college success.

Résumé
BEVERLY FOLGER
RFD #2, Box 931
Hurleyville, New York 12477
(518) 497-4328

POSITION SOUGHT: Market/Management

SUMMARY OF
QUALIFICATIONS:

Marketing Executive, 10 years experience. Increased sales
volume 50% in 9 months by opening new areas with merchandising
seminars. Successfully negotiated overseas buying based on
production projections, inventory needs and sales.

EXPERIENCE:
1973-1977

Marketing Director, RST LEATHERWORKS, INC. Faced with a twofold
problem, the company's lack of exposure and the dealer's reluc-
tance to handle a high-priced line, I launched a series of merchandising seminars combined with hospitality suites. Covering
38 states in a nine-month period, I opened new areas, showed the
dealer how to sell the product and sales increased a full 50%.
I was invited to join the executive board of a highly respected
Washington lobbyist group, thus establishing the company's
reputation in the industry.

1972-1973

Director International Marketing and Sales, XYZ Company. I introduced the company to the Japanese ball-bearing market at a time
when Japanese production capacities appeared to be consumed by
existing corporations. I was able to successfully negotiate
prices and delivery of merchandise and market it domestically.
One sales contract that I personally negotiated was equal to the
company's gross volume of the previous year.

1967-1972

Production Control Director, APX CORPORATION. Originally hired
as Customer Service Manager, I initiated systems where none had
existed. Sales volume increased by 4 times its original strength,
and I became production control director, responsible for the
planning and buying of a six-million-dollar inventory, traveling
to Spain and England to accomplish this. I reduced an obsolete
inventory of specials which was in excess of one million dollars
to less than $50,000. I was called upon to close sales where
previous negotiations had hit a snag.

1965-1967

Customer Service, LPQ CHEMICAL CORP. As one of four in customer
service, I handled problems of production and delivery. I was
elevated to head of the department in 5 months.

PERSONAL:

Born U.S.A. 1935
B.A. Cornell University, 1957.

(Techniques to overcome the perceived "weakness" of no recent employment were discussed at length in chapter 4.)

However, she *is* currently employed and *has* been since 1979. For reasons known only to Beverly, she elected not to put her recent experience down. Why not? Because the work she wanted to do (marketing), and which she had done for ten years, is not what she's doing now. Like Larry Spooner, Beverly wants to make a significant career change. What did she do in trying to extricate herself from this nonmarketing job?

1. She approached her friends, relatives, and business associates, asking for marketing contacts.
2. She spent one and one-half hours updating her résumé—no one else proofread it or criticized it.
3. She called several executive search firms and employment agencies and sent each a copy of her résumé.
4. She answered ads appearing in one major Sunday paper for three weeks.

She got only negative responses—either "Thank you, but no, thank you" form letters from companies she wrote to directly (or no response at all), or "Don't call us, we'll call you" from the agencies.

Like Larry Spooner, Beverly concluded that "it's a lousy job market; the companies are discriminating against me because I'm a woman and over forty." Some of her feelings are probably accurate. However, the negative responses she was getting were mainly the result of the way she was marketing herself. Considering Beverly's circumstances (working in a nonmarketing job), using an action letter instead of a résumé would have worked much more in her favor. See chapter 7.

A Second Look

By reviewing Beverly Folger's original résumé a second time, we can begin to understand her motivations. Her résumé shows no work experience since 1977. But, as we mentioned previously, this is not the case. She has been working full time since April 1979. Beverly, however, chose not to reveal her current position because she dislikes her job and feels it doesn't fairly represent her capabilities. Whether this is true or not, leaving her current employment out of her résumé works *against* her getting interviews because anyone who reads Beverly's résumé would jump to their own conclusions (mostly negative) in order to explain that big gap in her work history.

☞ *Insiders' Tip:* Résumés should answer questions, *not* raise them.

Most people reading her résumé would assume one or all of the following things:

1. She got fired from her last job, has rotten references, and can't get work now.
2. She decided to stay home and be a homemaker and is now bored and wants to earn some pin money.

3. She had a nervous breakdown and was incapacitated for four or five years.

4. She got divorced and couldn't take the pressures of a job.

None of the above is true, of course, but these four reasons are unfortunately typical of what would go through a potential employer's mind when confronted with a résumé like Beverly's.

☞ *Insiders' Tip:*   Avoid chronological gaps in your résumé; they will always work against you.

Beverly was a woman on the right track but unaware of it. Her original résumé (what there was of it) was actually pretty good, and it was done more or less in the P-A-R format. What if you are on the right track and don't know it? You will probably do one of two things: (1) either get on the wrong track and wind up in a dead end (this results in your staying in your present position and continuing to be unhappy) or (2) stumble onto another job.

It's critical that your written marketing materials work in your favor and not against you. Beverly learned this lesson the hard way. In addition to showing a large, unexplained gap in her work history, she showed her date of birth and year of college graduation. This information blew her out of the water. That is, the weaknesses of her résumé sabotaged its strengths, a common practice among inexperienced résumé writers. (See chapter 4 on résumés.) What Beverly Folger has to do is identify areas of work she likes best, know what she's best at, and build upon it.

Beverly selected marketing as her career path. Here is her revised résumé, which accentuates what she has to sell.

BEVERLY FOLGER
RFD #2, Box 931
Hurleyville, New York 12747
(518) 497-4228

SUMMARY OF QUALIFICATIONS:

Results-oriented Marketing Executive with 14 years of experience. Creative problem-solver, expertise in closing sales and motivating distributors and staff; excellent communications skills, both oral and written; comfortable dealing with superiors, peers, subordinates, and clients.

BUSINESS EXPERIENCE:

1979 to present	AAA MANUFACTURING, Hurleyville, New York as <u>Manager, Customer Service</u>, for this metal-working manufacturer.

- Currently redesigning all company catalogues, price sheets and other sales literature.
- Select graphics and type and write copy.
- Hire outside freelancers.
- Breaking down technical language of catalogues into laymen's terminology.
- Responsible for setting up and disseminating product literature to clients and to specific, targeted direct-mail lists.
- Created a telephone sales order form that can feed the information gathered on-line into a computer.
- Arrange for attendance at and cover important regional and national trade shows.

1973-1977	RST LEATHERWORKS, INC., Mahwah, New Jersey, as <u>Marketing Director</u>. Faced with a twofold problem, the company's lack of exposure in the motorcycle aftermarket and dealers' reluctance to handle a high-priced line of leather outerwear, I launched a series of merchandising seminars combined with hospitality suites to encourage purchasing/sales.

- Personally covered 38 states in only 9 months, directing a national sales force of 4.
- Opened new regions and instructed dealers on how to sell the product line.
- Invited to join the Executive Board of the Motorcycle Institute Commission, a highly respected Washington, D.C., lobbyist group, establishing the company's reputation throughout the industry.
- Organized and ran all national industrial and trade shows.
<u>Result</u>:
- Increased sales by 48% to $18 million.

1972-1973	XYZ COMPANY, Bellemore, New York, as <u>Director, International Marketing & Sales</u>.

- Introduced the company to the Far East ball-bearing market at a time when their production capacities appeared to be consumed by existing corporations.
- Successfully negotiated prices and delivery of merchandise which was then marketed domestically.
- Managed the efforts of three sales representatives.
<u>Results</u>:
- One personally negotiated sales contract equaled the company's total gross volume of the previous year.

1967-1972	APX CORPORATION, Huntington, New York, as <u>Production Control Director</u> for this ball-bearing manufacturer.

- Planned out and bought a $6 million inventory, traveling to Spain and England.
- Purchased balls and bearings in Western Europe and the Far East.
- Reduced obsolete inventory in excess of $1 million to less than $50,000.
- Called in to close important sales when prior negotiations had reached a deadlock.
- Opened a warehousing and docking facilities port in Wilmington, North Carolina.
- Initially hired as Customer Service Manager to implement systems where none had existed.

Results:
- Increased sales volume from $1 million to $4.2 million.

1965-1967	LPQ CHEMICAL CORPORATION, Rye, New York as <u>Customer Service Department Head</u>.

- Handled production and delivery problems as one of four Customer Service Representatives.
- Due to outstanding performance, was promoted to Department Head in only 5 months.

EDUCATION:

B.A. Marketing; Minor: Advertising, CORNELL UNIVERSITY, Ithaca, New York. Graduated in the top 25% of the class. Dean's List; Varsity Tennis; Student Government.

INTERESTS:

Skiing, horseback riding, tennis, travel.

REFERENCES:

Available upon request.

Larry Spooner and Beverly Folger had been kidding themselves. They had not committed themselves to the time and effort involved in marketing their skills. But by applying themselves to the methods in this book, they were able to design marketing programs that worked.

To make a significant switch, or even to change jobs so that the next step is the right career step, you have to do some serious work!

- Make a want-ad analysis according to the above techniques.
- Draw good conclusions about the most important factors of the job titles you've selected.
- Compare these conclusions against your work history, expressed in P-A-R terms, in order to conclude if a career move is practical or not.
- If switching is not practical, select a new job title and repeat the want-ad analysis.
- If it is practical, review chapters 4 and 7 on how to develop your actual "marketing" pieces: action letter and résumé.

As an aid to help you follow these steps in their proper sequence, we have provided you with the detailed flowchart at the beginning of this chapter. Use it as a reference.

WANT AD ANALYSIS WORKSHEET

Ad Title(s) 1. Financial Analyst	5.	Sources of Ads:		
2.	6.	1. Sunday New York Herald		
3.	7.	2.		
4.	Industries Represented			
Number of Ads	1. Consumer Products	4.		7.
Dates of Ads 2/2/82	2.	5.		8.
Salary Range	3.	6.		9.

Job Requirements/Skills Education/Location, etc.	Frequency in Ads	Number of Ads	%	Jargon
1. 1–3 years' experience	1			
2. MBA Finance/Accounting preferred	1			
3. Liaison to subsidiaries, divisions & hq.	1			
4. Reporting on finance and managerial issues	1			
5. Coordinate periodic reporting	1			
6. Coordinate budgeting and long-range planning	1			
7. Financial statement analysis	1			
8. Review of capital projects	1			
9.				
10.				
11.				
12.				
13.				
14.				
15.				
16.				
17.				
18.				

WANT AD ANALYSIS WORKSHEET

Ad Title(s) 1. Financial analyst 5.		Sources of Ads:	
2. Financial analyst 6.		1. Sunday New York Herald	
3. Financial Business analyst 7.		2.	
4.	Industries Represented		
Number of Ads (3)	1. Consumer Products 4.		7.
Dates of Ads 2/2/82	2. Chemical/Pharmaceutical 5.		8.
Salary Range	3. Printing/Textile Inks and Paints 6.		9.

Job Requirements/Skills Education/Location, etc.	Frequency in Ads	Number of Ads	%	Jargon
1. 2–3 years experience, 1–3	111			Entity accounting
2. MBA or CPA preferable	111			EDP
3. Liaison between sub. division and parent company for financial mgmt. rept.	1			Interface
4. Reporting on finance and managerial issues	1			
5. Coordinate periodic reporting	1			
6. Reporting, budgeting and long range planning	1			
7. Financial statement analysis	1			
8. Review capital projects	1			
9. Work on projects alone (Self-motivated)	1			
10. BS Finance & Accounting required	11			
11. Internal consulting	1			
12. Interface (liaison with) senior management	11			
13. Computerized systems experience	11			
14. Prepare specs, schedules, and documentation	1			
15. Train operating personnel to use systems	1			
16. Judge projected investments for results	1			
17. Work as part of team	1			
18. Entity accounting	1			

(continued)

Job Requirements/Skills Education/Location, etc.	Frequency in Ads	Number of Ads	%	Jargon
19. Foreign exchange experience	1			
20. Capital expenditure evaluation/analysis	1			
21. International operations experience	1			
22. Buy vs. lease experience	1			
23. Creative and analytical	1			
24. Good oral and written skills	11			
25. Location = New Jersey (international job)	11			
26.				
27.				
28.				
29.				
30.				

Conclusions

Top Four Job Tasks or Skills

1. _____

2. _____

3. _____

4. _____

Minimum Education Required_____Salary Range_____

Minimum Experience Required_____Travel Requirements (%)_____

Geographic Limitations_____

Other_____

WANT AD ANALYSIS WORKSHEET

Ad Title(s)	Sources of Ads:
1. Financial Analyst 7. Financial Analyst 2. Financial Bus. Analyst 8. Financial Analyst 3. Financial Analyst 9. Financial Analyst 4. Financial Research Anal. 10. Financial Analyst 5. Financial Analyst & Reports Manager 6. Assistant Director Finance	1. Sunday New York Herald 2.

Number of Ads	10	Industries Represented

Number of Ads 10	1. Consumer products 4. Record Company 7. Hospital
Dates of Ads 1/19, 2/2 2/9, 2/16	2. Chemical/Pharmaceutical 5. Consumer 8. Shipping Company
Salary Range Mid-Teens	3. Printing/Textiles 6. Industrial 9. Publishing

Job Requirements/Skills Education/Location, etc.	Frequency in Ads	Number of Ads	%	Jargon
1. 2–3 years experience	111	3	30	Entity accounting
2. MBA or CPA preferable	11111111	8	80	EDP
3. Liaison between subsidiary division and parent company for financial mgmt. rept.	1	1	10	Interface
4. Reporting on finance and managerial issues	11	2	20	Interactive computer programs
5. Coordinate periodic reporting	1	1	10	Foreign exchanges
6. Reporting, budgeting and long range planning	1	1	10	General ledger
7. Financial statement analysis	1111	4	40	ROI
8. Review capital projects	1	1	10	
9. Work on projects alone (self-motivated)	1	1	10	
10. BS Finance & Accounting required	11111	5	50	
11. Internal consulting	1	1	10	
12. Interface (liaison with) senior management	11	2	20	
13. Computerized systems experience	11111	5	50	
14. Prepare specs, schedules, and documentation	1	1	10	
15. Train operating personnel to use systems	1	1	10	
16. Judge projected investments for results	11	2	20	
17. Work as part of team	11	2	20	
18. Entity accounting	1	1	10	

(continued)

Job Requirements/Skills Education/Location, etc.	Frequency in Ads	Number of Ads	%	Jargon
19. Foreign exchange experience	1	1	10	
20. Capital expenditure evaluation/analysis	1111	4	40	
21. International operations experience	11	2	20	
22. Buy vs. lease experience	1	1	10	
23. Creative and analytical	11	2	20	
24. Good oral and written skills	1111	4	40	
25. Location = New Jersey (International job)	11	2	20	
26. 1–3 years' experience	11	2	20	
27. Research, writing, and coordinating develop. of fin. advisory bulletines for mgmt. & clients	1	1	10	
28. Review and analyze cargo and terminal reports worldwide	1	1	10	
29. Develop and maintain general ledger and subsidiary systems	1	1	10	
30. Supervise Payroll & Billing departments	1	1	10	
31. Required to write interactive computer programs	1	1	10	
32. Design and maintenance of computerized financial systems	1	1	10	
33. Knowledge of statistics–economics	1	1	10	
34. Operations analysis	1	1	10	
35. Analyze marketing and sales support plans	1	1	10	
36. Prepare artist-profitability studies	1	1	10	
37. Analyze pricing strategies	1	1	10	
38. Analyze cost-of-sales accounts	1	1	10	
39. Analyze ROI	1	1	10	

<u>Conclusions</u>

Top Four Job Tasks or Skills

1. Analyze financial statements (40%)

2. Computer knowledge (50%), but suspect all want it

3. Capital expenditure evaluation and analysis (40%)

4. Good oral and written skills (40%), but all probably want this.

Minimum Education Required BS Finance or Accounting (80% preferred MBA's)   Salary Range Only one said mid-teens but this was a beginners job. Estimate: Most are low $20's

Minimum Experience Required = 1–3 years (50%) [1 year (20%) + 2–3 years (30%)]   Travel Requirements (%)

Geographic Limitations 100% — All in N.Y. Metro, 60% in N.Y.C., 40% in N.J., Westchester or Connecticut

Other

WANT AD ANALYSIS WORKSHEET

Ad Title(s) 1.		5.	Sources of Ads:		
2.		6.	1.		
3.		7.	2.		
4.		Industries Represented			
Number of Ads		1.	4.		7.
Dates of Ads		2.	5.		8.
Salary Range		3.	6.		9.

Job Requirements/Skills Education/Location, etc.	Frequency in Ads	Number of Ads	%	Jargon
1.				
2.				
3.				
4.				
5.				
6.				
7.				
8.				
9.				
10.				
11.				
12.				
13.				
14.				
15.				
16.				
17.				
18.				

Job Requirements/Skills Education/Location, etc.	Frequency in Ads	Number of Ads	%	Jargon
19.				
20.				
21.				
22.				
23.				
24.				
25.				
26.				
27.				
28.				
29.				
30.				

Conclusions

Top Four Job Tasks or Skills

1.

2.

3.

4.

Minimum Education Required_____Salary Range_____

Minimum Experience Required_____Travel Requirements (%)_____

Geographic Limitations_____

Other_____

6. Switching to Beat Inflation

"There is yet time enough for you to take a different path."

—From a Chinese fortune cookie,
  Hunan Restaurant, Berkeley Heights, New Jersey

How to Know When to Look for a New Job

There are many signs that tell you when to begin looking for a new position. Some of these include boredom (work has become repetitive, and a promotion or lateral move to another area is not possible for too long a time); insufficient responsibility or freedom; working for a slow-moving superior; not earning enough money; few, if any, psychic benefits. There are many more reasons to seek new employment, but one major thing to consider is future compensation, particularly with the double-digit inflation of the 1980s.

Many people who are fearful of changing jobs stay in mediocre (or worse) job situations because they allow themselves to be locked up in "golden handcuffs," the other benefits they receive besides their regular salary. Some golden handcuffs are as follows.

PENSION PLAN:	I have only two and a half years to go before I'm fully vested.
PROFIT-SHARING PLAN:	I think I'll get about 12 percent of my salary additionally this year if the company does well. But I have to stay through December 31.
COMMISSIONS/BONUS:	I'll be able to make another $4,800 if my big sale goes through next month.
TUITION REFUND:	I'm in college right now, and my company reimburses me for my tuition.
HEALTH PLANS:	This dental plan is really good, and both my kids will need braces next year.
COMPANY CAR:	Maybe my next job won't give me an automobile and I'll have to buy a $7,000 or $8,000 car. I can't afford that.
EXPENSE ACCOUNT:	A new job probably wouldn't give me as liberal an expense account.
STOCK OPTIONS:	I just became eligible for 1,000 shares of stock. If I leave now I can't exercise my option.
MEMBERSHIPS/DUES:	My present employer pays my country club dues; maybe my next one wouldn't.
VACATIONS:	I get 4 weeks a year now; maybe a new employer would only give me 2.
PARKING SPACE:	My parking space shows I'm a high-ranking corporate official. A

	new employer might not have facilities for this.
SENIORITY:	I'm well respected here. If I leave, I have to start all over in gaining credibility.
LIFE INSURANCE:	My family gets a lot of money if I die. Maybe the new employer has a mediocre plan.

If you see yourself in any of the above, really think twice about what you're doing, for you could be kidding yourself. We are not suggesting you become a job hopper, but if you have had for some time a nagging feeling that your work life could be better, look inside yourself to see if you are doing yourself a disservice by wearing one or more of these golden handcuffs. You can recoup all your benefits and sometimes more when negotiating with a new employer.

How to Calculate Your Salary Shrinkage

"Shrinkage?" you say. "How can my salary be shrinking? I'm earning double what I earned ten years ago!" Well, let's see. Take the case of Helen Santucci, an accounting manager at a medium-sized commercial bank. In 1968 Helen earned $11,000 and in 1981 she made $25,000. It looks as if she's more than doubled her salary in thirteen years, but we'll check out the value of this increase, using a business formula, employing the Consumer Price Index (CPI) to calculate her earnings growth.

Below is the Consumer Price Index Table from 1967 through 1981. You can obtain an updated table from any regional office of the Bureau of Labor Statistics, part of the Department of Labor, or call the main office in Washington, D.C.: (202) 272-5160.

CONSUMER PRICE INDEX TABLE

Year	Index	Year	Index
1967	100.0	1974	147.7
1968	104.2	1975	161.2
1969	109.8	1976	170.5
1970	116.3	1977	121.3
1971	121.3	1978	195.4
1972	125.3	1979	217.4
1973	133.1	1980	246.8
		1981	272.4

Helen Santucci's 1981 salary in terms of 1968 dollars is figured as follows:

$$\frac{\text{Gross 1981 salary} \times \text{1968 CPI}}{\text{1981 CPI}} = \text{1981 salary expressed in 1968 dollars}$$

$$\text{Substituting her salary figures we get: } \frac{\$25,000 \times 104.2}{272.4} = \$9,563.14$$

Helen's 1981 salary in constant 1968 dollars is a resounding $9,563. She has actually lost $1,437 in gross earnings, a truly outstanding reward for thirteen years of growth in ability, skills, and experience. It's worse than it looks, for this $1,437 is gross dollars, *not* after-tax dollars.

Here's another interesting case in point. Andy Miller went to work at a major bank in New York City in 1970 as an operations manager in Securities Processing. Salary: $12,000. In 1973 he joined another financial institution, also in New York City, and is currently a vice president there. Salary in 1980: $45,000. In talking to Andy while writing this chapter, Linda Kline mentioned the Consumer Price Index Table formula. Andy asked her to see how well he had fared over ten years. Below is the calculation:

$$\frac{\overset{\text{(1980 salary)}}{\$45,000} \times \overset{\text{(1970 CPI)}}{116.3}}{\underset{\text{(1980 CPI)}}{246.8}} = \$21,201 \text{ (Andy's 1980 salary expressed in 1970 dollars)}$$

On the surface he seems to have done well, certainly better than Helen Santucci. But let's look closer.

Andy's gross salary has almost quadrupled ($12,000 to $45,000), yet his 1980 salary of $45,000 is equivalent to only $21,200 in 1970 dollars. In other words, if he'd been earning $21,200 in 1970 he would have lived as well as he does today on $45,000. The difference between the $12,000 he earned in 1970 and $21,200 is only $9,200 (gross). In fact, his increased purchasing power in real dollars is probably around $5,000, taking into account his high tax bracket at $45,000 as against a much lower one at $21,200 and paying increased social security taxes. And this $5,000 purchases much less than it did ten years ago. Now Andy has a better understanding of why his standard of living has not increased appreciably over the past ten and a half years. He understands—he certainly isn't happy about it!

Isn't it time you took your job search seriously?

The Four Major Types of Career Moves

If you've decided to switch, you have four alternatives: (1) moving up (same job area, same organization), (2) moving up (same job area, new organization), (3) same organization, different job, (4) new organization, different job.

As far as monetary compensation is concerned, this is generally what happens in these four areas:

(1) *Same Job Area, Same Organization.* A merit increase for moving up in *the same area, same organization.* Many companies try to combine a yearly merit review with a promotional increase. If this happens, the increase could exceed 15 percent.

(2) *Same Job Area, New Organization.* A 16 to 33 percent increase if you're a senior executive, for moving up, since the employer has to steal you away by making it financially attractive for you to release some of your golden handcuffs for theirs.

This is the best place to negotiate good things for yourself.

From *Compflash* (a compensation review published monthly by the American Management Association), April 1981:

What are the trends among managers earning between $18,000 and $75,000? National Personnel Associates, a network of independent employment agencies that specialize in jobs in this range, reports these interesting observations garnered from surveys of member firms:

- An estimated 29% of these managers have a résumé circulating.

- About 9% of the managers who are offered a new job turn it down because their current employers made an acceptable counteroffer....

- Seventy-two percent of applicants to management-level personnel agencies are currently employed and they get 81 percent of the jobs. Successful job-changers receive a compensation package averaging 18 percent better than unemployed applicants who are equally qualified.

☞ *Insiders' Tip:*   Do not leave your present employer while looking for a new job if it is at all possible not to. You're more valuable and have more bargaining leverage if you have to be persuaded to leave.

From *INC.* magazine, January 1981:

Executives making $30,000–$45,000 got pay increases averaging 16% if they switched jobs in the first half of 1980, a survey by a Chicago-based executive search firm found. The more they were paid, the greater the increase. Those in the $46,000 to $60,000 range got 18% more, those making $61,000 to $85,000 got 21%, and those earning $86,000 to $110,000 got 26% raises. And the heavy-weights earning over $110,000 averaged 33%, the firm says.

(3) *Same Organization, Different Job.* You might initially have to take a lateral move at no dollar increase or a slight one of 5 to 6 percent. If this is the case, contract up front *before* you move into the new position for a quick merit review within three to six months. This is the time when you are in a position to negotiate.

(4) *New Organization, Different Job.* You *may* have to move laterally, take a slight decrease, or get only a slight increase. This is the area that's almost impossible to figure, as it depends upon how radical a switch you are making and how well you market your skills. Again, contract in the beginning for a quick review. In fact, if possible, get it *in writing*. If not, *you* put it in writing.

☞ *Insiders' Tip:*   When any organization extends you an offer of employment, it should be in writing. (Remember, the road to hell is paved with good intentions.) Assuming you had a positive verbal discussion about a quick three- or four-month review, but it is not mentioned in your offer letter, accept the offer as follows:

Dear Mr. Cooper,

I'm pleased to accept your offer of $31,500 for the position of Marketing Manager. As you know, this is a lateral move for me financially, and, as we discussed, I'll be looking forward to my 3-month merit review.

I'll be starting on Monday, May 12, and I will call you early next week to arrange the physical, etc. . . .

Should You Accept a Pay Cut to Switch?

It depends.

If your career has been following the usual series of events such as annual or merit raises, an occasional promotion, and increased responsibilities typical for your industry, and you are satisfied with your future prospects, you should *not* accept a pay cut when switching positions.

But, if your next salary increase threatens to put you at the very top of your field, and your future career prospects in this field are limited (or you desire to change careers), a change (with a possible pay cut) may be the only way out of a dead-end situation. Take one step backward in order to take two steps forward. Try to switch out before your next pay jump or you may be too expensive for any employer to consider hiring you.

Organizations are reluctant to hire people at much less than what they earned before, even if the candidate says he/she is willing to accept a large salary decrease. Why? No one *likes* to earn less than they did before, and employers are always afraid that if the person is not ecstatic with the new position, the combination of lowered pay and a job that's not as terrific as anticipated will cause the person to make an early exit. And then—the organization has to start the interviewing and selection process all over again with its attendant negatives (departmental morale decline, lost sales, decreased profits, additional recruiting costs, et cetera.). So, rather than take the risk, employers just say, "No, thanks."

However, if you are determined to change and you know what your dollar value is for the job you're pursuing, you can agree to accept the lower salary but contract (in writing), before starting, for a three-to-six-month merit review.

Consider the case of Maureen Dempsey, a supervisor of social workers for Cook County in Chicago. After twelve years of work experience she switched to a large brokerage firm to head up their brand-new employee counseling department. She left her old job at $23,500 and started at $21,000 at her new one.

The chart opposite illustrates what she can expect over an eighteen-month period.

As you can see, in only eighteen months Maureen is financially ahead of her old job even though she took a $2,300 salary decrease to start at the brokerage firm. In addition, her future career prospects are much greater in industry.

Salary as Supervisor of Social Workers	Salary as Manager, Employee Counseling	Date/Explanation
$23,500.00	$21,000.00	6/15/80 / Maureen changed jobs.
	$22,800.00	12/14/80 / 6-month review (negotiated as part of written hiring agreement); 9% increase ($1,890).
$25,438.75		1/2/81 / Contractual increase of 8.25% ($1,938.75).
	$25,476.57	6/10/81 / Maureen's annual review: 11.3% increase based on an "Excellent" evaluation ($2,586.57).
	$25,476.57 + ($1,250) = $26,726.57	12/23/81 / Company bonus paid at Christmas ($1,250).
$27,435.69		1/2/82 / Contractual increase of 7.85% ($1,996.94).
	$29,680.20	1/15/82 / Merit and promotional increase to Director, a 16.5% increase ($4,203.63). This increase is based on her *base* salary of $25,476.57 (not including the Christmas bonus).

Questions to Ask Yourself: "Another Job or My Next Career Move?"

If you have made the decision to find a new position, you must plan how to go about it.

1. If you are seeking a career move, not just another job: You must be able to articulate, in P-A-R format, both at your interviews and on your résumé, the *problems* you were hired to solve in the past, the *actions* you took to solve them, and the *results* you achieved. See chapter 3, "Product Analysis (Know Thyself)." You must discuss these things succinctly and demonstrate how ready you are to make your next move *upward*. In summation, you must do considerable self-assessment and then be able to convince a new employer of your appreciable worth.

2. If you wish to stay in your present company and move up in the same job area: You must speak to your immediate supervisor and perhaps to his or her manager. There may be no place to promote you to or no allocations available to create a new position. You then have three choices: (a) stay where you are and wait for an opening to occur; (b) leave for another position at another company; (c) move laterally into a new job area in the same company.

If waiting for a new position to open up will take too long according to your career timetable, you'll have to leave your present employer for another or move to a new job area within your organization, if a spot is available.

If your company has no openings in other areas in which you have an interest (or you're interested in a particular job area and the existing management doesn't want or need you), then you have to put out outside feelers for a new job, new employer.

3. What kind of organization do you want to work for? Very large, medium-sized, small (under 500 employees), very small (under 100 employees), start-up, perhaps risky (under 50 employees)? Your decision here will determine the thrust of your marketing attempts.

☞ *Insiders' Tip:*   It's easier to move from a large company to a small one than the other way around unless you have an incredibly specialized (usually technical) background that a future employer wants.

Smaller companies are generally less sticky about degrees, too. You can get to be the vice president of Marketing without an M.B.A. or other advanced degrees in a smaller firm much more easily than you can in a multinational giant.

So, if your academic credentials won't have Exxon or Procter & Gamble camping on your doorstep pleading with you to join them, try a smaller organization. In a smaller company you can gain exposure to areas that you wouldn't if working at a giant. At smaller companies you gain varied experience; at larger ones you get prestige from having the "name" behind you. In 1980, small businesses (defined as 500 employees or less) employed the majority of all workers.

4. If you receive an offer from an employer who wants you to relocate, are you prepared to move?   If you are, then your opportunities for finding employment greatly increase. However, this is true chiefly if you are at a manager's level or higher, or you are viewed as having managerial "potential." The new employer generally picks up part or all of your relocation expenses. If you do have to relocate yourself fully or in part, the expense is tax-deductible.

Even if you are willing to or really want to relocate, it may be difficult to do so. Many areas of the country have prejudices against people who are not from their part of the country. For example, if you are a Californian, have been educated in the Southwest, and work for a California-based organization, you will probably have some difficulty convincing a northeastern company that you are a hard worker and possess the requisite "killer instinct." Valid or not, you will be viewed as too "laid back," more interested in whether you have a swimming pool at your apartment complex than whether their union's going out on strike. Be prepared to bring up these issues first, even if your interviewer does not. The people who interview you may not mention these concerns, but they sure are thinking about them!

If you are not willing to relocate, don't interview with employers who will inevitably want to move you. Keep in mind, however, that relocation is often a fact of life for managers in big organizations and that you may be hurting your long-term career. Employees at IBM often say that the initials I.B.M. stand for "I've Been Moved."

From *Homequity's* Relocation Issues and Trends, April 1981: "Housing is an enormously costly asset or investment to buy, finance, maintain and sell. . . . On average and depending on the area of the country, values are no longer appreciating at the 12-18% per year level. . .but more in the range of 4% to 9%, and in some locations are declining by as much as 5%. . . . Within the last three years, a person who allotted $700 for a mortgage payment was able to afford a $94,000 home. And today? That amount of inflated money only covers the payments for a home valued around $65,000. Real incomes are still not keeping pace with rising inflation. . . ."

5. Should you visit local employment agencies if you don't want to relocate?   By all means. When you are seeking new employment, list yourself with several firms that have some expertise in your job area. Some of these agencies may want you to list yourself with them exclusively, but unless you have 100 percent faith that only one can find you a wonderful opportunity in a short period of time, use several. *You* are the one who's looking. If you have a good background, believe us, they'll market you.

6. *Will executive search firms be interested in you?*   Perhaps. Even though executive recruiters (often called head-hunters), unlike employment agencies, do not let you visit them unless they have sought *you* out, most of them will accept your résumé (even if they say they won't) and put it in their extensive files if your background's of interest to them. Remember, though, executive search firms work for the corporations, *not* for the candidate. They couldn't care less that you are seeking employment. Most of their targeted candidates are people who haven't even been thinking about making a job change. They will never try to "market" you, whereas employment agencies will if they feel you are salable. Laws governing executive search firms differ from state to state, but most bona fide executive recruiters generally don't handle positions paying under $30,000 or $35,000 even if their state allows them to go lower.

Executive recruiters often have out-of-state clients, so your desire not to relocate will decrease your potential value to the recruiters even if they are interested in your background.

7. *Should you answer ads in newspapers and trade journals?*   Definitely yes. Remember that job hunting is a tough business. Do anything and everything that will help you get your next desired position. But be judicious: you could be answering a blind ad placed by a division within your present organization.

8. *Should you write letters or send résumés directly to potential employers?*   Again, yes. Leave no stone unturned. Limit your letters geographically only if you cannot or will not relocate. See chapter 7 on action letters.

9. *Should you ask people you know for help in your job campaign?*   Certainly. Most job seekers, over 70 percent, get their jobs through contacts. And put your trust in strangers. They will often be more helpful than friends and family members who think they know you too well.

10. *Should you think about starting your own business?*   Yes, think about it, but do some in-depth homework before you leap into this abyss. It takes expertise to develop a needed product or service, money to finance the beginnings, and even more money to carry you through some rough times, which are guaranteed to be there. Just because you sold two quilts to friends last Christmas does not mean that you have a viable business venture. Keep in mind that you are better off earning $30,000 working for someone else than starving to death at $9,700 just to be able to say it's your own business. Most small business ventures fail within the first two years because they are undercapitalized, undermanaged, or both. Banks are not equity lenders; you will probably have to finance your own start-up. You have to produce three years' worth of financial statements showing a good progression upward in profits before a bank will loan you a dime (this is particularly true if you market a service instead of a product).

The Six Hottest Transferable Skills for the 1980s

Now that we've discussed some very valid reasons why you should think about making a career move, here is a list of highly transferable skills that most employers look for when hiring.

If you possess some, most, or all of these in your work or volunteer background you will be more valuable to many potential employers.

Public Speaking

If you belong to any professional associations, become active on some committee and be sure to talk publicly, even if it's only to introduce other speakers at a meeting. It's not frightening at all once you do it a few times. Then, you'll be able to lead discussions or to lecture. If you don't belong to any professional association, join one or two. If public speaking terrifies you, take a course at Dale Carnegie or join Toastmasters International. They'll teach you how to overcome your trepidations.

Budget Management

If possible, grab hold of any budget you can, even if it's a tiny one. Manage the dispersal of the funds, and keep accurate records. Having some fiscal control experience is always a plus.

Managing/Supervising

Even if you do not have people directly reporting to you, take responsibility for a group effort, if possible. And don't forget volunteer experience if you haven't supervised at work. Managing is managing, whether or not you're paid for it.

Interviewing

Interviewing doesn't have to take place only when hiring someone. Obtain information by direct questioning of others. If you belong to any organization, get involved with its newsletter (or start one) and interview people for articles. Offer to screen candidates for your boss, even if doing so is not part of your job description. In your personal life, interview several accountants or attorneys before you pick one. Develop a list of specific questions to ask each person you see.

Instructing

Teach a class at night in your local adult education center, at the "Y," or at a professional association. Remember that most "teaching" occurs in the daily exchanges between people (persuading others to your point of view). Any position of leadership where you are in the limelight gives you a chance to teach concepts and methods. And, you don't have to have a Ph.D. or any degree in order to instruct; you can teach cookie baking, automobile repair, horseback riding, bridge, anything!

Writing

Write business letters, reports or memos at work. Write for a club or professional association's newsletter, write letters to the editor of newspapers and magazines, start a departmental newsletter if you can get your boss's permission, try to write an article for a magazine. Get yourself into print—you don't have to be the next F. Scott Fitzgerald to put pen to paper!

7. Action Letters: A Little Goes a Long Way: The Direct-Mail Marketing Approach to Career Changing

"Words are like sunbeams; the more they are concentrated, the deeper they burn."

—RICHARD C. BORDEN

There's Gold in the "Junk Mail" Format

In 1935 Richard C. Borden wrote a book entitled *Public Speaking as Listeners Like It*, which outlined a simple four-step method of presenting information. Though the book was aimed at public-speaking situations, the method of presentation had application 'way beyond its intended audience. Borden's formula for presenting information soon spread to radio advertisements, mail solicitations, magazine ads, and, by the early 1950s, television advertising.

Richard Borden's "Golden Formula" consists of the following: part I, Ho Hum Crasher (or "hook"); part II, Why Bring That Up?; part III, For Instance (other examples); part IV, So What?

This formula was so successful that it became the foundation of what is now the $4 billion direct-mail marketing industry. Since its initial appearance in 1935, the Golden Formula has stood the test of time and remained virtually intact for almost fifty years. Quite an achievement! Over the years, his formula has been called by different names—including AIDA (Attention, Interest, Desire, and Action)—and is widely used among advertising sales personnel. Regardless of its label it remains, in essence, Richard Borden's Golden Formula.

This successful formula can also be applied to job-hunting letters.

Part I, the Ho Hum Crasher, is designed to catch the audience's attention. In a public-speaking situation, the audience challenges the speaker to get and hold its interest. When writing a letter, you have the same problem: capturing the attention of the reader. However, *your* audience is not bound by the actions of a larger group. The courtesy afforded your letter is about ten or fifteen seconds in duration, only long enough for your reader to finish all or most of your opening paragraph. To encourage further reading, your Ho Hum Crasher must hook your audience.

Part II, Why Bring That Up?, addresses the question of your audience: "OK, you have my attention. So why bring that up?" You must give your reader the connection between your opening paragraph and its situation. Be specific. Identify your interest in a particular job. You must guide your reader in the direction in which you want him or her to go: that is, toward a more complete understanding of your work experience.

Part III, For Instance, includes additional paragraphs (examples), describing your work experience, each in the P-A-R format. These should answer the question raised in part II. This part makes up 80 percent of your action letter.

Part IV, So What?, is the concluding paragraph of your action letter. Here you briefly review your educational experience (or lack of it) and your salary experience, and ask your reader to respond with a specific action: to grant you an interview. Follow asking for the interview with a sentence telling the reader that you will call within a week or ten days if the reader doesn't call or write first.

This four-step procedure is used (with slight adaptation) almost everywhere as the way to present information quickly, accurately, and in a forceful, convincing manner. Look at this example from direct-mail advertising.

CUSTOM PUBLISHING COMPANY
120 North 14th Street
Kenilworth, New Jersey 07214
201--944-7300

Build up the skills and effectiveness
of your supervisors with this new, easy-to-use
training program from Custom Publishing.

The experienced supervisors in your organization are key people. They need to be kept up-to-date on the best supervisory skills and practices. Now Custom Publishing and David Cooper have teamed up to help you meet this responsibility with a new training program.

The Art of Supervising Audio Cassette Program helps in three important ways:

First--it's PRACTICAL. Each of the ten sessions is loaded with information your supervisors can start using on the job right away.

Second--it's ECONOMICAL. The complete program--fifteen hours of practical training--is only $165.00. And the materials needed by each supervisor cost less than $8.00 each (even less when you take advantage of our quantity purchase discounts!).

Third--it SAVES YOU TIME. This program is self-contained. It virtually eliminates administration time. Leaves you free to concentrate your efforts in other areas. Ideal for self-instruction, but equally effective for small group training.

The best way to learn about The Art of Supervising Audio Cassette Program is to see it for yourself. Simply fill out the enclosed reply card and I'll send you the complete program for a ten-day preview. See if you don't agree that this is the easiest, most economical way to train supervisors you've come across in a long time.

Sincerely,

Alexander Ufer
Marketing Manager

Direct or Junk Mail

This letter was sent to training and development professionals by a major book publisher as part of a direct-mail marketing campaign to promote the sale of a new program.

A personal testimony

*The Joys of Junk Mail**

There was a time when I threw it all out—the piles of pamphlets, circulars and ads that always seemed to come at least in duplicate and averaged as much as one to two inches of paper per day. Now I not only read some of it—I also keep some of it and find that I refer to what I save when preparing for a meeting, a workshop or a trip. I am sure that I probably don't do with the material what the sender intended—a brochure for a seminar was sent to encourage me to attend, NOT to keep me current on what is happening in the field—but I certainly do use it!

And much of the unsolicited mail that I receive really does not deserve to be included under that rather derisive category of "junk mail."

*Women Business Owners of New York, *Womanventure*, May 1981.

You can apply the analysis to magazine advertisements, radio spots, and direct-mail pieces. The Golden Formula has withstood the critical test of time and proved successful in a variety of areas. Our experience has confirmed that, when applied to your job search, the Golden Formula can have spectacular results. Lloyd Feinstein, one of this book's authors, used this approach to obtain his last three jobs. You can too!

The action letter below is typical of how the four-step format would be applied to a job candidate's history. By carefully examining this action letter you will see how the want-ad analysis and the P-A-R formula can be combined with this four-step format to create possibly one of the strongest marketing instruments for your own job search.

Dear

As Assistant to the Vice President for International Finance at a major Chicago bank, I conducted an extensive survey of the reactions of the major European newspapers and perodicals to the 1977 Spanish elections. To assess the financial implications of the elections and their impact on the bank's investments, I organized the articles by date, country, and within each country by political reaction; conceptualized, then composed, individual reports for each country; translated pertinent articles as appendices to the report, which was submitted to the bank's Board of Directors.

I am writing because your organization may be in need of a person with my background and experience for your Management Trainee Program in International Corporate Lending. If so, the following accomplishments may be of interest:

- I produced financial reviews for extending a line of credit, joining a syndication, increasing or decreasing a line of credit, or letting the credit line lapse. Also I analyzed balance sheets and income statements against institutional guidelines. To add depth to the analysis, I consulted credit file data, dispatch telexes in both French and English to our six shareholders for their assessment and approval, and obtained recommendations from other key financial institutions. The completed reviews were submitted to the Vice President.

• As Project Coordinator for a photocopying survey, I interfaced with management and line staff to explain the bank's need to evaluate current copy demand. I supervised employee compliance with the guidelines of the survey. I produced daily reports evaluating the use of various types of photocopying "jobs." Monitored discrepancies between machine metering and employee logs. I prepared a summary report for the Purchasing Director which recommended the most profitable investment in photocopying services. This resulted in a yearly savings of approximately $14,000 for our department.

• Using information supplied by the Vice President, I compose and supervise the preparation of all correspondence for his signature (produced in both French and English). I translate correspondence, reports and telexes for dissemination among various members of the International Finance Division.

I graduated from Hunter College, New York City, with a B.A. in 1973, speak French and Spanish fluently, and am matriculated in the University of Chicago's graduate evening division to obtain my M.B.A. My salary requirements are competitive. I would be glad to discuss my experience further in a personal interview.

Respectfully yours,

Barbara R. Wilkinson

The counseling sessions that eventually helped to produce Barbara Wilkinson's action letter were characterized by her generally low opinion of herself. On numerous occasions she would say, "But I'm really only an executive secretary!" As a result of the give-and-take of the questioning session, and after reviewing her completed action letter, Barbara came away with a greater appreciation of her own worth. So did her new employer!

Why Barbara Wilkinson's Action Letter Is a Do!

The letter employs the Golden Formula and her key paragraphs are in the P-A-R format. Paragraphs describe her major job accomplishments. Results are quantified when possible. P-A-R paragraphs are arranged from strongest to weakest (high interest to low interest). Salary is discussed but not disclosed. The letter is kept to one page in length with proper use of space.

Analysis of a Typical Action Letter: The Golden Formula

As with the résumé, an action letter has only a few seconds to catch the attention of your reader. Therefore, it is critical that your opening paragraph (the Ho Hum Crasher) address the greatest need of your audience. To identify this need consistently, simply do a thorough want-ad analysis of the job title of greatest interest to you. In this way, you can be sure that your opening paragraph will hook the largest possible audience.

Generally, the opening paragraph, the Ho Hum Crasher, is a P-A-R paragraph with a slight adaptation to identify where you are (were) employed. It comes in two variations:

1. One that identifies your employer.

As Sales Manager for the Rock Island Water Company I maintained the highest level of equipment rentals by handling customer-service problems in person (or by phone). In addition, I reviewed account records and questioned fleet drivers to establish the basis for service interruption. Rectified problems through Delivery, Service, Billing, and Credit departments, which yielded less than 1% attrition per month, the lowest in the company.

2. One that disguises where you work. This format is recommended if you feel your switch would be difficult and knowledge of your current employer would work against you.

As Sales Manager for a major service company, I maintained the highest level of equipment rentals by handling customer-service problems in person (or by phone). In addition, I reviewed account records and questioned fleet drivers to establish the basis for service interruption. Rectified problems through Delivery, Service, Billing, and Credit departments, which yielded less than 1% attrition per month, the lowest in the company.

Identifying the Parts

Current employer, not named   Action

(As Sales Manager for a major service company) (I maintained the highest level of equipment rentals) (by handling customer-service problems in person [or by phone]). (In addition, I reviewed account records and questioned fleet drivers) (to establish the basis for service interruption.) (Rectified problems through Delivery, Service, Billing and Credit Departments) (which yielded less than 1% attrition per month, the lowest in the Company.)

Results   Problem   Action (continued)

From this example, you can see that the sequence of the P-A-R paragraphs can be adjusted to meet a specific need. So long as you cover the "Problem," "Action" and "Results" somewhere in your paragraph, feel free to experiment with sequencing.

The second part of our Golden Formula (Why Bring That Up?) is what we call a stock paragraph. It has only two variations, to be used in a cold-canvassing letter or in response to a specific advertisement.

(1) Cold-canvass

I am writing because your organization may be in need of a man (woman) with my background and experience. If so, you may find the following accomplishments of interest.

(2) Advertisement

I am writing in response to your advertisement for a (title of ad), which appeared in the (date) edition of the (name of newspaper or publication). Your organization (company) may be in need of a person with my background or experience. If so, you may find the following accomplishments of interest.

The third part of your action letter, the "For Instance," will always form the bulk of your presentation. It is composed of three to five paragraphs in the P-A-R format. These are usually very tight, short paragraphs with "punch," which correspond closely to the needs identified in your want-ad analysis for a particular job title. The placement order of these paragraphs should follow the order of need determined by the want-ad analysis.

The first "For Instance" example is from the training and personnel areas.

To improve interviewing skills, I designed and developed a six-hour seminar entitled "Employment Interviewing for Managers." I instructed managers throughout the corporation in questioning and listening techniques. This highly participative seminar was keyed to the accurate completion of a man-specification form. To date, 68 key managers and administrators have completed the program.

The second "For Instance" example is from the employee-relations area.

To increase the effectiveness of employee communications hospitalwide, I negotiated the purchase and adaptation of the American Airlines customer treatment program. I selected and trained 20 discussion leaders, then supervised the implementation of the 14-week program for 5,100 employees. Evaluation included questionnaires, interviews, and analyses of (random) employee job performance, which resulted in an average improvement of 22% above baseline data.

The next "For Instance" example is from the sales management area.

To expand lead sources for new business, I analyzed the Service Department's reports. Trained 4 route drivers to produce leads for new business in exchange for a sliding commission. This produced an increase of 35.6% for the service men and 17.8% for the route driver. Gross revenues increased $22,338 in only 5 months.

The final part of the Golden Formula is the "So What?" Here the reader is asked to take specific action: to invite the person in for an interview. In sales jargon this is the "close," where the seller (writer) tries to close the sale. A number of additional objectives are also achieved: brief review of the job searcher's education (or lack of it), discussion (but not disclosure) of the salary issue, and follow-up both on the reader's part (call the applicant in for an interview) and the applicant's part (telephone as follow-up to the action letter).

The "So What?" paragraph has two variations: one that reviews the writer's formal education, and the other, which attempts to overcome the educational deficiencies in the writer's background. With this exception in mind, the rest is a stock paragraph.

(1)   Degreed Writer

I am a 1978 graduate of Ohio State University, B.S. in Chemical Engineering, and am currently enrolled in the M.B.A. program at the University of Southern California. My salary requirements are competitive. I will be glad to discuss my experience further in a personal interview and to that end will call your office within the next ten days to set a time to meet.

(2)   Nondegreed Writer

My on-the-job education progressed from Marketing Assistant to Product Manager Trainee to Assistant Product Manager on two regional snack foods with sales volume of $1.7 million. I was then promoted to Associate Product Manager for a $5.2 million line of confectionary and helped increase sales to $7.3 million in 14 months. My salary requirements are competitive. I would be glad to discuss my experience further in a personal interview, and to that end will call your office within the next ten days to arrange an interview.

The phrase "and to that end will call your office within the next ten days" should not be used when sending your action letter to a blind ad. It should be used only when cold-canvassing or when you've been referred to a specific person and you have a name and title.

To summarize the Golden Formula, it consists of:

Part I, Ho Hum Crasher: One P-A-R paragraph, slightly adapted.

Part II, Why Bring That Up? Standardized paragraph in two variations: (a) for answering an ad; (b) for direct communication with an organization (cold-canvass).

Part III, For Instance: Three to five P-A-R paragraphs.

Part IV, So What? Standardized paragraph in two variations: (a) for college graduates; (b) for noncollege graduates.

The Dos and Don'ts of Action Letters

To help familiarize you with the action letter, here are annotated examples of both strong and weak letters.

Action Letter "Do"—Retail

Dear Mr. Pitoski:

As buyer of fashion jewelry and fashion accessories for a major Baltimore retailer (6 stores), I developed vendor relationships characterized by continuous verbal and written communication, which led to my planning ads and inventories with vendors and documenting ad agreements. I also negotiated for return privileges or markdown money with 72% of my manufacturers.

I am writing because your organization may be in need of a woman with my background and experience. If so, the following accomplishments may be of interest:

• Developed and monitored my department's allocation of dollars via planned sales and inventories, maintained turnover, and increased gross margin on a semiannual basis. This resulted in an 11.4% average annual increase over the eight-year period from July 1970 to June 1977.

• Instructed and supervised department managers with pertinent selling information relating to current trends and fashion predictions. Utilizing sales trend meetings, illustrations, and written communications, I explained the rationale for selection and the function of the merchandise geared toward telling the merchandise story to the customer.

• Maintained and nurtured a close relationship with local newspaper fashion editors to assist in free publicity for the store. Selected merchandise for newspaper ads and approved art and copy.

• Selected merchandise and solicited vendor cooperative advertising for a Mother's Day and Christmas catalogue, which resulted in a 60% sell-thru for the former and 75% for the latter.

• Instructed and supervised the development of 6 executive trainees, which resulted in the promotion of all 6 to assistant buyers in various locations within the store.

My on-the-job "education" progressed from sales to supervision to promotional buyer in daytime dresses with a volume of $600,000 per year. I was then promoted to the Loungewear Department and achieved record sales of $1.1 million yearly. In my current position, in the Fashion Jewelry and Fashion Accessory Department, sales have reached $1.5 million annually. My salary requirements are competitive. I would be glad to discuss my experience further in a personal interview and will call you next week to set up a time for us to meet.

Sincerely,

Andrea Luciano

Why This Action Letter Is a "Do"

It shows specific attention to the bottom line (profits) and a concern for increased sales. She uses action verbs to describe her experience, and her results are quantified. She lists her major accomplishments in the areas of managing people and interpersonal skills: key elements for any successful manager. She shows evidence of creativity (free publicity). She has addressed her education problem (lack of it) head-on and turned it into a positive accomplishment.

Action Letter "Don't"—Personnel

Mr. Nelson Wilson
4071 Pine Bluff Road
Waco, Texas

Mr. Joseph P. McConnell   June 17, 1981
Chairman of the Board
530 Route 93
Phoenix, Arizona

Dear Mr. McConnell:

I saved a manufacturing firm $10,000 a year by recruiting a uniquely qualified senior executive at a salary well below that budgeted for his position.

Your company may be in need of an employment of a recruiting specialist. If so, you may be interested in what I have done in this field.

As Director of Recruitment I have been responsible for the hiring of dozens of employees per year, ranging from entry-level to Regional Vice President.

I developed an effective recruitment program at a cost of approximately 10% of salaries, utilizing advertising, direct recruitment of identified candidates, and other sources.

I worked with department and group managers to determine actual requirements of positions to be filled and developed job analyses and descriptions.

I personally interviewed and evaluated candidates prior to referring them to specific managers and assisted those managers in interviewing candidates when such assistance was needed.

During the staffing of a major midwestern plant, I successfully located nine specialists and managers in an industry with a very tight labor market.

I recruited a project engineering manager for a plant located in the Caribbean where management had determined that a manager from a minority group was needed.

I am fully familiar with equal employment opportunity and other legal hiring requirements. I am equally comfortable communicating in written or verbal form.

I have a Bachelor of Science degree and have attended New York University's M.B.A. program.

If you desire to discuss my experience in greater detail, I would be pleased to do so in a personal interview.

Very truly yours,

Nelson Wilson

Why This Action Letter Is a "Don't"

There is no mention of where this person worked. By mentioning plant and manufacturing, the reader could conclude that this person is experienced only in technical recruitment. He failed to follow the P-A-R format. Job performance only partially qualified. He gave no indication that he knows how to manage a staff—he apparently is a one-man show, since he has to handle all levels of recruitment. Many of the statements relate to mundane, typical parts of the job requirements for any recruiter, rather than major accomplishments. He failed to give time parameters on his assignments—were they done in one month or a year?

Action Letter "Do"—Marketing/Sales Trainee

320 N.E. 83rd Street
Orlando, Florida 33831
October 3, 1980

Mr. Paul Hurtley, President
PDI Drugs, Inc.
6301 Peachtree Street
Atlanta, Georgia

Dear Mr. Hurtley:

As Sales Representative for a Japanese distributor of three American drug manufacturers, I increased my sales volume 175% and reduced accounts receivable by 41.4% in 24 months.

I was hired after getting my M.B.A. by the CEO to turn-around and manage his small, unprofitable export company. The strategies I created and implemented produced a profit in only seven months.

I came to America one year ago to start a new career and a new life. Since my arrival, I have obtained my work permit and become one of the top salesmen of a line of home humidifiers. To implement my career strategy of obtaining a position more closely suited to my skills and abilities, I took the above interim position. I now desire a long-term relationship. Thus, your company might have need of an ambitious and personable professional (age 32) to fill the position of:

1. Sales Representative
2. Assistant Product Manager
3. Export Manager Trainee
4. Import Manager/ Buyer Trainee

I feel that I am realistic about my recent arrival in this country. Still I bring an unbroken record of accomplishments. My wife is a medical technician and we have two young children.

I would be happy to meet to discuss my joining your organization. Hoping to hear from you in the near future, I remain

Very truly yours,

Horacio M. Falik

Why This Action Letter Is a "Do"

It is results-oriented, a strong letter even though it is not in a strict Golden Formula (it is more chatty and less formal). It is written in a friendly style that is not formularized. It comes across as honest; it tells us he has been in this country one year and has the proper papers. Probably he had this letter professionally developed, for it is too well written for a nonnative speaker of English who has been in this country only one year.

Action Letter "Don't"—Health Care

```
                                        73 Portland Road
                                        Mamaroneck, New York


Director--Administration
Bellevue Hospital Center
First Avenue & 27th Street
New York, New York  10016


Dear Sir:

    I am a dedicated, highly motivated Health Care Manager/Researcher with an M.P.H.
degree in Systems Management and seven years of experience in both laboratory manage-
ment and data processing systems research.  I have made large contributions in all
areas under my responsibility.  These include increasing the cost-effectiveness and
quality of systems research.  I know I could make a strong contribution in your
company.  Therefore, I would welcome the opportunity to join your staff.

    I am an expert in:  laboratory management and data processing administration in
a laboratory environment; techniques to optimize the design and functioning of equip-
ment used in laboratory systems research.  I am also an authority in the field of
Health Care Systems Management.

    I have received awards from management for cutting laboratory costs by 42%.
This was done by changing procedures and ending dependence on commercially avail-
able equipment and reagents.  This has resulted in the laboratory maintaining its
high level of research and productivity while reducing manpower by 12%.

    I thrive in a difficult environment.  I am an expert at solving abstract prob-
lems.  I am calm, calculating and good at details.  I prefer to work in a group
environment of highly intelligent and well-motivated individuals.

    I can help your organization and would like to meet to discuss my experience
further.  To that end, I will call you within ten days to set up a time for us to
meet.


                                        Respectfully,


                                        Thomas W. Brooks
```

Why This Action Letter Is a Don't

It's a good example of "overkill." To the reader, remember that self-praise stinks ("I am dedicated," "an expert," "highly motivated"). Positive conclusions such as these should be deduced from a reading of your action letter (soft-sell technique). Instead of saying that he made "large contributions," Brooks should have described them in P-A-R format and allowed the reader to draw the conclusion. Avoid making promises ("I can help your organization"). Your P-A-R paragraphs will more than convince the reader of your potential within their organization. He is a lazy job hunter; he failed to find out the name of the Director of Administration. Although he concludes his letter with "Respectfully," he doesn't sound as if he would be very respectful.

Summary

The key difference between a well-written, *successful* action letter and an unsuccessful one is that a successful action letter generates interviews. Wherever possible, describe yourself as a person who can get things done through others rather than doing it all yourself. The world is full of Indians; it is short, however, on chiefs. The P-A-R paragraph below was done properly, but it describes a doer, not a manager. However, if there are three or four other paragraphs in this letter, the writer can show team effort somewhere else.

To produce an accurate monthly vacancy report covering 5,692 budgeted positions, I compared wage and salary's files against both a printout of budgeted positions and an existing table of organization. Corrections were made regarding job number, job title, and distribution code. This manually compiled report was organized by department and job title within each division, showing budgeted positions, number filed, number vacant, percentages of each, and the vacancies compared to previous reports.

Unless you're just entering the world of work, work in a job that doesn't require supervision of others to be successful, or possibly reentering it after a long absence, keep in mind during your job search that it's important to project an image of yourself as a *manager of others*.

A Portfolio of Action Letters

We have added here, on the following three pages, three sample action letters. Notice the similar structures; this format is adaptable to almost any field of employment. All employ the Golden Formula, and all project managerial skills and experience. Each is aimed at the specific potential employer, not the world in general.

Sales Management

1877 Manor Drive
Rochester, New York 14211

(716) 438-4012

Dear Mr. DiGeronimo,

As Sales Manager for a major equipment leasing company, I maintained the highest level of leasing by handling customer service problems in person (or by phone). In addition, I reviewed account records and questioned distributors to establish the basis for service interruption. I rectified problems through Delivery, Service, Billing, and Credit Departments, which yielded less than 2% attrition per month, the lowest in the company for the past eight years.

I am writing because your organization may be in need of a man with my background and experience. If so, you may find the following accomplishments of interest.

- To expand lead sources for new business, I analyzed the Service Department's reports. I trained four distributors to produce leads for new business in exchange for a sliding commission. This produced an increase of 35.6% for the service staff and 17.8% for the distributors. Gross revenues increased $22,338 in only 5 months.

- To motivate the sales force, I devised an incentive program that paid $2.50 for each new lease. To reinforce the program's effectiveness, monthly summaries of the program were mailed to the sales force's spouses. The program resulted in new business increases of 10.48% ($100,445) in my territory and the adoption company-wide of the program.

- To control all areas of accounts, I managed the sales force of 16 and reorganized the support staff of 9 people engaged in order entry, expediting, customer service, and records maintenance. Additionally, I had extensive interface with EDP. This resulted in an average annual net gain in accounts of 18.7% from 1973 to 1981.

My on-the-job "education" progressed from owner/operator of a dry-cleaning firm to mutual and life insurance salesman and then sales manager. My salary requirements are competitive. I would be glad to discuss my experience further and will call your office within the next ten days to arrange a personal interview.

Sincerely yours,

Howard R. Olsen

Customer Service

263 Washington Ave.
Apt. 6
St. Paul, Minnesota 52101

March 5, 1982.

Mr. William Wedemeyer
Manager of Customer Service
Sharp Electrical Corporation
4129 Route 1
Rochester, Minnesota 53614

Dear Mr. Wedemeyer:

As Customer Service Representative for the electronics division of an international conglomerate, I handled consumer complaints while maintaining cost containment guidelines. I interfaced with dealers, servicers, field engineers and customers to determine accuracy of complaint. I evaluated complaint profiles against past cases, which resulted in the identification of possible areas of design change and increased customer satisfaction evidenced by 47.3% weekly increase of "thank you" responses.

I am writing because your organization may be in need of a woman with my background and experience. If so, the following accomplishments may be of interest:

- To record and handle customer telephone inquiries promptly and accurately, I upgraded an existing format so relevant data could be compiled quickly, verified, and acted upon. After implementing this format, the department logged an increase of 18% complaints resolved within the initial contact or with one follow-up. Based on this data, the format was adopted nationally throughout our 9 division service centers.
- To increase the number of dealers authorized to sell our product line, I assisted the Division Sales Manager in the inspection of prospective stores to determine their suitability as company representatives. I prepared reports summarizing market potential, sales volume, location, display facilities and availability of repair service. As a result of my recommendation, 6 new dealers were authorized to carry our line. In each case, we outsold competitive lines within 6 months.
- I conducted frequent seminars and daily telephone contact to maintain close relationships with independent authorized service companies.

I am a graduate of Centenary College for Women in Louisiana. My salary requirements are competitive. I would be glad to discuss my experience further in a personal interview and will call you within two weeks to arrange a mutually convenient time.

Sincerely yours,

Joanne England
(201) 962-4716

Executive Assistant

400 East Main Street
New York, New York 10010

October 17, 1979

Mr. John P. Roland, Vice President
QRZ Corporation
26-38 Hudson Street
Charlestown, New Jersey 08314

Dear Mr. Roland:

As Executive Assistant to the Controller of a national retailing chain of ex-clusive stores I was directly responsible for overseeing the smooth functioning of an office of 12 professionals and clericals. In addition, I hired, trained and managed all clerical staff. I dispersed payroll, purchased equipment and supplies, managed the daily operations of the A/R Department of 4 people, and reported to the Corporate Controller.

I am writing because your organization may be in need of a person with my back-ground and experience. If so, you will find the following accomplishments of interest:

   *Reduced staff from 18 to 12 while maintaining efficiency.
   *Reduced corporate costs by over $100,000 annually.
   *Implemented a system reducing A/R backlog from 54 to 29 days.
   *Made transition from manual to computer system in less time than allocated and
     under budget by $12,300.

My previous experience was as the Administrative Assistant to the president of a medium-sized chemical company. There I set up, staffed, and supervised a technical library, redesigned 3 reporting forms, eliminating processing by 23% and reducing costs by over $65,000 a year; designed, developed, and dispersed an in-house news-letter that is still being produced.

My formal education includes a B.A. in Psychology and Economics from S.U.N.Y. at Albany in 1968 and in-house IBM courses at employers'. My salary is competitive.

I would be happy to discuss my experience further in a personal interview.

Sincerely,

Susan E. Jones

(212) 491-6314

8. The Interview: Many Are Called but Few Are Chosen

"Never measure the height of a mountain, until you have reached the top. Then you will see how low it was."

—DAG HAMMARSKJÖLD, MARKINGS

If you're like most people, the prospect of facing a job interview makes your palms sweat and your heart go into mild palpitations. This can immobilize otherwise articulate people in their ability to communicate effectively.

However, one consolation is that most people will be empathetic to your situation. Whether they're in the personnel department or your future boss they, too, had to go through the same process to get their jobs. Keep in mind that the company you're seeing had a reason to invite you in: the résumé or action letter you sent closely fitted an existing opening; a search firm or employment agency felt you could be right for their client; or you were highly recommended by someone whose opinion the people you are to see respect. But it is best to be prepared for all kinds of people and all types of interviews—then you will achieve your goal, *the* right position.

Company recruiters regard interviews as a way of measuring their own ability to assess candidates and to "sell" qualified candidates on working at their company. But always note that what you consider qualified and what any company representative views as qualified may differ. This does not mean that *you* are unqualified for the type of position you seek. It *can* mean that you are at the wrong company.

For most applicants the interview process is a proving ground for career goals and personal self-esteem. The successful job interview validates that a college degree, special training, or prior work experience *means* something. There is so much ego-involvement for both interviewer and applicant, it is small wonder that you may become a little edgy. Much of this anxiety can be dispelled, though, if you understand the whole interview process and do not regard yourself as a victim or suppliant.

Executive recruiters know that most people applying for jobs have at least two to four interviews at each company and have to interview at approximately nine or ten different companies before one offer is forthcoming. And the offer you get is one you may not want to take. This is true if you are staying in your present field. If you are attempting a major career change, many more interviews than ten will be necessary.

Preinterview Attitudes

Since the interview is so important, no matter how calm you want to appear, you will probably have some anxiety. But it is important to keep in mind certain facts that may get lost in the adrenalin-filled interview.

The acceptance of a position is a major event. It commits you and a company in the way a marriage does, so it is essential that you conduct an interview carefully and rationally. You should not lose sight of the fact that it is a major step in career development and you have certain rights in relation to the interview. You have the right to ask questions to determine if the position is a good fit for your career goals and personal values; in fact you had *better* ask questions! You have the right to get paid a fair salary; you have the right to ask to meet your coworkers and subordinates, not just your immediate superior (ask about this only after it is clear that you are going to be extended an offer or after one has been made); you have the right to ask to see your personal work area (again, only if you are getting or have received the offer); you have the right to work in a nondiscriminatory environment; if you are a woman, it is *illegal* for someone to ask you about marriage plans, children, or who cares for your children while you work. You have all kinds of rights. Look upon interviewing as a positive time in which to explore many possibilities. And when possible, if you still feel a little shaky about all this, start with what we call "throwaway" interviews. Practice interviewing at organizations you don't care about much, just to hone your skills at fielding questions. Take any reasonable interview. Save your important interviews for when you have finished practicing. You can also interview for information about a field before you interview for jobs in it.

The following questions and answers do not cover everything you will ever be asked, but many of these questions come up at some point in almost every interview. You should become skilled at answering them.

There is more than one good answer to each of these questions, but we have prepared the ones we know (from experience) work.

The Four Stages of the Typical Employment Interview

There are four major stages in all employment interviews. Awareness of these stages will enable you to handle better and control the interviewing process.

Stage I. Chitchat Time or Breaking the Ice

An interview is an interaction between two strangers, not unlike meeting someone for the first time at a cocktail party. One key thing to remember is the importance of the *firm handshake*. Women readers, pay close attention to this: firm handshakes are *crucial*. Don't arm-wrestle your interviewer to the floor, but be sure your handshake says: "I am comfortable, I am in control."

The interviewer should take the initiative in beginning the dialogue; you are the respondent. Even though you may wish to get down to basics right away, view this time as a relaxation technique for both of you. Remember, most interviewers, particularly if they're *not* in Personnel, are not so skillful that they are comfortable meeting strangers either! The responsibility is on you to make *them* comfortable.

This "chitchat" allows you to assess quickly the communications skills of the interviewer, both verbal and nonverbal, which will facilitate conversation flow later on.

Stage II. Information Exchange

Once some form of rapport has been established through chitchat, the second stage is focused on exchanging information. Presumably the person you're seeing will have read your résumé before your arrival and will have prepared topics for discussion based on your background. You did provide one, didn't you? And it is in the P-A-R format, isn't it?

This is the ideal situation, but don't count on finding it 100 percent of the time. Some people will read your résumé for the first time while you sit across the desk from them pretending not to notice.

The interviewer should also share information with you on the company in general and the position for which you are applying in particular. If this information is not given, ask! It is necessary to have this information in order to proceed to stages III and IV.

It is now your interviewer's turn to communicate relevant information regarding job fit. Be aware that his or her job is to match candidates as closely as possible to specific positions. You, therefore, must have done your homework on the company and the specific position available and must have decided on the best way to verbalize matching your skills and experience to the job. Provide descriptive, assertive (but concise) statements to your interviewer, using a fair number of action verbs. Do not run off at the mouth. Doing so is boring and indicates a lack of concise thinking ability.

Stage III. Expanding the Focus

In stage II, the interviewer and you gained some general insights into the rightness of the match. During stage III experienced interviewers zero in on critical information. This part will be much more detailed, regarding very specific qualifications. Together, you will explore aspirations, personal goals, and work values. Stage III is where your responses point out differences from or similarities to what the company is looking for. Remember, the people interviewing you probably had other résumés somewhat similar to yours to review. They have to make a determination about your "fit" for the particular position. They can only do this on the basis of *what* you say and *how* you say it.

It is at this stage that a clear difference appears between your hoping the interviewer likes you and your understanding that this is a *mutual* decision-making process.

It is also here that a skilled interviewer will become less involved in the process and the interviewee will take charge to amplify background, skills, and experience. You must gain more information by asking direct questions about the specific position, determining whether it meets your needs. *You* must successfully control this part of the interview. You should ask questions regarding mobility, why the job is open, where the person is who had the job before, how many people you would manage, if you would have support staff, if you have budget control, et cetera. This is the only way you can determine if the position is or is not for you. If you feel positive about what you hear, by all means show your enthusiasm.

☞ *Insiders' Tip:*   More jobs have been lost at this point than at any other because a candidate didn't want to appear excited.

Stage IV. Wrap-up or Tying Loose Ends Together

This part of the interview allows both of you to clarify any information needed and make some final comments tying the interview together. Here again, if you are interested in the position, state it very clearly.

Unless it is volunteered to you, ask what the next step is in the interview process. This assumes that you have a good feeling about how the interview went and that you are sincerely interested in pursuing the position. Ask about the length of time before you will be called back for a second round of interviews, scheduling a time, et cetera.

If your first interview was with a company recruiter, you may not get much feedback regarding your chances at this point, as he or she will discuss you first with the hiring manager, but some information may be gleaned. If you are a good "people reader" you should now be able to tell fairly well how good your chances are to go on and have further interviews.

Remember that "chemistry," NOT qualifications, is usually the factor in personnel selection.

Since you were called in for an interview, you may assume that you are at least minimally qualified for the position. But it's the *intangible* factors that cause offers to be made, *not* the tangibles. As with job performance, it has much less to do with how well you do your job than how well you are *perceived* to do it.

If you are a fairly conservative person and everyone you have seen while interviewing is in jeans and wears shirts open to the navel and lots of gold chains, you can safely assume you would not be too happy working at this company even if a job was offered. People are often rejected for positions because of their style, not because of an inability to perform the work. If you don't proceed beyond Personnel at a corporation, it could be just that. It also could be that your interviewing skills were not up to par, but we will work on this! When you are turned down for a position (and it happens to everyone), do not internalize the rejection by thinking you are unqualified. Your first interviewer may perceive that the personality fit is not right.

It is much better to be rejected for a job than to take one that's wrong and want to leave three months later. Most people leave for style and personality mismatch reasons first, position, title, and money later.

☞ *Insiders' Tip:*   Those of you who will get the job of your choice will be the best qualified at *getting* jobs (interviewing skillfully). However, success does *not* mean you are the most qualified candidate for the job. Please recognize this distinction.

Tested Questions for the "Structured" Employment Interview

The following questions are divided into four distinct areas: Work Experience, Education/Training, Personal Factors, and Home Environment. *Some* of these questions will be asked at nearly every interview you have; others will show up less frequently, but you should be prepared to answer all of them concisely, articulately, and in a relaxed and friendly manner. Practice interviewing with friends, business associates, and sitting in front of a mirror. This last method is very useful, as you can see your own gestures and expressions and modify them accordingly, if necessary. The "a" answers to the tested questions are poor ones; "b" answers are the better responses. None of the answers to "b," the best response, are hard-and-fast, but if you are asked that question, the answer you give should be similar (in your own words). This question-and-answer format is not that of one person taking one interview. Rather, it is a list of common questions that are often asked at interviews, giving one poor answer and one good answer to each question. At interviews, they won't appear in this order.

I. Work Experience

1. *How did you originally get your present (last) job at XYZ Company?*
   (a) I was interviewing through my college's placement office and XYZ was interviewing on campus. I guess I lucked out.
   (b) After researching the companies coming to campus to interview for marketing people, I decided that XYZ most closely had what I was looking for: an excellent training program, a track record of moving their qualified trainees along, a good salary, and a chance for me to make a contribution early in my career.

2. *Can you describe your present responsibilities and duties?*
   (a) I spend a good part of my day talking with other people to get the information I need about my reports. I also supervise one or two clerks.
   (b) I gather data for my marketing research reports from outside vendors and the in-house marketing people. Then I organize it and submit it for typing early so I can get it back for editing and a final draft before the end of the day. My assistant works closely with me on this. I then finish my reports and submit them to my manager, the vice president of market research. I also make oral presentations at weekly departmental meetings.

3. *What do you particularly enjoy about working at XYZ?*
   (a) The people are very nice there and I could finish my work by five P.M. most of the time.
   (b) I learned quite a bit at XYZ and I feel I made some significant contributions to my department and the company. The people in my department are quite supportive and helpful, from my boss to the clerks. Reviews and promotions were fair, and everyone pulled together. But I'm ready for a more responsible position now.

4. *What did you like least at XYZ?*
   (a) My boss used to yell at us a lot if our work wasn't done exactly the way he wanted. He made me nervous.
   (b) I didn't feel that management delegated enough. My manager was not always clear when giving directions and occasionally would lose his temper. However, I found that if I approached him to ask for clarification, he was helpful. But I knew I could do more than I was allowed; I wasn't being challenged or worked hard enough.

5. *What would you consider your biggest accomplishment at XYZ?*
   (a) I did a large study with almost no backup in a very short time. It surprised my boss, but he took credit for my report.
   (b) I researched, collected data, and published a key report for my department head. He needed it to make an important presentation to top management and was extremely pleased that my report was very thorough and would probably help us get the extra budget money we'd requested. I got the report to him four days early so he had a chance to go over it and prepare for his presentation. We did get our excess budget approved, by the way.

6. *Did you have any disappointments at XYZ? Did anything turn out less well than you planned?*
   (a) I spent a lot of time doing a report and then my boss didn't use it in the marketing plan. I was really angry that I wasted my time.
   (b) I had spent about six weeks working on a report for my manager which was to

be included as part of our department's yearly marketing plan. However, at the last minute the whole focus changed, and my part was entirely eliminated. My boss spoke to me, praising my work, but explained that now she couldn't use it. Naturally I was disappointed, but these things happen to everyone, and she was considerate enough to let me know she understood how I felt.

7. *What personal progress did you make at XYZ Company?*
   (a) I got to know a lot of people and it helped my social life.
   (b) I had several important relationships at XYZ that enabled me to work more effectively. I developed a good mentor relationship with my boss. He taught me many of the subtle workings of a corporation that I needed to know. I now understand quite a bit more about organizational structure and the inner workings of a big company.

8. *How has your job changed since you were hired at XYZ?*
   (a) They keep piling on the work and I don't get any overtime for it. But I keep plugging away.
   (b) I have had two raises in less than eighteen months and have been given much more responsible work. The department's responsibility has grown and sometimes it's difficult to get support help, but when projects have short deadlines I give them highest priority so they can be completed on schedule or early.

9. *What are your reasons for leaving XYZ?*
   (a) I didn't get promoted last review. In fact, my annual raise was minimal. They're a cheap company.
   (b) I feel I can make a greater contribution at another company. XYZ provided a terrific training ground, but it's a fairly conservative firm and promotespeople rather slowly. My boss has been trying to get me a promotion for over five months. In her own way she's encouraged me to look outside. She knows I'm not being developed quickly enough, but her hands are tied.

10. *How would you describe your most recent superior? What are his or her strengths and limitations?*
    (a) My boss is basically an okay guy but he's not one to mix much with his people. He gets temperamental a little too often for me.
    (b) My manager is a quiet man who allows us to work without interference. But he is approachable and supportive when we need clarification or explanations. His limitation is his style; management doesn't regard him as a high-potential leader. As a day-to-day boss, though, he's excellent.

11. *For what things have your superiors complimented you?*
    (a) My boss told me she liked my sense of humor.
    (b) She told me that my reports were always timely and well written and that she viewed me as a high-potential employee in her division because I was a team player and a leader. She said I exercised good judgment, and she made me acting manager in her absence even though several other people are senior to me.

12. *For what have your superiors criticized you?*
    (a) My boss says that when I'm under a time pressure my work is sometimes sloppy.
    (b) I've never really received criticism unless it's been to slow down. My manager commented that with my energy level he's afraid I'll burn out. (He was

kidding.) I like to work with time constraints on me; I perform well under deadlines and pressure.

13. *How would your employer describe you?*
   (a) He'd say I was an easygoing person who got along well with everyone. I never make waves.
   (b) My manager regards me as one of his two key people. He knows he can count on me to do professional work and that I can motivate the less effective people. He views me as a results-oriented, supportive leader within his department.

14. *Did you find some aspects of your job difficult to perform?*
   (a) I sometimes had trouble understanding what my boss really wanted.
   (b) No. If anything my work wasn't challenging enough after my first six or seven months at XYZ. My manager has said he found it difficult keeping me challenged and busy enough.

15. *How did you solve problems that you encountered on your job?*
   (a) I just dug in and did the best I could. Sometimes I was right, sometimes not.
   (b) I concentrated on what I perceived the problems to be and usually solved them myself. Occasionally I would seek my manager's advice to be certain I was right. I don't like to waste time by going off in the wrong direction if it's avoidable. I found very few problems; the ones I encountered generally came from unclear directions.

16. *Did you and your superior ever disagree on work matters?*
   (a) My boss always wanted me to do things his way. Sometimes I would do it my way because he was wrong a lot.
   (b) Occasionally—but it was a matter of style rather than content. My manager's detail-oriented and even though I handle details well, I am basically a conceptual person. However, whenever he's questioned any report, I found he was amenable to most of my ideas once we discussed them.

17. *In what way has XYZ prepared you for greater responsibility?*
   (a) I've been there for three years now and my work is getting repetitive. I know I'm ready for more responsibility.
   (b) In my three years at XYZ I have been assigned increasingly responsible work. I've had three promotions, my last one to supervisor, just ten months ago. But promotions from the level I am at now will be slow in coming—XYZ is conservative. I need more responsibility and challenge than what I see available in the near future. I'm ready to be a manager now but, in my personal timetable, it won't be possible to achieve it at XYZ.

18. *What is your impression of your former/present employer?*
   (a) It's a nice place to work but they're kind of stodgy.
   (b) XYZ is an excellent employer, particularly for someone right out of school who needs a supportive but conservative management style to learn the ropes of corporate life. However, once a person gets self-confidence and is able to make decisions, XYZ doesn't always keep pace with a high-powered employee.

19. *How long have you been looking for other employment?*
   (a) About four or five months, but there's not much around. Employers all want advanced degrees these days, but I have been called back to a couple of places.
   (b) I've been actively looking for about four months. I'm going back for in-depth interviews at two companies next week and one the week after that.

20. *What position are you seeking now?*
   (a) Well, I was a marketing assistant at XYZ. I think I'd like to be a marketing supervisor now.
   (b) I'm seeking a position as a marketing supervisor in a large organization or marketing manager in a smaller one. My present title is marketing assistant, but I am really the department supervisor. My marketing manager put me in charge of three assistants, but he can't get me a title change or a raise for at least six more months.

II. Education/Training

1. *What made you decide to attend PQR College?*
   (a) It was close to home and when I got some scholarship money it meant I could quit my part-time job.
   (b) I selected PQR over three other schools because of its excellent sociology department. This was the first criterion. Even though I was offered less scholarship money at PQR than at two other colleges I felt the quality of its education was superior. I made up the money difference through part-time and summer work.
2. *What determined your choice of major?*
   (a) Well, I always liked people and I felt sociology was a good major for that.
   (b) The study of people always fascinated me, and even though I knew it could be limiting for career marketability, I majored in sociology. While at PQR I took five business courses and two years of calculus and I'm currently enrolled in an evening program for my M.B.A. I feel very strongly that the study of society and people has made me an astute "people" person, an ability that's important in any organization.
3. *How would you describe your academic achievements?*
   (a) I did average work at school overall. I had to work part-time, so my grades suffered. I would've done better except for that.
   (b) I did much better my last two years of college because I really applied myself. In fact, my best academic years were when I held two part-time jobs instead of one. I discovered I perform best under reasonable pressure and deadlines.
4. *What made you decide to become a sales representative?*
   (a) Well my dad's in sales and he always made a lot of money. Also, I don't think I'd like to be behind a desk all day.
   (b) I've always been good at convincing people to my point of view and I know I can apply these skills to business. I'm also very ambitious and sales is both challenging and financially rewarding.
5. *Did you participate in extracurricular activities while at school?*
   (a) I belonged to the English Lit Club and I played field hockey for two years.
   (b) I was elected dormitory representative and attended monthly meetings with the six other dorm reps to discuss mutual problems and devise solutions. As vice president of the English Literature Club I arranged for three writers to come and speak to us. I also played intramural field hockey and worked from twenty to twenty-five hours a week. I limited my activities to these three things because of my work schedule, as I was determined also to make good grades.

6. *How did you spend your summers while in college?*
   (a) Oh, I kind of hung around a lot. Occasionally I babysat or ran errands at my family's business.
   (b) For three summers I worked as an administrative assistant at a small leather goods firm. I became familiar with accounting, sales procedures, and how a small business operates. Before that job I looked after two children for twenty-five hours a week and on weekends I worked as a waitress at one of the better restaurants.

7. *What were your vocational plans when you graduated?*
   (a) I really didn't know what I wanted to do so I took a job as an administrative assistant at a local company in their marketing department just to earn some money. I wanted to move into my own apartment.
   (b) With a B.A. in sociology there were many jobs I couldn't get but I knew I wanted a marketing career. I obtained a job at XYZ as administrative assistant to the vice president of Consumer Marketing. Through the company's tuition-refund program I matriculated evenings for my M.B.A. and need only three more courses to graduate. That's how I was promoted to marketing assistant last year. I intend to continue in consumer marketing, which is why I'm now looking for a position as an assistant product manager.

8. *Have you had any other schooling or training since college graduation?*
   (a) I'm taking some business courses at night but they're kind of boring. I guess an M.B.A. will help, though.
   (b) I took several business/math/stat courses at college and have just completed 30 percent of my M.B.A. in Finance at JKL University evenings. I will get my degree in about one and a half more years.

9. *How do you think college contributed to your development?*
   (a) I think it made me grow up and now I'm not afraid to be on my own. I learned a lot.
   (b) It was my first experience away from home, on my own. I learned how to solve problems, get my own jobs; I met different people and benefited from their experiences. I learned how much I *don't* know yet. It has made me hungry to keep developing and growing.

III. Personal Factors

1. *In general, how would you describe yourself?*
   (a) I'm an easygoing person who gets along well with everyone.
   (b) I'm a hard-working person and very results-oriented, but I'm not temperamental. I enjoy challenges and do my best work when there's some kind of deadline to meet and the work is interesting.

2. *What are your outstanding qualities?*
   (a) I am punctual, orderly, and I don't hassle people.
   (b) I can motivate people and convince them to my viewpoints; I'm organized and methodical and can work problems through to completion and on time. I work well with people and have a good sense of humor.

3. *What do you see as your personal shortcomings?* (Give one good answer and you probably won't have to give another!)
   (a) I sometimes don't react quickly enough to getting work out on time—I find it hard to motivate myself.

(b) My biggest personal failing is being impatient. I like the challenge of working hard and don't like to work with people who don't feel this way. However, I'm realistic enough to know that many people are not self-motivated, so I have learned not to express my displeasure.

4. *What traits or qualities do you most admire in an immediate superior?*
    (a) My boss should be easygoing and not jump all over me if I make a mistake. I'm only human.
    (b) I admire superiors who are fair, who can accurately assess the strengths and weaknesses of their staff, and give out work equitably while challenging lower people to improve. I also like a boss with a sense of humor—that can be a saving grace when work gets tense at deadline times.

5. *What has contributed to your success up to the present time?*
    (a) I don't make any waves where I work. Everyone likes me.
    (b) I'm a highly motivated person (which shows) and I do my work well. I'm liked by my peers, superiors, and subordinates and my boss knows she can count on me. I'm pretty sure that's why I've received my last two promotions earlier than expected.

6. *What disappointments, setbacks, or failures have you had in your life?*
    (a) I wanted to go to graduate school but my test scores weren't so great and I didn't get in where I applied.
    (b) I can't think of anything very dramatic. I disappointed myself and my swimming team in college by losing a major race that cost us the year's championship, but I'd hardly call it a major upset in my life. Basically my life's been fine; I've tried to plan it as best I could and I deal logically with problems when they come up.

7. *What are your long-range goals and objectives?*
    (a) I'd like to make a lot of money and be famous someday.
    (b) I'd like to be in top-level management (vice president or president of a division) in a capacity that affects the bottom line (dollars) of that company. If I can achieve this, I know the monetary compensation will be there.

8. *What kinds of situations make you tense or nervous?*
    (a) If my boss yells at me I usually get uptight.
    (b) I rarely get tense or nervous. Sometimes I get a little edgy if I'm waiting for the go-ahead from my boss on a proposal I've submitted that's important. But it doesn't affect my performance or my interaction with others.

9. *If you could live your life over again, what changes would you make in your life or career?*
    (a) I wish I'd been born into a wealthy family so I wouldn't have to worry about money so much.
    (b) I'm pretty happy with my life. Most things have turned out the way I wanted them to because I believe in planning. I think that for my age and educational level, I'm doing well. I like my work very much and I do want to keep learning and contributing.

10. *When you consider joining an organization, what factors do you take into account?*
    (a) I have to like the "looks" of a place and feel that the people I'll be working with are pleasant.

(b) I consider several factors. Will I be learning what I expect to on the new job? Will it allow me to grow and be valuable to my employer? Will the position satisfy my immediate and middle-term goals (that is, mobility, compensation, type of work)? Will I respect my boss and benefit from his or her tutelage? Are the people I'll be working with my style? Et cetera.

11. *What do you want in your next job that you're not getting now?*
   (a) I'd like to get more recognition from my boss for my contributions.
   (b) I will only take a position that has a clear-cut career path. I'm a career person, not a job seeker. I want to be in a position where my superiors give me recognition when I earn it and where I can make contributions to the company.

12. *What position would you want to be holding in five years? Ten years?*
   NOTE: This can be a tricky question. Unless you're very sophisticated and know the titles in *this* particular company don't answer this very definitely, as titles often differ from company to company even within the same industry. Try to avoid naming a title, and give a "general" answer instead: "I'd like to be in a solid middle-management position in the Finance/Marketing/Personnel Department within five years." For ten years, say, "I would hope to be somewhere in top management, perhaps a director or vice president."

13. *What do you see as an advantage to working at XYZ?*
   (a) I think I could learn a lot in the position we discussed and everybody seems nice here.
   (b) I'm impressed with the management style and with the people I've met. I think my background dovetails nicely with the position you wish to fill and yet it gives me room to grow and to make new contributions. I'm impressed with the way XYZ helps its employees follow certain career paths.

14. *In what area of XYZ do you think you can make the biggest contribution?*
   (a) I think I'd fit into several areas well. I'd leave that decision up to you now that you know my background.
   (b) I think I could contribute significantly in sales because of my prior accomplishments. Even though I have experience in other areas, sales is where my deepest interest lies and where I plan to build my long-range career.

15. *What changes and developments do you anticipate in your field?*
   (a) I haven't really thought much about it. I guess if there were new things to learn I'd pick them up.
   (b) If marketing, like most fields, changes rapidly as companies become increasingly sophisticated, then specific changes are hard to predict but I've noticed a shift in companies' management toward regarding [Personnel/ Engineering/R & D/et cetera] as more important. I intend to be up to date on things related to my work; I'd be happy to take courses if needed. I read several professional publications in my field now and would continue to do so.

16. *What kind of support would you need to make your best contribution at XYZ?*
   (a) I'd like my boss to praise me once in a while for good work.
   (b) I'd like to be assured of support from my peers, superiors, and subordinates. If we work as a team to do the job well, that's support. I can work well alone, too, but I'd need feedback on how I was doing. As far as general support goes, I presume I'd have a secretary or access to one when needed.

IV. Home Environment

NOTE: These questions are somewhat psychologically oriented. The interviewing person is generally trying to find out how stable you are, via questions on your home life. Even if your mother was an alcoholic and your father spent ten years in a maximum security prison, do *not* reveal any of this to a company representative. It has *nothing* to do with *your* ability to perform well.

1. *What can you tell me about your childhood and home upbringing?*
   (a) My mother doted on me because my father wasn't home too much. They got divorced when I was seven years old. I guess I was spoiled.
   (b) My childhood and adolescence were very happy. My mother was very supportive of me and encouraged me to better myself and try new things. I know that's why I'm self-assured today.

2. *What are your recreational and leisure-time interests?*
   (a) I play cards once a week with friends or go to the movies.
   (b) I have many interests but pursue only a few because of my work schedule. I jog every morning for thirty minutes and play tennis once or twice a week. I also love photography [or coins, or collecting rare books].

NOTE: Make certain that some of the activities you cite are competitive and people-oriented such as tennis, backgammon, chess, racquetball, or squash.

3. *Do you belong to any social, civic, or professional clubs?*
   (a) No. I don't have any time for organizations and most of the ones I know are boring.
   (b) I am active in my town's politics, and I belong to two professional organizations [name them]. I hold an office in one [name it].

4. *How do you spend your vacations?*
   (a) I usually hang around or visit my family in Chicago.
   (b) I try to take unusual vacations because I love doing new things. One vacation I rafted down the Colorado River and on another I went on a one-week theatre tour in London. This year I'm going to Peru.

5. *If you had more time, are there any activities in which you'd like to participate?*
   (a) Not really; I like my free time to do what I want.
   (b) I am pursuing much of what I like now. If anything, I sometimes feel overcommitted, particularly since I head two committees in three organizations. But I love it.

6. *Are there any other aspects of your qualifications which we haven't covered, relevant to the position you and I discussed today?*
   (a) No, you covered what I wanted to say.
   (b) I think we have covered all I need to know about how my experience and abilities fit your position. However, I'd like you to know that I am impressed with what we've discussed and with your company. I'm very interested in this job. I hope that I made a favorable impression and that you will seriously consider me for this position.

The last thirty seconds of an interview can be as awkward as the first thirty. Everyone, interviewers included, has most difficulty in keeping beginnings and endings flowing smoothly.

When an interview is about to end, the interviewer invariably will ask if you have any questions. Make certain to have one or two, if only clarification of a point (such as who reports to whom in the department, how large it is). Ask a question; never allow the conversation to die by saying, "No, I don't have any questions." Always ask something relevant to the conversation just past and then make one or two very positive statements about enjoying the interview and hoping that you are one of the candidates being considered for the position. *Ask for a business card*, shake hands, and leave. Write a thank-you note within forty-eight hours, reexpressing your interest.

NOTE: *Concerning Proper Dress for an Interview:*

1. Always dress one level up from your position. If you are a secretary, dress like an office manager. If you are a sales representative, dress like a sales manager; if you are a director, dress like a vice president.
2. Always look professional. Do not wear the latest fashions from *Vogue* or *Gentleman's Quarterly* to an interview, no matter how much they cost. You have to convey the message of being in style but not trendy.

Men should wear suits (navy, gray), collegiate striped ties and white or blue cotton shirts, black (and polished) tie shoes (wing-tips are best), over-the-calf-length black or navy socks, and no ostentatious jewelry. Wristwatches should be conservative and college rings are now a no-no! (We don't make the rules, you know.)

Women should wear tailored suits when possible, silk or very good polyester blouses (preferably white or light solids), dark pumps (no slingbacks, sandals, or boots). If the weather's terrible, wear boots to the company, carry your shoes with you, and change. Wear sheer pantyhose (no colors or decorations), and carry a briefcase or large pocketbook, but not both (if possible). Jewelry should be in good taste; wear only one ring per hand. No clunky bracelets, no rhinestones. Earrings, if you wear them, should be small—no dangles. The company people you meet should remember that you looked terrific but not be able to remember what it was you were wearing.

If you are just starting out from college and are somewhat strapped financially, get one or two dark (but not black) suits and one or two blazers in navy, gray, et cetera. Blazers are good with any wardrobe and if combined with the correct skirts and blouses convey almost the same image as a two-piece suit (but not quite). NEVER wear a pantsuit to an interview. Even though most organizations have relaxed their dress codes, pantsuits, no matter how expensive, are inappropriate at interviews.

Pantsuits, or more comfortable clothes, may be worn once you get hired (only if other people on your peer level and above wear them; if your peers do and your boss doesn't, you shouldn't either if you are looking for a rapid promotion). Depends on your organization's attitude.

I know all this talk about dressing properly sounds hokey. It basically is—however, it is also reality. You can't change an organization to your way of thinking before you get hired. So, play their games (because that's what they are) and get your job. Once you're established and respected, you can try bending rules if it's important to you. It's hard or impossible to do this if you are not there. Get there first.

Stress-oriented Interviews with Questions and Answers

Sometimes potential employers ask questions designed to trick you or put you on the defensive. Do not become defensive. Look at these questions for what they are and learn how to answer them properly. Their reason for asking: the job you're being interviewed for is a stressful one. Can you handle it? The interviewer is checking your responses.

1. *What do you know about our company?*

Before the interview, you'd better learn a lot about what they do, such as products produced, company size, income, profits, reputation, and image. Companies in the news are easy to research, because they are usually "public" companies (their stock is traded on one of the three stock exchanges), and therefore their records and performance have to be public knowledge. Libraries are good reference sources for information about public companies. You can also request that an annual report be sent to you. Privately held organizations are harder to research because they don't have annual reports. If it's a local organization, check its reputation in the community.

2. *Why did you leave your last job? (or Why are you looking to leave?)*

A sure question in *every* interview. Try to give a "group" answer: "When the contract was canceled/the territory was made smaller/a major supplier left town, our complete division was let go." This is if you are not employed (and if it's true).

(a) If you are still employed, explain that upward mobility is limited, you like to work hard and the work is not challenging enough, you want to make more money, you want a "line," not a "staff," job because that's where the work is most demanding, promotions come quickly, and the positions are more financially rewarding.

NOTE: Line jobs are in *sales, marketing* or *production;* EVERYTHING else is staff. Line positions *directly* affect profits; staff areas such as personnel, public relations, or administration may contribute to profits but only indirectly. Staff jobs are carried as company overhead and are usually the first areas where people are laid off in times of hardship. Remember that this is generally true; nothing is *always* true.

(b) If you are currently unemployed ("between jobs"), be prepared to discuss it, but don't be defensive. *Good answer:* "My job was very demanding, both in the amount of work and the time spent at work. Interviewing was just about impossible, so I carefully planned this time to seek a new position and I put away adequate funds to tide me over for several months until I find the right position."

(c) *If you were fired:* if it was for nonperformance, insubordination, or your hand was caught in the company till, you'll have a hard time explaining this away. Keep in mind that most people get fired because of a clash in personality or management changeover, or they were pawns trapped in a high-level corporate chess game where top management was out to "get" a particular executive and the fired person, as part of that person's group, fell too.

Do not carry on in negative terms about your former employer; doing so makes you, rather than the employer, look terrible. If possible, make somewhat light of your firing: you can always joke and say that you now know how Lee Iacocca of Ford Motor Company felt when Henry Ford fired him. Many people who'll be interviewing you have been fired at some point in their careers. It's much more common than you think. You may say (if it's true): "My boss left the company and the new person brought in from outside hired people who previously worked with him. I was one of six people dismissed." Or "Management decided not to upgrade my position, and there was nothing else open in the company I wanted to take after interviewing in several areas," or "My position's not being refilled, as far as I know," "My position's been divided up and three people are now handling it," or "My manager knew I wasn't happy, suspected I was interviewing, and asked me about it directly. When I told him I was looking outside, he asked me to resign."

(d) Make certain you know what the people you give as your references are saying about you. You should know this whether you have left voluntarily or were terminated. Have a friend who's working at another company call up to check out your references as if she or he were interested in employing you. This way, if there are any negatives, you can call your former employer and work out better things to be said about you or change references. Always be certain to give prospective employers names of people most likely to give you good references. Before you leave a company, speak to key people and ask if they will give references for you. Never "surprise" them later on. *Get permission.*And call any past employers you wish to use, too.

3. *Don't you think that, with your background, you are overqualified for this position?*

This is the time really to sell yourself, unless you don't want the job. Show that your so-called overqualifications would be the employer's plus. "Overqualified" can mean they think you're too old but cannot legally say so.

NOTE: This may be a ploy by the employer to suggest a low salary or a polite way of telling you you won't "fit in." If you really are interested in the position, continue to show how you can be of value by relating incidents from past employment that apply to the job under discussion. However, if you suspect you are overqualified, don't push for the offer. If you did get it, you'd be bored and start looking to leave too quickly.

---

4. *Why should we hire you? We feel that the aerospace/industrial marketing/ consumer marketing industry isn't useful experience for our business.*

Point out the similarities between your past or present position and the one you are seeking: schedules to meet, sales objectives to achieve, budgets to prepare, personnel requirements to fill, et cetera. Show how your experience can be of great value to the employer even if it's from a different field. This is particularly important going from nonprofit to profit, industrial to consumer, financial to consumer businesses, and similar ones. This is a situation in which you *must* speak in the business terms of the company interviewing you. (Every industry has its own jargon; know the terminology of the industry you're seeking.)

5. *Our experience with aerospace/industrial/legal/sales/production people has not been good in this area of our work. Why should I hire you?*

Stress that with your knowledge and past experience, and your interest and familiarity with their company, you and the company are a good match. Demonstrate that your work can help them because your past experience relates to the job. *Give examples!* You may also suggest (carefully) that people have to be judged as individuals and not as a group.

6. *What did you like least about your previous/present job?*

This question is intended to see how you react. The interviewer wants an honest answer. Reply in a positive way; *never* speak negatively about your present employer. Talk about how you like to work hard and say that length of time on the job at your company appears to be more important than achievements and that promotions are slow for *everyone.* Mention that meeting deadlines and schedules is important to you or you do not feel that your employer utilized your strengths enough. You are capable of harder work. Raises were not always based upon performance. Convey the message that you had much more to give to your company than they were able to use.

7. *What are three of your strong points?*

Know more than three. Relate them to the company and to the particular job you're discussing now.

(a) Ability to convince people to your point of view. (This is good for *any* position that is people-oriented.)
(b) You're organized and goal-oriented when selling/working on projects, and so on.
(c) You're persevering, but if a project's going wrong, you know when to change the course of action.
(d) You are able to manage and motivate people.
(e) You have excellent skills in personnel selection.
(f) You work equally well on your own or as a member of a team.

8. *What are three of your weak points (looking for a negative reaction)?*

Turn any weaknesses into a strength; a weakness *has* to become a plus. The answers below are all correct to use.

(a) "I tend to be impatient. What I mean by that is I am very results-oriented."
(b) "I'm somewhat impatient if I'm part of a team effort and the other people don't work hard."
(c) "When schedules are pressing, I sometimes get in there myself and work with my subordinates. This isn't supposed to be great management, but I like to have important work done on time."
(d) "I am not very tolerant of sloppy work (laziness)."

NOTE: Give one good answer and you'll probably not have to give the other two. But be prepared to give three.

---

9. *What kind of salary are you seeking?*

This question can be tricky unless before the interview you have the information from an executive search firm, employment agency, or newspaper ad. Know what you're worth, what the position *should* be paying, and what the job pays in related companies. But always give a range, don't ever mention one specific figure. If you've been sent to the employer by a search firm or employment agency, they will have told you the salary range ahead of time.

For example, *don't ever say,* "I'm looking for $14,500." Do say, "The positions I've been interviewing for have been between $14,000 and $17,000, $25,000 and $30,000, $33,000 and $40,000." Don't box yourself in. The employers then know that you have to be offered at least your minimum if they want to hire you. Try to be firm on your minimum; don't go lower. If you know that $18,800 is your rock-bottom minimum, and it's also an industry salary average, don't settle for $18,300; you'll never make it up by "good work" later on. Tell the employer that you have another offer for $19,000 and even though you would rather work at his/her company, $18,800 is the minimum acceptable salary you could consider.

If they want you enough they will come up with the extra dollars. Believe us! Companies are not used to people (women in particular) bargaining. It's supposedly "unfeminine" for women to consider money important. But you will also lose respect for not being "business tough" if you cave in and settle for less than what you are worth. *Hold out for what you want* (but *know* what you are worth in the marketplace prior to interviewing).

10. *What is your present (or last) salary?*

Try to convey that your previous salary (if low) has nothing to do with how you will perform the job you are now discussing. In fact, one of the reasons you're seeking new employment is for better pay.

It's unethical but not illegal for a company to get a salary history from your employers. Certain industries are well known for paying less than others (publishing, retailing, nonprofit organizations, educational institutions, and hospitals are examples).

Example: If you are a manager of accounting at a publishing firm, earning $19,000, and your counterpart at an industrial company earns $26,500 for the same work, you should use $26,000 or $27,000 as a minimum acceptable base for yourself if you are seeking a position in an industrial firm.

Again, stress that you have been interviewing for positions with a range, such as $14,000 to $18,000, $28,000 to $33,000, $65,000 to $72,000.

11. *What is your philosophy of life?*

This is a subjective psychological question about business philosophy, not your personal credo. Keep to business-related information only. This is a "reaction" type of question. Turn the question to your advantage by asking your interviewer if she or he wants a specific or general answer. Your personal philosophy of life can be lengthy. Your answer depends largely on whom you are talking to. But don't worry too much about this one; it doesn't come up too often.

12. *Do you have any objections to a psychological interview or tests?*

Answer should be, "No, I don't mind." Only *extreme* symptoms are looked for. Tests are often given when you're interviewing for sales positions or at high-level managerial positions in a company that uses an industrial psychologist. If you object to the taking of a test, you will go no further in the interview process. A good source on tests is *Brain Watchers,* by M. Gross (Random House, 1962). It's out of print, but may be available in libraries.

13. *Don't you feel you are a little too old/young for this job?*

Legally, no one can say you're too old (if you're forty or over). Rely on your past work experience to support this question. You may not know enough at this stage about the job's specifics to answer properly. If you don't, try to get more information by asking the interviewer a question about the experience level of others in the job. Then relate your pertinent experience to that answer.

14. *How do you (or your family) feel about possible relocation to Toledo/Chicago/Boston/St. Louis?*

Be able to say that you have thought about and discussed the possibilities of relocation before seeking a new position, and it's perfectly all right; your family is willing and supportive. If you cannot relocate (you're in college or graduate school, your husband/wife is a doctor or lawyer with a practice here, et cetera) say so.

This may be a "de-selector" question, especially if asked early in the interview. You may not ultimately have to move, even if you are willing to. But if you really cannot move, say so. If you can move but don't want to because you just spent $800 for wall-to-wall carpeting in your living room, you'd better rethink your priorities: a better position with a bright future or staying where you are because you like your apartment. (You can always reseam your carpeting!)

15. *How much money do you expect to be making five years from now?*

Since no one knows what the value of money is going to be in five years, do NOT fall into the trap of telling what you think you'll be making. Do NOT EVER give a dollar figure! You *can* mention abstracts like "I expect my salary to be at least double (triple, quadruple) what it is today."

Talk in terms of job satisfaction from doing your work well; you know the financial rewards will follow. A good answer to this is "I don't know all the titles and salaries in your particular company [unless you are in the exact same industry], but I would expect to be somewhere in upper-middle management with a salary commensurate with my responsibilities and abilities." Or "If I perform well as your marketing manager I would expect to increase my responsibilities, eventually becoming a marketing director, then a vice president. I presume my promotions and merit increases will be based on performance."

If you *know* the titles, then "I expect to be a sales manager, group product manager, assistant vice president, office manager, senior administrator, production manager, controller, executive secretary, senior systems analyst, account executive, senior auditor, head buyer, merchandise manager, editor, senior research associate, personnel manager, with a salary level appropriate for that position."

16. *Tell me about yourself.*

Don't spend much time in answering this, as it is usually related to personal issues and can be used as a trap question. Keep the reply work-related. Tell something about yourself that *directly* applies to the job for which you are interviewing; have it come out in the form of a helpful experience—something *you* can do for the employer. Relate an incident or two from your past work that points up your strengths.

17. *Why do you want to work for our company?*

Talk about the kind of firm it is (financial, consumer products, nonprofit, industrial, and so on) and say that you have always wanted to work for this type of company. Verbalize how your background can contribute to them. Give one or two *short* examples of ways in which you can benefit them, based on your work experience and abilities (including "style"), not "Well, I've heard good things about how you treat your people, I have a friend who works here." Let the interviewer know this is a serious decision for you.

18. *Why do you want this kind of position in our company?*

Know why ahead of time or postpone your interview until you do. If necessary, briefly reiterate your special skills and experience and tell how they relate well to the position under discussion. Answer in terms that will be of interest to the *employer*, not to you. NEVER convey that you are out of work and hungry, or that you know they pay 100 percent tuition for M.B.A. degrees and you plan to get one. Everyone wants to hire a winner, a contributor.

19.   *What can you contribute to us if we hire you?*

Don't presume to "tell" (lecture) the interviewer on what you can do for them; you do not know all the problems they are trying to solve. However, you should have enough information on the company and the job for which you are interviewing to relate incidents of successful solving of a past employer's problems. Make certain it relates well to their industry and to the position you are discussing.

20.   *Would you be willing to accept less than you are now/were earning?*

This is a tough question. If you are career switching you may have to accept the same or even a lower starting salary if you need specific training before you can perform your work adequately. However, contract up front to get a raise and/or performance review in three or four months to bring you up to your present salary. You should try to get this in writing. Many employers are reluctant to put "possibilities" in writing, but if the person hiring you has verbally agreed to a review after your training period is completed, when you receive your offer letter *accept the position in writing* and mention your three-month performance review.

If, however, you are seeking a position in the same or a closely related field, *never* take less money. If you have to take a similar salary, again, contract for a quick performance review. This can be hard to do if you are unemployed and have been for a time, but realize that you rarely, if ever, make up the money differential if you settle for less money when you go in.

21.   *After talking about this job, I'm not certain that I see a good fit. If you had your chance at any job here, what would you really like to do?*

WARNING! This is a *trick* question, usually asked by personnel people to disqualify candidates. If you have just spent forty-five minutes talking about your avid interest in finance/marketing/administration or whatever, and then answer this by saying, "Gee, I'd really like to be a purchasing agent," you have just signed your death warrant. The interviewer will know that you really don't know what you want to do and that you will probably accept any half-decent-sounding job at any company that offers you one. The proper response is, "I'm sorry you don't see me as fitting into your marketing/ finance/administrative position, because *that's* where my interest lies. I don't know every job title in XYZ, but if you think I'd fit somewhere else, I'd be happy to hear about it. However, I want you to know that I am seeking a position as a financial analyst and if you don't think I'm suited for XYZ, I will continue to look at other organizations." By responding this way, you have restated your deep interest in a particular job and have not mentioned any others. You have shown that you are open-minded to other possibilities (but only after you have thrown the ball back into the interviewer's court without commitments).

22.   *What other kinds of companies are you interviewing?*

Another "disqualifier," again, usually asked by Personnel. If you are asked this and you are at a bank interview, answer that you are looking at "financial institutions." Do not tell the interviewer that you have been interviewing in the health-care field, consumer products, et cetera. Conversely, if you are interviewing at a consumer company, don't tell them of your long-standing interest in the financial community. To a potential employer it can indicate that *in spite of what you say,* you have not determined what it is you really want to do or where it is you want to do it. This is not a capital crime, but if you want a particular job, play the game by its established rules. Interviews are at best adversary relationships, and corporate representatives generally seek reasons to screen you *out,* not in. Company people look for ways to turn you down, not to hire you. Know this in advance, and you will be prepared to beat them at their own game, using their rules. Interviewing can be a lot of fun.

The point of having an interview is to get an offer. (You don't have to accept one if you don't want the job.) You will not get an offer each time you have an interview, but if you learn to field these questions in a comfortable manner, you will definitely increase the percentage of interviews to offers by at least 60 percent. Interviewing is an art form; you need practice to become proficient at it. Remember to take those "throwaway" interviews (interviews at organizations in which you don't have a deep, deep interest) first if you feel you need practice. Sometimes one of these firms will surprise you and offer a terrific position, but, in general, use them to sharpen your interviewing skills. Then move on to interviews with companies that interest you more.

If you work in the creative fields of art, design, advertising, writing, public relations, and so on, your portfolio is often the key to your success in switching positions. *Who* you know in public relations is often more important than what degree, if any, you received. The same holds true for graphic designers and people who write advertising copy and other creative pieces.

When about to embark on interviewing, make key selections from your portfolio (often "less is more"). If you're to interview with a consumer package goods firm, don't bring your ads and layouts from a chemical company, but select the ones from the cosmetic, toiletries, and fashion firms instead.

Often the people who judge your portfolio wonder if you actually did the work. Obviously, you should show only your own work. However, if your portfolio does not represent the kind of job you're seeking, you can put together a few layouts/ads/designs, et cetera, that show you understand what the company is looking for, and that even though you have *not* done this work, you know how to do it. Back it up with what you have done.

As a creative person, you can market yourself in the P-A-R format by following this sequence of verbal presentation:

(Problem)   1.   What the company wanted done (why you were hired).
(Action)   2.   What you did and how you solved their problems.
(Result)   3.   Why you did it that way and what it yielded.

Employment Contracts

Most of us have heard of employment contracts, those almost mythical agreements between high-level executives and higher-level executives. Employment contracts are generally drawn up when an executive is taking on a risky "turnaround" job (attempting to make healthy a failing company or division within a specific time frame), but they are also used more routinely than you might think and at lower levels than president or vice president. Many times you can negotiate an agreement or ask that a termination clause regarding severance pay (or relocation costs or bonus) be put into your hiring package along with the rest of your benefits. You can opt for a good severance package if laid off or fired (unless it is for cause).

We have spoken to many executives who said they would have been very willing to include severance and other agreements, but the person being hired *never asked!* It can't hurt to ask; if the answer is "no," you're no worse off than before asking. But don't ask until the offer's been made!

9. Campaign Mechanics: Virgos Have an Edge

"It is not enough to have great qualities, we should also have the management of them."

—LA ROCHEFOUCAULD

"There are always jobs for people who go about looking for jobs in the right way."

—THOMAS SOBCZAK

In your job search, it is not necessary to be a Virgo to be well organized. It may help, but it is not a prerequisite. What is required for conducting a well-balanced, organized job campaign? Some record-keeping techniques, attention to detail, persistence based on your motivation to succeed, and some specific advice. In this chapter the elements from previous chapters are arranged in such a way as to maximize your chances of obtaining job interviews.

Penetrating the Job Market Successfully

Assuming that you now have or soon will have an excellent résumé and action letters, how do you use them to your best advantage? Answering help-wanted ads is one way. Additionally, it is important to let everyone you know—friends, relatives, neighbors, and business associates whom you trust—that you are seeking a new employment opportunity. Remember that personnel agencies and executive search firms (15 percent) and job advertisements (15 percent) represent only 30 percent of all job openings at any one time. Unless you are not in a hurry to change jobs, to switch successfully in the least amount of time it is necessary to have a strategy to reach the 70 percent of the job market that never advertises, the "hidden" job market.

Where does this "hidden" job market come from? It comes from constant change. Just as a river is constantly flowing, depositing silt, changing its width and even its course, so do organizations change. The manpower of any organization is *always* in a state of flux. People leave through resignations, retirements, firings, illness, leaves of absence, or death. Correspondingly, this means that organizations hire all the time. A late 1981 survey reported that in the manufacturing sector of our economy there is a 4 percent employee turnover *each month*. This means that in a period of only two years and one month the work force of an entire industry completely turns over.

This constant change in the workplace generates jobs in the hidden job market, where your action letters can generate job interviews for you.

To penetrate both the open and hidden job markets, we have provided you with a flowchart for each strategy you choose to use in your search.

1.   *Answering the Want Ads: Open or Blind Ads*
2.   *Cold-Canvassing: Reaching the Hidden Job Market*
3.   *Employment Agencies and Executive Search Firms*

Accompanying each flowchart is an analysis of the individual steps in the chart. In addition, you are provided with a list of questions and answers that are frequently asked about the job campaign.

To complete our discussion of the mechanics of the job campaign two important topics, often overlooked, are discussed: networking and tax deductions.

Answering the Want Ads: Open or Blind Ads*

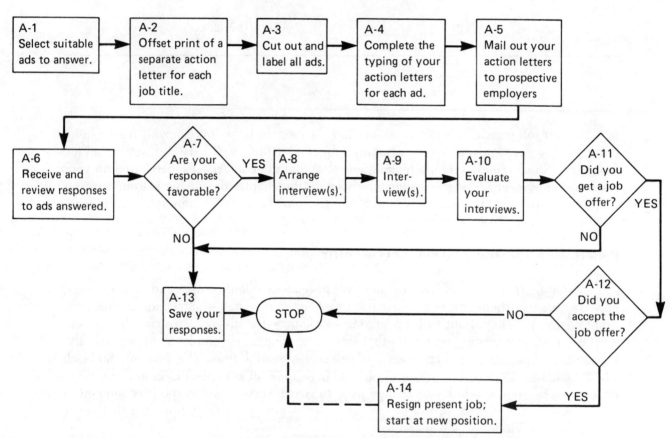

*This flowchart assumes (1) individual job title selected and want-ad analysis completed, (2) work experience matches top four items in want-ads analysis (chapter 5), (3) action letter offset printed using the "Golden Formula" (chapter 7) and the P-A-R format (chapter 3).

Box	Title	Comment
A-1	Select suitable ads to answer.	On a daily basis follow the classified and display ads in your local newspapers. Also follow a few national newspapers such as the *Wall Street Journal*, the *New York Times*, or the *Washington Post*. Pay particular attention to advertisements that appear in trade publications in your area of specialty.

Box	Title	Comment

A-2 Offset print or make good Xerox copy of a separate (typed) action letter for each job title.

Avoid going overboard on the number you have offset or make on a word processor. Fifty to one hundred copies of each separate action letter are probably sufficient. After you have determined the effectiveness of your letter, larger numbers can be printed. (With luck, you won't need to do this.)

Test your letter's success in obtaining interviews before printing larger numbers. Three to six interviews granted per hundred letters sent is considered successful and the standard to shoot for in your own search. Retain receipts from printing services for IRS reporting; these costs are tax-deductible.

Be sure to use your own typewriter or one to which you have easy access. It is necessary that the typeface of your salutation should match the body of the letter.

If you answer only four or five ads from each job title selected, type them individually to save printing costs.

A-3 Cut out and label all ads.

Record-keeping is very important in your job campaign. Cut out each ad you answer, and on the back of it record the date of the ad, the name of the publication, and which action letter was sent in reply to the ad. The back of your ad should look like this:

> 10/18/81
> *Los Angeles Times*
> Action Letter #2

Place each answered ad in an envelope labeled by ad title and date of ad. Keep each week's same-titled envelopes together. This way you can be sure to find any specific ad when you need it at a future time.

Example: If you answered six ads for Financial Analyst during the week of October 12, 1981, label the envelope, "Week of 10/10/82—Financial Analyst," and, after marking the source of each ad on its reverse side, put all the ads into this one envelope.

Open Ads

A-4 Fill in on your offset, word-processed, action letters specifics for each ad.

Using the same typewriter you used to write your action letter, fill in the following:

1. Dear Mr. or Ms. Jones: This should be 2 spaces above your opening paragraph; no more, no less.
2. Count 2 spaces *above* the "Dear Mr./Ms." That's where the last line of the organization's address (city/state/zip) goes. Count backward from that line to leave yourself 4, 5, or 6 spaces for the advertiser's name, title, company, street address, etc.
3. Your home address goes on the top right-hand side of the paper.
4. Type the date 2 spaces below your address.

It is not necessary to type a separate letter for each ad. Use your printed action letter instead. It is not critical to the success of your job campaign that your "Why Bring That Up?" paragraph identify the specific ad you're answering. Typing "Re," followed by the ad title and the ad's date will do nicely. (Skip 2 spaces.)

Box	*Title*	*Comment*

If the person named in an ad to whom letters and résumés are sent is in Personnel (and you've answered a marketing ad), try to determine (by phone) who the head of marketing is and send two letters: one to the personnel person (as requested) and one to the person who will probably interview you if you are selected to be interviewed. That way, if Personnel rejects your letter, the head of marketing may not.

Blind Ads
A-4

For blind ads, those that give only a box number and address, follow the instructions for answering open ads, but make these adjustments.

1. The "inside address" lists the box number and address and looks like this example which appeared in the *New York Times:*

> X7127
> *TIMES*
> New York, NY 10108

2. Because you don't know to whom you are writing, the "salutation" should be: "Dear Advertiser."

Open and Blind Ads

A-5   Mail out your action letter.

Avoid sending the traditional cover letter and résumé, even if it's requested and even if your résumé is in the P-A-R format. Remember, your objective is to obtain an interview, NOT to provide the prospective employer with your detailed job history. Filling in the particulars of your work experience should be done within the context of the interview. Don't let the employer jump to conclusions about who you are (or aren't).

Most companies take at least two to six weeks to reply. This allows them time to pass your action letter on to the department that's hiring. Use this waiting period to develop mailing lists from your library research.

A-6   Receive and review responses to ads answered.

Read each response carefully for follow-up. Match up, then staple the appropriate ads to your responses.

A-7   Are your responses favorable? (Yes)

Favorable responses (requests for you to arrange interviews) require careful and timely follow-up.

Are your responses favorable? (No)

See A-13 and review the chapters on action letters and the want-ad analysis. You may have to polish up your marketing materials.

A-8   Arrange an interview.

Allow a minimum of three to five days to research the prospective employer and, if possible, the department in which the job occurs before taking the interview.

Use *Standard & Poor's* directories to obtain general information on the company (this works for large publicly held organizations only). The *Dun & Bradstreet Reference Book of Corporate Managements* will provide data on key executives (who may interview you). Try to review an annual report and/or a "10K" for detailed financial information. Ask a local stockbroker or the librarian at a university or college business school for this information. Major public libraries have

Box	*Title*	*Comment*

business sections, sometimes with their information on microfilm or microfiche. This can be very valuable to you. Ask the librarian for magazine articles on the company or specialty directories on the industry.

Researching the prospective employer will prepare you to answer properly a key question always asked at the interview, "Why do you want to work for our organization?"

When arranging your interview date, try to get more information from the person making the arrangements at the organization. He or she may be privy to the position's salary range even if it wasn't stated in the ad. Ask what the salary range is. It will save you valuable time if you discover the salary range is 'way under what you're earning. You may choose to cancel the appointment. But don't do that unless you can verify that the salary range discussed is accurate. If you decide to cancel the interview, tell the person you're speaking to that you'd love to see his/her boss, but your salary requirements are higher than their range. Also tell this person that you'd like to speak to the interviewer. If the interview "arranger" won't put you through, ask for the name and title of the person you were supposed to see (tell the person on the phone it's to send a thank-you note). Then call or write to this individual to verify the salary information given to you over the telephone by the assistant.

A-9   Interview(s)

It is critical that you have carefully reviewed the chapter on interviewing prior to your interview and that you have researched the company thoroughly.

Act normal at the interview. Be yourself. If you act phony during the interview, you will be forced to maintain this facade during your employment. Explain your background and do so using the P-A-R format. You will appear well organized and logical and you won't lose your train of thought. Tell the interviewer what he or she needs to know, not what you think will please him or her. Exaggerations can hurt you later on. Remember that you are interviewing the organization just as much as they're interviewing you. You have to determine if you want to work there even if an offer is extended. So be objective *and* perceptive.

Present yourself as a specialist with a good generalist's knowledge of your discipline.

A-10   Evaluate your interview(s)

After each interview, list (on paper) any questions you had trouble answering. Develop acceptable or better responses for future interviews.

Were you in control of the interview? Did you feel comfortable? Did you carry your part of the talking? Did you ask intelligent questions about the job's content, work environment, career growth, et cetera? At the end of the interview did you express an interest in the position (if so disposed)? Did you ask when you would next hear from them? Did you thank the interviewer?

Send a brief thank-you letter as follow-up. If you are really interested in it, *ask* for the job in your thank-you letter.

A-11   Did you get a job offer? (Yes)

Evaluate the job offer carefully. It should be a logical next step in your career, not just a change of scenery.

Box	Title	Comment
	Did you get a job offer? (No)	Try to determine why no offer of employment was made. Was there a problem at the interview? Remember, the more interviews you take, the better you get at it. Nevertheless, don't dwell on rejection. You can't take it personally. You generally must have eight or ten interviews in a row, even if you're staying in the same field, before one offer is extended. And, that offer may *not* be the one you want!
A-12	Did you accept the job offer? (Yes)	If you accept an offer, protect yourself and request that it be put in writing. *Note:* Though most verbal job offers hold up, from the time you accept a new position, give notice to your present employer, and begin your new job, things can change in an organization. If your offer is *not* in writing, it could be withdrawn and leave you without *any* job, old or new.
	(No)	If you decline an offer, be gracious, thank the person who extended it, and follow up by sending a thank-you note. You never know when you may need information from this organization or where the person you declined will be working in two years! Leave a good impression. Evaluating a job offer will depend on individual circumstances. However, some basic guidelines can be followed:

- Negotiate your starting salary, job title, whom you're reporting to, the date of your next salary review, benefits, et cetera.
- If the salary offer is lower than hoped for, but you've decided to take the job, negotiate an early salary review (three months or six months instead of annually).

Note: Future career and salary growth are more critical than an initial high starting salary (if the other factors are there).

Box	Title	Comment
A-13	Save your responses.	Retain them for future reference. These responses can provide valuable information (names, job titles, addresses, phone numbers, et cetera) if you decide to do another job campaign in the future.
A-14	Resign your present job; start your new position.	Professional courtesy requires giving an employer at least two weeks' notice upon resignation. If you are involved in a major project or are at a director level or higher, consider giving three or four weeks' notice. Your new employers shouldn't mind the delay since they would benefit, expect, and get this same courtesy in the future. Some organizations make you leave right away. Know about yours before you resign.

Cold-Canvassing: Reaching the Hidden Job Market

Of the different strategies for finding a job, cold-canvassing with an action letter offers the greatest potential for success. There are two reasons for this view: You can go after 70 percent of all existing but unadvertised job openings (this greatly increases your prospects for a successful switch); over the last ten years it has become quite evident that the direct-mail, action-letter approach to changing careers is the single most effective technique available. It is the only method that allows you to separate yourself from the great majority of people, who rely solely on the résumé approach.

A word of caution, however, about the cold-canvass technique. In the years ahead, the use of word processors and mailing lists is expected to become more widespread. So states the *Wall Street Journal*, "Résumé Floodtide Posing Problems in Job Market," February 24, 1981. In the unsettled decade of the 1980s, large numbers of job hunters will turn to word processors as a means of canvassing the entire world! To distinguish yourself from this growing herd, avoid this "canned" approach by using the P-A-R format and by remembering the importance of recanvassing your mailing lists.

Cold-Canvassing: Reaching the "Hidden" Job Market

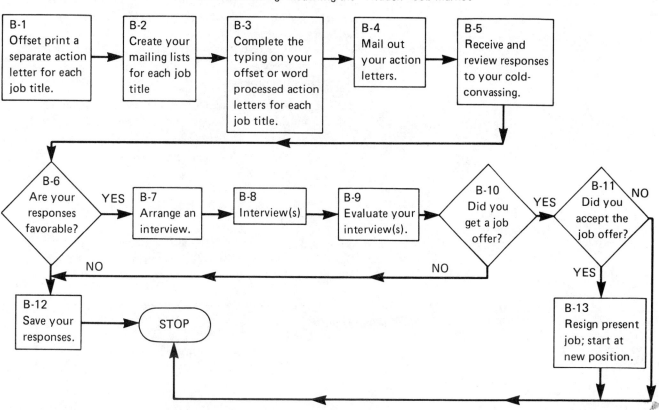

Box	Title	Comment
B-1	Have offset printed or word-processed a separate (typed) action letter for each job title.	See A-2 under "Answering the Want Ads."
B-2	Create your mailing lists for each job title. (Also use these sources for researching prospective employer.)	Reference librarians are your best resource. Use them! That's why they are there. Local libraries are usually limited. Instead, seek out a large city library or the library of a college or university school of business administration.

Some key resources include:

- *Standard & Poor's Register of Corporations*
- Dun & Bradstreet's *Million Dollar* and *Middle Market* directories
- Dun & Bradstreet's *Reference Book of Corporate Managements*
- Industrial directories (by state)

Box	*Title*	*Comment*

- *Fortune* magazine's 1000 top corporations (see May, June, July issues)
- *Inc. Magazine's* top 100 small corporations (May and July issues)
- Individual indexes (also good for researching a particular company) including *New York Times Index, Wall Street Journal Index, International Index, Reader's Guide to Periodical Literature, Business Periodical Index, Magazine Index, Newspaper Index*
- The *Yellow Pages* of telephone directories of major cities
- *Advertising Age*
- Association directories

Type each employer's name and address on a separate 3 × 5 index card. It should look like this:

Mr. William Spencer, President
Citibank, N.A.
399 Park Avenue
New York, New York 10043

The index-card format allows for ease of filing and sorting.

Record your job campaign history on the back of each index card. Simple record-keeping would look like this:

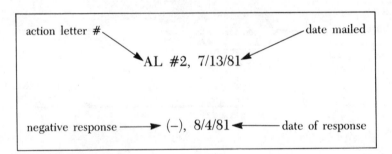

Box	*Title*	*Comment*
B-3	Complete the typing on your action letters for each ad.	See Section A-4 under "Answering the Want Ads."
B-4	Mail out your action letters.	Exhaust the mailing on your preferred job title before beginning a second mailing. Wait six to eight weeks before sending out your second mailing. This should be sent out to the same mailing list. The proper person to send it to, either the president of the company or the hiring individual (if known), will usually remain the same. Remember, you can mail to more than one person at a company.

Avoid sending your action letter to the Human Resources (Personnel) Department unless you're seeking a job in Personnel. The main function of a personnel recruiter is to screen out candidates.

Avoid sending the traditional cover letter and résumé. Your objective is to obtain an interview, NOT to provide the prospective employer with your detailed job history.
See Section A-5 under "Answering the Want Ads."

Box	Title	Comment
B-5	Receive and review responses to your cold-canvassing.	Read each response carefully for follow-up.
B-6	Are your responses favorable? (Yes)	Favorable responses (requests for you to arrange interviews) require careful and timely follow-up.
	Are your responses favorable? (No)	See A-13 for explanation.
B-7	Arrange an interview.	Before going on the interview, always allow at least three to five days to research the prospective employer and, if possible, the department where the opening occurs. An executive recruiting firm specializing in finance searches reported in the October 1980 issue of *Inc. Magazine* that the first person interviewed for a job almost never gets it. The person with the best chance of being hired is the last person interviewed. Therefore, don't rush your job campaign. Be sure to research your prospective employers carefully and fully. See Section A-8 under "Answering the Want Ads."
B-8	Interview(s)	See Section A-9 under "Answering the Want Ads."
B-9	Evaluate your interview(s)	See Section A-10 under "Answering the Want Ads."
B-10	Did you get a job offer? (Yes)	See Section A-11.
	Did you get a job offer? (No)	
B-11	Did you accept the job offer?	See Section A-12.
B-12	Save your responses.	See Section A-13.
B-13	Resign present job; start new position.	See Section A-14.

Employment Agencies and Executive Search Firms

Employment agencies can be a double-edged sword. They work either for you or against you, depending on how you use or abuse them. The most productive way to take advantage of the services provided by employment agencies is to take an active rather than a passive role. This means: do your homework. Prepare several want-ad analyses to help define your career goals, create your reference résumé in P-A-R format as a way of illustrating the breadth of your background and experience, and develop several specialized résumés in P-A-R format. The latter would be adjusted to reflect interviews the employment counselor hopes to send you to. By developing these materials in advance of your initial visits to employment agencies, you will be better able to explain your background and work experience both verbally and on paper. Coming across to employment counselors as a knowledgeable job applicant is the best way of convincing them of your qualifications.

If you are trying to make a radical change from teaching to training or social work to public relations, for example, employment agencies won't do much, if anything, for you. Most agency representatives work on commission or on a draw against their future commissions. If they interview twenty-five people a week, they will rank these twenty-five in order of most placeable to least placeable. If you are not working in the *private sector* (business), and all their job openings are in the private sector, they will select only those three or four candidates of the twenty-five who have business experience and ignore you, your calls, and your letters. It is difficult to place someone who wants to switch careers. You know that from trying it yourself. Companies all want to hire people with experience similar to the job they have open. And, since they will pay a fee to the employment agency, they expect the agency representatives will not go out on a limb for a stranger (you) if pushing you for an interview could mutilate their meal ticket. The same holds true for executive search firms, only more so. They will never try to help you switch from one career to another or even help you move up if you are staying in the same field. They are on contractual arrangements with their clients and paid before and during a search. They are not at all inclined to help *you*. They find their own candidates; candidates do *not* go to them for help. Executive search firms handle mostly jobs that pay in excess of $30,000. At these salaries, where the client organization pays 30 percent (or more) plus expenses to the search firms, they demand very specifically experienced people from very narrowly defined industries. Executive search firms are used to filling difficult and, often, politically sensitive positions.

Employment Agencies

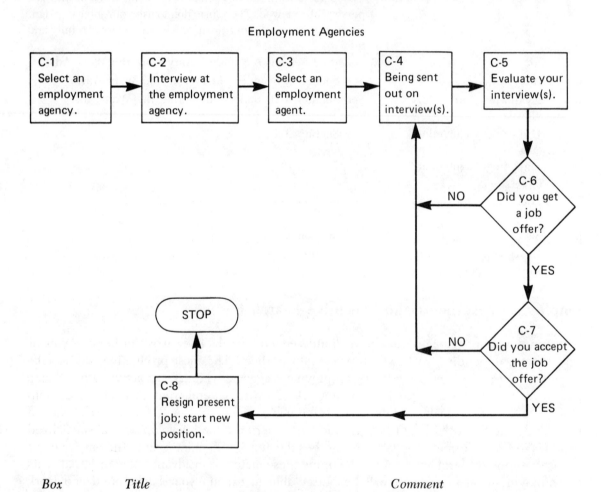

Box	Title	Comment
C-1	Select an employment agency.	Select an employment agency that concentrates in your particular specialty. For example, if you're a product manager in a packaged-goods company, you should use an agency that specializes in marketing. Some agencies have offices in many cities throughout the country. To locate agencies that cover your particular specialty, use the *Directory of Executive Recruiters* ($12 prepaid from Consultant News Publications, Templeton Road, Fitzwilliam,

Box	Title	Comment

Box   *Title*   *Comment*

NH 03447). The directory lists agencies alphabetically by job function, industry, and geography.

Personal references from coworkers in your specialty and your professional associations are quite good and shouldn't be overlooked. Agencies that advertise in association publications are another good source.

If you're interested in relocating to a new city, your best bet is to select an agency in that city. This will prevent the agency from having to split the placement fee (with the agency in your old location). It will work harder on your behalf.

C-2   Interview at the employment agency.   Dress is important. Dress as you would for a regular job interview. (See above, page 195.)

C-3   Select an employment agent.   Good agencies have specialists who know your particular discipline. Their expertise often comes from their having been employees in your job category (they know the jargon), placing many previous candidates like yourself, and/or having an extensive network of business contacts.

To evaluate an employment counselor at an agency, test his/her knowledge of jargon in your specialty. Does the person have an in-depth knowledge of the developments in your field—at least what's happened in the last three to five years? Does the counselor know the job content? And most important, are you treated in a professional manner?

When you are being interviewed at an agency, the counselor may become your agent. For this reason, bring your P-A-R résumé, which summarizes your experience in *one* job area. As your agent, your counselor should provide constructive criticism of your résumé, interview style, and manner of dress.

If a rapport has been established, be prepared to bare your job "soul" to your employment agent. Honesty, along with completeness, is very important. Your agent must know the negatives in your job history (why you were fired, frequency of job changes, and so on) if you are to be placed quickly, or at all. Be prepared to act on your agent's criticism of your career and the way you interview. Remember, your agent knows what can increase your marketability.

In return, your agent should be professional, honest (won't ask you to lie), knowledgeable, enthusiastic, thorough, and persistent. You should have a good gut feeling about your agent. If not, select a new one.

C-4   Go out on interview(s).   When an agency sets up an interview for you, always take the interview. If you must cancel (emergency only), alert both the agency and the employer. Otherwise you could jeopardize your relationship with the agency and its relationship with the employer.

Very carefully review the chapter on interviewing prior to your interview.

See Section A-9, "Answering the Want Ads."

C-5   Evaluate your interview(s).   See Section A-10.

Since the main function of employment agencies is to find people for jobs, not jobs for people, be cautious in your assessment of each job opportunity. A good employment agent

Box	*Title*	*Comment*
		should be as concerned as you are with how well you "fit" with the prospective employer. In the last analysis, however, if you have a gut feeling that the "fit" is wrong and not for you, be sure to follow your instincts and reject the position. If you don't, experience has shown that you will usually regret it!
C-6	Did you get a job offer? (Yes)	Evaluate the job offer carefully. It should be a logical next step in your career, not just a change of scenery.
	Did you get a job offer? (No)	Review the circumstances with your employment agent. See Section A-11.
C-7	Did you accept the job offer? (Yes)	See Section A-12.
	Did you accept the job offer? (No)	The decision to turn down a job offer should be discussed fully with your employment agent, who will then communicate it to the employer.
C-8	Resign present job; start new position.	See Section A-14.

Questions Frequently Asked about a Job Campaign

1. Should I delegate mundane aspects of the job hunt, such as typing and researching employers, to others?

NO! Maintain complete control over your job campaign; *do not* delegate any part of it, including typing (unless you cannot type) to others. This applies particularly to those of you who are between jobs. Doing all aspects of the job campaign can be very therapeutic. It will provide you with a sense of purpose at a time when your self-esteem may not be as high as you'd wish.

2. Is there value to reading trade publications in your area of specialty?

YES! Besides usually listing employment opportunities, these publications contain articles on companies that are expanding their product lines and services. Companies love to trumpet their accomplishments in the trade press. This will give you a head start on most of your competition.

3. Why should I send my action letter to the president or chief executive officer; aren't they too busy to read my letter?

NOT TRUE. In most cases, your letter will be read and you will receive a personal response (even if it's done through a subordinate). One of the rights a high-ranking executive retains is the right to read his or her own mail. People who have made it to the executive suite got there by learning to delegate well. Throughout their careers they have usually delegated everything, with two exceptions: the right to hire and fire, and the right to go through their own mail. So, send your action letter to the people who head organizations you wish to work for or to the person who could be your boss (such as the national sales manager, director of human resources, or the controller).

4. Should I send my action letter to the Human Resources Department (Personnel) or the personnel director?

NO! Avoid the Human Resources Department, if possible, unless you're seeking a position in it. Since the final hiring decision is seldom made there for other areas, send your action letter to the president, or chief operating officer, or the person who could hire you. These are the people who approve the creation of new jobs or the filling of existing ones.

Besides, when your letter or résumé is passed downward from a president, it will receive more serious consideration than if recruiters from Personnel sent it upward.

   5.   When answering want ads, will I be called for a interview if I send an action letter, rather than a résumé?

YES! Conventional wisdom holds that if you answer a want ad without supplying "a résumé and complete salary history," your response will not be considered. This simply is not true. A *well-prepared* action letter will get you more interviews than the traditional résumé-and-cover-letter approach. Still skeptical? Try this approach. Divide your want ads and send a cover letter and résumé to one half and an action letter to the other half. See which generates more interviews. You will probably be surprised at the results.

   6.   Should I send a follow-up response to companies or organizations that failed to respond to my initial inquiry?

YES! (Unless you answered a blind ad; box numbers hold for only about three weeks.) After six weeks send out the same action letter, or a slightly altered one, to all advertised organizations that failed to reply (either positively or negatively) to your original mailing. Your rate of interviews should not change. If your action letter is well constructed, in accordance with our previous instructions, it should draw between three and six interviews per hundred letters sent out.

   7.   I always wanted to work for this particular organization but have never had the courage to apply because my background and experience are not traditional for the job. What is the best approach to take?

DON'T HOLD BACK! Instead, apply to those organizations for whom you have always wanted to work. For small organizations, stress contributions to growth. In larger, more established companies, stress your qualities of cooperativeness and working as part of a team. Always demonstrate your results quantitatively.

   8.   If requested to by a prospective employer, should you agree to complete a psychological test? Or take a lie-detector test?

IT DEPENDS. If you really want to work for a particular organization and it requires such a test, take it, but keep in mind that this test *may* be an indicator of how employees are treated on the job (probably with suspicion).

   9.   How should I handle the issue of references?

To ensure that the people you ask for references do right by you, follow these guidelines:

   (a) Get permission from everyone whose name you intend to offer as a reference.
   (b) Provide each person with your job objectives, names of the companies that are likely to be interviewing you, your desire for an honest appraisal of your abilities, and a list of your major accomplishments.
   (c) Choose references that match or somewhat match the jobs you're going after. Try to provide the name of an ex-employer in the same type of work as the person interviewing you.
   (d) Avoid giving prospective employers "to whom it may concern" reference letters from previous employers. They carry little or no weight because they are usually too general. Companies prefer to obtain specific information on a potential employee and usually use the telephone to get it.
   (e) Avoid listing your references on your résumé or in your action letter. Instead, use the phrase "references are available on request."
   (f) Your list of references, when requested by a potential employer, should include name, address, telephone number (work, and home if known), business connection, and job title of the person to be called.

10. Instead of having my action letter(s) offset printed, could I save this expense and instead use a word processor or good copying machine?

YES, YOU CAN. But try to avoid using copying machines. The effort you put into development of your P-A-R action letter(s) deserves to have the letters look original. The cost of offset printing is relatively inexpensive, in most cases cheaper than paying for word-processing or other kinds of copies.

11. What is the most difficult aspect of the mechanics of a job campaign?

Maintaining the momentum of your job campaign *after* you have been asked in by *one* potential employer for a job interview. This is particularly true if the position is one you are excited about and really want. Most of us jump to the conclusion that the job will soon be ours. Unfortunately, this is almost never the case. It usually takes several weeks, sometimes months, for all parts of the hiring process to come together.

If you stop your job campaign in anticipation of this one position, you will lose valuable time and future opportunities. Avoid the temptation to stop your campaign when you are granted an interview, even if it's *the* interview. Keep your letters going out on a regular basis each week. Remember you must have eight to ten interviews going on more or less simultaneously to get one or two offers. You'll maintain much greater salary leverage if you are being seriously considered for *more* than one position.

12. How do I know that the action letter I've developed will be effective in getting me interviews?

YOU DON'T KNOW UNLESS you mail it out to employers! You can, however, test-market your action letter. Here's how. Have it (and your résumé) reviewed by friends or business associates who are knowledgeable about you. Avoid anyone who will patronize you: that is someone who you suspect is not enthusiastic about your impending career change. Another useful source to test-market is employment agencies. Record and analyze their criticisms and review your résumé if you trust their judgment. Your résumé and action letter must always reflect some level of experience in the top four items tallied up in your completed want-ad analysis if you are to be seriously considered for a position in your selected career area.

If you are not getting a minimum of three interviews for every hundred letters sent out, your opening paragraph may not be strong enough. If you suspect it isn't, rewrite it or substitute a new opening. Try trading your opening paragraph for one of your "for instance" paragraphs.

13. You've just been fired or laid off, and you are feeling somewhat sorry for yourself. To cheer yourself up, is it a good idea to take a vacation *before* starting your job campaign?

ABSOLUTELY NOT! Going on vacation before you start your job campaign can be the worst possible action. Any severance pay and/or unemployment compensation you receive from your previous employer should be used to finance your job search, not two weeks in the Bahamas. *After* you have located a new position, allow yourself a week or two for a well-earned vacation *before starting* your new job, as it will take six to twelve months before you qualify with your new employer for time off.

14. After an interview should I send a letter of thanks to my interviewer(s)?

YES! Your letter should be brief (one page only) and should always cover (1) your appreciation for the opportunity to meet with them and for their courtesy and time, (2) a summary of the substance of your discussion, and (3) an expression of continuing interest, if it exists.

15. When requested, should I fill out a company's job application?

Generally, YES. If you are seeking a high-ranking, executive position it's perfectly acceptable to complete only those questions that may not be covered by your résumé. Return the application stapled to a copy of your P-A-R résumé prior to your interview (or, if it's requested, after it). If you receive a "no, thank you" letter in response to an advertisement, but you are sent a job application to complete, disregard it. This is usually a waste of time. An organization requesting the application probably wants it to fulfill some governmental Affirmative Action requirement. The application almost never leads to an interview, so use your time in a more productive manner.

16.   Will the state of the economy affect my chances of switching jobs successfully?

NO. Many people have used the argument that because the economy is bad, they can't conduct or even attempt a job change. This is patently untrue. It is a myth spread by lazy job hunters. Experience has convinced us that there is no such thing as a bad job market; there are just bad marketing materials and insecure people. If you have followed our recommendations and are still unsuccessful, it may be because of the quality of the materials you are sending out. Are there spelling and/or grammatical errors in your materials? Has anyone other than yourself proofread your action letter or résumé? You may also consider test-marketing your materials (see question 12). Even in the Great Depression of the 1930s, 75 percent of the working population was still working—perhaps not in the exact jobs of their choice, but only 25 percent of the work force was totally unemployed. At a current unemployment rate of 8 percent or 9 percent, there are plenty of jobs of choice around if you are willing to make the effort to find one. It's all up to you.

Networking: One of the Prime Ways to Switch Jobs

"Network" as described by *Webster's New Collegiate Dictionary*, 8th edition: "an interconnected or interrelated chain, group, or system."

The term *networking* sprang up in the late 1970s and is often associated with the women's movement. However, the noun *network* is used exactly as the word *contacts* has been used over the years by men speaking of "the old boy network."

If you are considering a fairly radical career change, it is important to network with individuals and groups who work in or are familiar with the field in which you have an interest. For example, if you are a teacher and you are considering a career in personnel you should do the following things:

(1)   Talk to anyone you know who has a job in personnel.
(a) If you don't know anyone, ask friends, relatives, or business associates to introduce you to someone they know.
(b) Ask those people (that person) how they got their jobs, what they do on a daily basis, how much can you expect to earn in a year, two, five, ten years, and any other things that are important to you.
(2)   Rewrite your current résumé, using some of the jargon of the personnel field to present yourself better to a future employer (see "A Glossary of Jargon").
(3)   Take out library books on personnel and do some homework.
(4)   Do a want-ad analysis for three or four different kinds of personnel positions to see if your work background has enough of the specifications to obtain a personnel position and, more important, if you want to be in personnel, knowing what those requirements are.
(5)   Attend meetings or join ASPA, the American Society of Personnel Administrators, or the American Society of Training & Development, national organiza-

tions. They present many interesting, informative, and affordable workshops and seminars for members and nonmembers. Their chapters are located in and around large cities.

(6)   Many colleges, universities, YMCAs and YWCAs, career counselors, and so on, run workshops on a variety of topics (including personnel). Check out your local organizations.

☞ *Insiders' Tip:*   Remember, this process of networking brings you in contact with many people in the field of your choice. Over 70 percent of all jobs are obtained through whom you know, not what you know.

Another activity often overlooked by individuals who are considering a career switch is interviewing for information. Most people enjoy talking about themselves. Once a friend or relative has introduced you to a person who works in a field you're considering, ask the latter to refer you to someone else they know. After you see five or six people, you should have a pretty good idea what that field is all about.

A word of caution. Interviewing for information, while valuable, has its limitations and a pitfall or two. You can get so caught up in other people you may forget to begin interviewing for yourself ! When your Uncle Harry refers you to his friend Tom, a sales manager with 3-M Company, Tom has two thoughts in mind. Yes, he'll see you for twenty or thirty minutes because his good golf buddy Harry (your uncle) referred you, but he's a busy guy and also wants to get you out of his office as fast as possible (without appearing impolite). So what does Tom do? He gives you names of two salespeople he knows and tells you to call them and use his name. You call, and they see you and give you one or two more names to get you out of their offices as fast as they can. Don't be discouraged; some people will be genuinely interested in you and will be extremely helpful. We exaggerated this last bit a little, but not much.

In summary, networking is a highly effective way to generate interviews. Each person you contact knows at least three hundred people. Many people will sincerely want to help you but you must tell them how. Do this by (1) telling these people what you have accomplished (in P-A-R format, of course); (2) telling them what you want them to do; (3) informing them how they can help you in your search.

Finally, advise as many people as possible that you're seeking a new employment opportunity. Don't assume that your dentist or banker can't help. His or her sister-in-law or next-door neighbor may be just the contact you need.

Deep in the Heart of Taxes

One benefit of your job search, often overlooked, is the deductions you can take on your federal income tax return. These deductions apply whether you are unemployed or currently employed but looking to switch jobs, whether you find a job or not. To benefit fully from these legal deductions you need to (1) keep accurate records of *all* your job search expenses; (2) follow the Internal Revenue Service (IRS) guidelines exactly.

The importance of accurate and thorough record-keeping related to your job search cannot be overemphasized. As discussed earlier in this chapter, inadequate records can cost you in the interview process. Likewise, lack of attention to the costs incurred in your job search will prevent you from being able to take a substantial tax deduction. Here is a partial list of some of the expenses usually incurred in a job search. All of these expenses are tax-deductible but require proof of payment.

Type of Expense	*Type of Receipt*

Telephone calls:
- long distance
- local

- Telephone company statement
- Handwritten notes recording date, time, person contacted, phone number, and cost

Transportation (to and from the interviews, the library, et cetera)
- car

- tolls and parking
- bus or subway

- taxi, airport
- airline tickets

- Beginning and ending mileage readings multiplied by IRS allowed mileage rate
- Paid receipts (or keep a diary)
- Handwritten notes recording date, time, location of interview, cost
- Paid receipts
- Paid receipts

Professional counseling and/or résumé preparation

- Paid receipts

Reference materials, including books such as this one, typing paper and ribbons, envelopes and postage stamps (a major expense)

- Paid receipts

Services, including typing, word processing, printing

- Paid receipts

Temporary housing: hotel, motel, et cetera

- Paid receipts (If you have to relocate yourself, some of these expenses are tax-deductible. But since this is a complicated topic, be sure to consult an accountant.)

Expenses that are reimbursed by a prospective employer, such as air fare or hotels, cannot be credited for tax-deduction purposes.

If you have been fired or laid off, be sure to apply for unemployment compensation. Improve your cash flow when you are between jobs if you are collecting severance pay from your former employer (including any accrued vacation due you) by raising to a maximum of nine the number of exemptions you claim on your W-4 form. Doing this will reduce your federal income tax withholding. Though you will have to pay these taxes at a later date, you will be able to offset some of them with the deductions you've recorded during your job search.

Here is a brief list of government publications on taxes, available at any Internal Revenue Service office.

TITLE

Income Averaging	*Tax Information on Unemployment*
Index to Tax Publications	*Compensation*
Miscellaneous Deductions	*Tax Changes, Highlights of 198–*
Recordkeeping Requirements	*Your Federal Income Tax*

☞ *Insiders' Tip:* Do not forget or overlook expenses during your job search. It helps if you record them when they take place. An overlooked item can cost you tax dollars later.

To comply with IRS requirements, organize your home files. Be aware that most of us err on the side of keeping too much information rather than too little. An acceptable middle ground would include doing the following:

1. Use manila folders stapled along each edge to keep track of important or recurring tax-deductible expenses. Have another folder for responses to your mailings, and organize them by month, and within each month, alphabetically.
2. Store all records in one place rather than scattering them throughout your house. Don't leave any job-hunting information at your workplace; the wrong person may find it.
3. Pay particular attention to big-ticket items and be sure to get and retain airline tickets, motel bills, postage receipts, et cetera.
4. Review your records at least once a year to discard items no longer needed. Items used to support tax deductions must be retained longer (see below). January is a good time for an overhaul of your filing system, since it's just before you begin to work on your taxes.

How long should you save the supporting documentation for the deductions you claim from your job search? The statute of limitations on IRS audits is three years from the date a return is filed. If you filed a 1981 tax return on April 15, 1982, you should keep the return with its supporting documentation until at least April 15, 1985. Sometimes you must keep your records longer. For example, if you use income averaging, you must show your taxable income for the four base prior years. Finally, a word of caution. There is no statute of limitations in cases where the government suspects fraud, or where you have failed to file tax returns. In such cases, the IRS can demand records as far back as it chooses.

Bottom line: regardless of how simple or elaborate your filing system is, the essential thing is to know where everything is.

Summary

This chapter provided you with a structured framework for successfully managing your campaign. Specifics were presented covering the various job-hunting techniques: answering open and blind ads, cold-canvassing the job market using an action letter, and using employment agencies and executive search firms. Though our examples represent the ideal for each technique presented, they should be adapted by you to fit the particular circumstances of your campaign.

In making these adaptations, keep these points in mind:

1. Try more than one strategy at a time to improve your prospects for success.
2. Try the cold-canvassing strategy. It offers the greatest chances for effecting a successful switch.
3. Carefully plan each job strategy within the confines of your particular circumstances.
4. Follow through on your job plan in an accurate and thorough manner.

Remember to take advantage of your network of personal friends and business associates and to keep accurate records for tax purposes. You will have greater control over your job campaign and it will make you more self-confident. This assurance will generate more job interviews and increase your number of employment offers.

10. Educational Options, Financial Aids, and Reading Resources for Career Planning

"The first step in self-improvement is to admit our faults."

—Arnold Glasow

"Tolerate imperfection in others, never in yourself."

—Frank Tyger

Should You Go Back to School?

If you are currently employed, you probably know what additional education, if any, you need to move up in your career area. But for many people, particularly those contemplating major career changes, this issue of more (or new) education can be problematic and frightening.

What courses should you take if you plan to leave social work for a possible career in corporate personnel work? If you have a bachelor's degree in business, do you really need that M.B.A.? Do employers count seminars, workshops, or completed certificate programs as much as they would matriculation in an accredited college or university? Together we'll explore this rapidly expanding field of adult education, a buzzword of the 1980s.

FACTS: In 1977 more than 33 percent of U.S. college students were over twenty-five years old; 20 percent of all adults are presently enrolled in a postsecondary or training course; 67 percent of these 30,000,000 adult students are women.

If your future career goals are not yet crystallized, if you are interested in several fields, not one, you may want to take one or two noncredit courses in each area of interest before plunging into a degree program.

Most people who return to college choose majors according to their perception of the current labor market: to enter or move up in a particular field. But don't use graduate school to avoid looking for that new or first job. It's an easy self-deception. "I can't interview until I finish my next two courses; I don't know enough yet."

221

Some people take endless courses and degrees just to delay their job-hunting. This tactic is commonly called the sheepskin stall.

Remember that your personal life will be affected by time demands on you from school, work, and home (finding both time and place to do homework, socializing with family members and friends).

If you are now working and seek to advance, speak to your supervisor and/or to people who work in the area you wish to enter (if it is different from your present job area) about courses or a degree program that will help you.

If you have a mentor, seek out his/her advice or see your personnel department's training and development staff. If your employer has a tuition-reimbursement or advancement policy, check on that too. Most big organizations pay 50 percent to 100 percent of tuition depending upon the relevance of the subject matter to your work. Some pay 100 percent whether it's job-related or not. Check with your personnel department to be sure.

Many adult education programs offer associate's and bachelor's degrees geared to people who work:

Part-Time Study: many colleges offer credit courses in the evenings and weekends, and some have accelerated summer programs.

"Life" Credit (or Credit for Experience):   many degree-granting colleges and universities give credits toward degrees for "life experience," for knowledge gained in community service, independent study, volunteer work, homemaking, prior or present work experience, et cetera. They usually accept some or all of your past college credits, too, even if you never finished working for your degree and even if you attended college many years ago.

Some institutions give credits to people who have received acceptable scores on College Level Examination Program (CLEP) exams. For information on CLEP and its exams (nearly fifty different ones) write to: The College Board Publications Orders, Box 2815, Princeton, NJ 08540.

Thirty-three percent of this country's colleges and universities (almost a thousand schools) accept "life experience" in lieu of credits attained. You can get credit for as little as one semester to as much as three years toward a degree.

The Council for the Advancement of Experiential Learning (CAEL) has a toll-free number that will give you information on colleges in your area that award life credits. The person handling your inquiry will send you a computer printout on programs of interest to you at your request. Call (800) 638-7813; in Maryland call (301) 997-3535. The council recently compiled a directory of accredited schools that award life credits. Write to CAEL Learner Services, Lakefront North, Suite 300, Columbia, MD 21044. Cost: $3.50.

External Degree Programs: New York State has the *Regents External Degree Program,* which awards academic credits to people *countrywide* who can meet degree requirements through proficiency exams, independent study, completing courses at any accredited college or university, or through programs approved by business, the military, or the government. For information write to: The University of the State of New York Regents External Degree Program, College Education Center, Albany, NY 12230.

To get a complete listing of colleges offering external degree programs, write to the American Council on Education, Publication Department, 1 Dupont Circle, N.W., Washington, DC 20036, for *A Guide to Undergraduate External Degree Programs in the United States.* Cost: $10.50 plus $2.25 postage and handling.

Universities Without Walls: This used to be, until fairly recently, an association of thirty-one colleges and universities with headquarters at Antioch College, Yellow Springs, Ohio. It has now become the Union for Experimenting Colleges and Universities, with some independent affiliates.

The main difference between Universities Without Walls and the External Degree Program is that the former are community-based, whereas you could enroll in a New York State external degree program and be living in Atlanta or Laramie.

The UWW programs encourage a student-faculty mentor relationship. Make certain there will be an advisory aspect in your UWW program and, if your program operates out of a major college or university, make certain that you are allowed to avail yourself of that institution's classes and faculty.

To check out UWW programs in your area, call the CAEL toll-free number (800) 638-7813; (301) 997-3535 in Maryland.

Educational Brokering Centers: These are designed to help students (or people thinking about becoming students) to define their educational goals and to find out which institutions can best meet their goals. The EBCs also offer workshops, counseling, and general information; they are in 49 states at 465 centers. For information on the one nearest you write to the National Center for Educational Brokering, 1211 Connecticut Avenue, N.W., Washington, DC 20036, or send $3.00 for their publication: *1980 Educational and Career Information for Adults.*

Should You Get an M.B.A.?

That depends. It depends on your career objectives, the field you're in now, and whether or not your present employer (if you wish to stay but move up) puts a high value on an M.B.A. Many large corporations do; smaller ones don't as much, but since this degree has become very "in" over the last ten years, many more people are showing up with them at all kinds of organizations, large and small.

However, if you are contemplating a career change, a company change, or both, an M.B.A. may be a door-opener. If you're more than thirty-five years old, we don't recommend dropping out of the work force for two years to get one, unless you've been admitted to a place like Harvard or Stanford. If you are thirty-eight and drop out to get your M.B.A. at any school other than an Ivy League university, you probably will have more problems reentering at the age of forty than if you'd obtained your degree part-time evenings and started job-hunting when you had done half your course work. This is *not* a hard-and-fast rule; many people have left the work force for two years, have attended a not-so-prestigious university, and managed to get good jobs. But these people are the exception, not the rule.

If you're a "star" in your company they may sponsor you to get your M.B.A. full-time, but it's not likely, since most big organizations provide tuition refund help only for part-time evening degree programs. In the New York area, Columbia University, Graduate School of Business, has a two-year, all-day-Friday program that grants an M.S. in Business and is company-sponsored (but you work at your job Monday through Thursday!).

Send $4.00 to Empire State College, Saratoga Springs, NY 12866, for its *Innovative Graduate Programs Directory.* Double-check accreditation; not all graduate-school programs are accredited.

Company-Sponsored Training Programs

Most large companies sponsor in-house and external programs. They range from one day, to one week, several weeks, to one year and usually are specific and/or technical in content. They range from development of managerial skills to learning a specific computer language.

Sometimes you can receive academic credit for experiential learning if you have successfully completed company-sponsored courses—the longer ones, not a week or less.

Certificate Programs/Seminars

Certain fields, such as real estate and insurance, require certificates or licenses. However, most certificate programs are worthless unless they are offered as "executive education programs" by prestigious universities (among them Stanford, University of California at Berkeley, Columbia, Harvard, Northwestern, Wharton School at the University of Pennsylvania). Typically, "students" are company-sponsored managers with eight to ten years of experience. Many already possess M.B.A.'s or other advanced degrees, but their degrees are over five years old. These eight-to-ten-week courses are usually updates on present-day state of the art. If you feel you qualify, contact the appropriate person in your personnel department or get a copy of *Bricker's International Directory of University Executive Development Programs*, published by Samuel A. Pond, 425 Family Farm Road, Woodside, CA 94062.

Seminars are usually short and not accredited. However, it's a quick and fairly inexpensive way to determine your interest level in a field that you may or may not decide to pursue later on. Some seminar programs offer Continuing Education Credits (CEUs), equivalent to about ten semester hours. But many colleges and universities don't give credit for CEUs, although they may be lumped in with your "life experience" credits. When in doubt, don't take seminars that are under one CEU (ten hours) in length.

Continuing Education

Most colleges and universities offer interesting and valuable workshops, courses, and counseling programs for anyone contemplating a career change or reentering the work force. Don't overlook workshops and courses at your YMCA or YWCA or at professional associations. For instance, we've spoken of the American Society of Personnel Administrators in chapter 9. Or go to a program sponsored by the American Society of Training and Development or the Sales Executive Club. Some associations require you to be a member or an invited guest. Get yourself invited!

Warning

Do not go back to school until you have fairly well decided what it is you want to do. School can be a copout, a way to spend a year or two, supposedly offering you motivation and a sense of purpose, but in reality a way of stalling your commitment to find employment.

Even though the word *self-assessment* has become threadbare through overuse in self-help books, it is important to have clear goals and some ideas about how to pursue and reach them.

Do not become discouraged if, after taking some courses or even a degree in your "new" field, you do not get the job of your choice immediately. If you are closer to your goal, if the job you did get teaches you skills necessary for you to reach your ultimate aspiration, that's perfectly okay.

EXAMPLE: You are at point A in your career but have determined, through self-assessment and some courses at school, that you really want to be at point H. However, you may not be able to make the quantum leap from point A to point H in one move. But if you can go from point A to point D and point D places you in position to make the next move to point H, then that's terrific!

Most of us are harder on ourselves than on others. What is an acceptable attainment level or type of behavior in friends or relatives is unacceptable for ourselves. If you have decided to reach point H in one move and do not achieve it, then you perceive yourself as a FAILURE. But if a friend had not reached his "H" and had discovered that he was at "D" instead, you would say, "Don't be discouraged; you're on your way to H. Next time you'll make it." So don't set unrealistic goals for yourself. Life has a way of being disappointing enough. Where you can exercise control over yourself, do so.

The next aid we thought would be valuable was to provide you with a list of publications on financial assistance. Many of these references are from the Spring 1981 *Occupational Outlook Quarterly*. With luck, by the time *Career Changing* is published, all or most of these financial resources will still be available to you. But, with the federal government's extensive cuts in education, some scholarships, fellowships, and training programs listed in these publications may no longer be in existence. Please check out, very carefully, the ones in which you have an interest.

Selected List of Publications on Financial Aid

American Legion Education and Scholarship Program, *Need a Lift?* 1980. $1.00 prepaid. Available from the American Legion, Box 1055, Indianapolis, IN 46206. Provides information on careers and scholarships primarily for undergraduates who are children or spouses of disabled veterans.

Barron's Educational Series, Inc., *Barron's Handbook of American College Financial Aid*, 1977. $8.50 plus $1.50 postage. Available from Barron's Educational Series, Inc., 113 Crossways Park Drive, Woodbury, NY 11797.

———, *Barron's Handbook of Junior and Community College Financial Aid*, 1979. $8.50 plus $1.50 postage. Available from Barron's Educational Series, Inc., 113 Crossways Park Drive, Woodbury, NY 11797.

———, *You Can Win a Scholarship*, May 1981. Available from Barron's Educational Series, Inc., 113 Crossways Park Drive, Woodbury, NY 11797.

College Entrance Examination Board, *Paying for Your Education: A Guide for Adult Learners*, 1980. $3.50. Available from College Board Publication Orders, P.O. Box 2815, Princeton, NJ 08540. Pocket-sized guide designed to help adult learners obtain their financial aid. Contains a financial aid checklist, a calendar of important deadlines, a listing of other up-to-date sources of information and a glossary of terms.

Johnson, Willis L., *Directory of Special Programs for Minority Group Members, Career Information Services, Employment Skills Banks, Financial Aid*, 1980. $19.00 prepaid. Available from Garrett Park Press, Garrett Park, MD 20766. Information for minority students on financial aid, job retraining, and college awards, with a special section on programs for women.

National Center for Educational Brokering, *Inventory of Resources for Counselors of Adults: Financial Aid Information for Adult Students*, 1979. $1.00. Available from National Center for Educational Brokering, 405 Oak Street, Syracuse, NY 13203.

National Science Foundation, *A Selected List of Fellowship Opportunities and Aids to Advanced Education for United States Citizens and Foreign Nationals,* 1980. Free. Available from National Science Foundation, 1800 G Street, N.W., Washington, DC 20550.

Nies, Judith, *Women and Fellowships,* 1979. $2.00. Available from Women's Equity Action League, 805 15th Street, N.W., Suite 822, Washington, DC 20005. Information on how to apply for scholarships and fellowships at the graduate level.

Octameron Associates, *Don't Miss Out: The Ambitious Student's Guide to Scholarships and Loans,* 1980. $2.50. Available from Octameron Associates, Box 3437, Alexandria, VA 22302. Lists federal, state, and private sources of financial aid for undergraduate and graduate students, with a section on minorities.

Shlachter, Gail Ann, *Directory of Financial Aids for Women,* 1978. $15.95. Available from Reference Service Press, 9023 Alcott Street, Suite 201, Los Angeles, CA 90036. A listing of scholarships, fellowships, loans, grants, internships, awards, and prizes designed primarily or exclusively for women: women's credit unions; sources of state educational benefits; and reference sources on financial aid.

U.S. Department of Education, *Selected List of Postsecondary Education Opportunities for Minorities and Women,* 1980. $4.50. Available from the Superintendent of Documents, Washington, DC 20402. GPO Stock No. 065-000-0058-0. Information on scholarships, loans, and fellowship opportunities by field of study. Covers architecture, business, engineering and science, health, journalism, law, and others. Emphasizes, but not limited to, aid for minorities and women.

U.S. Department of Education, *Student Consumer's Guide to Five Federal Financial Aid Programs,* 1981-1982 ed. Free. Request current edition from the Bureau of Student Financial Assistance, P.O. Box 84, Washington, DC 20044. Describes Basic Educational Opportunity Grants, Supplemental Educational Opportunity Grants, College Work-Study, National Direct Student Loans and Guaranteed Student Loans.

U.S. Department of the Interior, *Career Development Opportunities for Native Americans.* Free. Available from U.S. Department of the Interior, Bureau of Indian Education Programs, Box 1788, Albuquerque, NM 87103. Lists approximately 100 sources of assistance for students who are one-quarter or more Indian, Eskimo, or Aleut.

Woodrow Wilson Fellowship Foundation, *A Selected List of Major Fellowship Opportunities for Black Students at the Graduate Level.* Free from Martin Luther King, Jr., Fellowships, Woodrow Wilson National Fellowship Foundation, Box 642, Princeton, NJ 08540. Advice on how to choose a school and obtain financial aid, including a bibliography and listing of fellowship programs.

The previous listings gave you some of the *publications* available on financial aid in general. The following information lists specific *sources* of financial aid available only to qualified women and minorities. (Sorry, all you non minority males!)

Selected Sources of Financial Aid for Women

Altrusa International Foundation, Inc., Founders Fund Vocational Aid Committee, 8 South Michigan Avenue, Chicago, IL 60603. Grants for programs leading to an occupational skill; emphasis on vocational, not academic, training. Women of all ages may qualify, but preference is given to older women. Applicants must have plans to start work within 12 months.

American Association of University Women, 2401 Virginia Avenue, N.W., Washington, DC 20037. Fellowships to assist women in their final year of professional training in law, dentistry, medicine, veterinary medicine, and architecture.

Business and Professional Women's Foundation, 2012 Massachusetts Avenue, N.W., Washington, DC 20036.
Sally Butler International Scholarships for women in graduate programs in education-related fields
Career Advancement Scholarships for women 25 or above who are returning to school either full-time or part-time after a break in their education
Clairol Loving Care Scholarships for women aged 30 or above for vocational, undergraduate, or graduate study
Loan Fund for Women in Graduate Engineering Studies, which provides loans to women for graduate-level programs in engineering with particular emphasis on master's degree programs
Second Career Scholarships for Displaced Homemakers, which provide funds for counseling and retraining

Danforth Foundation, 222 South Central Avenue, St. Louis, MO 63105. Fellowships for women whose education has been interrupted for three or more consecutive years who wish to pursue a graduate degree in teaching or education administration.

General Federation of Women's Clubs, 1934 N. Street, N.W., Washington, DC 20036. Scholarships and loans that are awarded by local clubs and state federations.

George R. and Eliza Gardner Howard Foundation, Box 1867, Brown University, Providence, RI 02912. Fellowships for women aged 30–40 pursuing studies in languages and literature, social sciences, history, philosophy, and fine, applied, and performing arts.

Kappa Kappa Gamma, P.O. Box 2079, Columbus, OH 43216. Scholarships for women pursuing undergraduate or graduate programs in physical therapy, occupational therapy, speech and hearing, learning disabilities, mental health, and social work.

National Association of Women Deans, Administrators, and Counselors, 1028 Massachusetts Avenue, N.W., Suite 922, Washington, DC 20036. Grants for women working toward degrees in personnel, guidance, and counseling.

Soroptimists International, 1616 Walnut Street, Philadelphia, PA 19102. Training awards to assist mature women to enter or reenter the labor market.

United Educators Foundation, Tangley Oaks Educational Center, Lake Bluff, IL 60044. Fellowships for full-time or part-time graduate students, particularly in the fields of education and library science.

Additional Sources of Financial Aid for Minority Group Members

Aspira of America, Educational Opportunity Center, 205 Lexington Avenue, New York, NY 10016

Bureau of Indian Affairs, Albuquerque Area Office, Division of Education, P.O. Box 8327, Albuquerque, NM 87198

El Congreso Nacional de Asuntos Colegiales, One Dupont Circle, N.W., Washington, DC 20036

League of Latin-American Citizens National Educational Service Center, 400 First Street, N.W., Suite 716, Washington, DC 20001

National Association for the Advancement of Colored People, 1790 Broadway, New York, NY 10019

National Urban League, 500 East 62nd Street, New York, NY 10021

United Scholarship Service, Inc., Capitol Hill Station, P.O. Box 18285, 941 East 17th Avenue, Denver, CO 80218

Now that you know all about scholarships, loans and fellowships, we thought that we would assemble a reading list for you, one that could be quite useful in career planning. After this list is concluded we will tell you why we selected these particular works and not some others.

Reading Resources Useful in Career Planning

Bird, Caroline, *The Two-Paycheck Marriage* (Rawson-Wade, 1979), $8.95.

Boll, Carl R., *Executive Jobs Unlimited* (Macmillan, 1979), $8.95.

Bolles, Richard N., *What Color Is Your Parachute? A Practical Manual for Job-Hunters and Career-Changers* (Ten Speed Press, 1980), $6.95.

Career Exploration in Marketing and Distribution. Stock No. 018-080-01733-4. $4.65 check or money order to: Superintendent of Documents, U.S. Government Printing Office, Washington, DC 20402.

Cohen, William A., *The Executive's Guide to Finding a Superior Job* (AMACOM [paperback], 1980), $5.95.

Dodd, Allen R., *The Job Hunter: Diary of a "Lost" Year* (McGraw-Hill, 1978).

Figler, Howard E., *The Complete Job Search Handbook: Presenting the Skills You Need to Get Any Job and Have a Good Time Doing It* (Holt, Rinehart, and Winston, 1980).

————, *Path: A Career Work-Book for Liberal Arts Students* (Carroll Press Publishers, 1979).

Harragan, Betty Lehan, *Games Mother Never Taught You (Corporate Gamesmanship for Women)* (Warner Books [paperback], 1979), $2.50.

Jackson, Tom, *Guerrilla Tactics in the Job Market* (Bantam Books, 1980), $2.95.

Lathrop, Richard, *Who's Hiring Who* (Ten Speed Press, 1977), $5.95.

Molloy, John T., *Dress for Success* (New York: Warner Books, 1978).

————, *The Woman's Dress for Success Book* (New York: Warner Books, 1978).

National Directory of Women's Employment Programs, Wider Opportunities for Women, 1649 K Street, N.W., Washington, DC 20006, 1979. $7.50 plus 60¢ postage.

Occupational Outlook for College Graduates, 1980–1981 Edition BLS Bulletin 2076. Stock NO. 029–001–02322–7. $6.00 check or money order to Superintendent of Documents, U.S. Government Printing Office, Washington, DC 20402.

Occupational Outlook Handbook, 1980–1981 Edition, Bulletin #2075, $8.00. Check or money order to Superintendent of Documents, U.S. Government Printing Office, Washington, DC 20402.

U.S. Department of Labor, Employment and Training Administration, *Senior Community Services Employment Program.* Fact sheet, free from the Employment and Training Administration, U.S. Department of Labor, Washington, DC 20213.

We could have named many other reading resources for you, but in our opinion, this list touches on the areas in which each of you may have an interest.

For a mature woman reentering the work force after a long absence, *Executive Jobs Unlimited* may not be as meaningful as the *Occupational Outlook Handbook* or *Games Mother Never Taught You*. For the middle manager seeking to move vertically, *Executive Jobs Unlimited* or *The Executive's Guide to Finding a Superior Job* is more important than *Path: A Career Work-Book for Liberal Arts Students*. For the recent college graduate, *Occupational Outlook for College Graduates*, or *Path: A Career Work-Book for Liberal Arts Students* will be more helpful than some of the books written for people with extensive work experience.

We suggest you get these books from your local library first, if they are available there. Those you find helpful you should then purchase as reference books. But be forewarned: there have been some terrible books published on job changing. This topic has been very "in" for the past decade, and we expect still further proliferation. The books we listed were written by professionals in the field of careers, not just someone or some group seeking to make a fast buck at your expense.

11. A Glossary of Jargon

> "'Twas brillig, and the slithy toves
> Did gyre and gimble in the wabe;
> All mimsy were the borrogoves,
> And the mome raths outgrabe."
>
> —LEWIS CARROLL, "JABBERWOCKY"

As we have mentioned throughout the book, jargon plays a critical role in your career search. Knowledge of a particular industry's "language" should show up on your résumés and letters and be used when interviewing. This demonstrates that you are an informed candidate. Without a fairly complete knowledge of your chosen field's jargon, you will be viewed by those who interview you as a novice and probably unacceptable as an employee. To help prevent this situation we have compiled a list of alphabetically arranged, job-related jargon words. We didn't include every jargon word for every industry, for we would be creating an entirely new book! The words in this glossary are ones you will often see in help-wanted ads and ones that we have used throughout this book.

Words you discover on your own may be abbreviations; if so, their definitions can usually be found at the back of any good dictionary. Terms not listed here are ones we found to be highly technical and used primarily in the engineering, computer, and telecommunications fields. Knowledge of their definitions is pertinent only if you already have some expertise in one of these fields.

As a person attempting to switch to a new field, you should have enough knowledge of less complicated jargon to help you get hired into your first position (assuming you interview well, dress appropriately, et cetera).

Abbreviations and words not explained here should be self-evident from their definitions. Now you are ready to "super-zap a sysjam" (spur-of-the-moment jargon for fixing a computer problem!).

Abbreviation	Term	Definition	Category
AAA	American Arbitration Association	Association that sponsors voluntary arbitration in labor, commercial and trade disputes	Labor relations
ACD	Automatic call distributor	Part of telephone or similar device that automatically dials into a terminal or specified phone	Telecommunications, general business
	Actuary	Person who calculates statistical risks, premiums, etc., for insurance	Insurance
ADEA	Age Discrimination Employment Act	Enacted by Congress to prevent age discrimination in hiring practices	Government term used in Personnel
ADP	Automatic data processing	Assembly, classification, recording, analysis, and reporting of information by electronic means	Computers

AE	Account executive	Person who manages a group of clients and/or accounts	Advertising, sales promotion, sales
Amex	American Stock Exchange	One of two exchanges where publicly listed corporations of certain worth trade their securities	Stock brokerage, finance
	Annual report	A yearly statement of the financial condition and operating results of publicly held companies written by them	General business
	Arbitrage	Buying and selling simultaneously the same commodity in two or more markets with the expectation of profiting from temporary differences in price	Finance, stock brokerage
	Arbitration	The hearing and determination of a case in controversy by a person chosen by the parties or appointed under a statutory authority	Labor relations
ASAD	Advanced structured analysis and design		Engineering
A/V	Audiovisual	Use of media such as slide presentations, film strips, to sell, motivate, educate, or train an audience	Personnel, sales, education
	Back burner	As in "put on the back burner." Expression meaning to delay something for future consideration	General business slang
	Bargaining unit	Term for labor union that represents a group of union employees	Labor relations
BOM	Beginning of month		Accounting, finance
	Bottom line	Slang for "final analysis." On an organization's balance sheet or financial statement a totaling of its profits or losses	General business slang
BOY	Beginning of year		Accounting, finance
	Break-even point	The level of output at which an organization's revenues and its costs are equal. At this point net profit is zero.	Accounting
	Broker	Any person acting as intermediary between a buyer and seller of real or personal property or services	Insurance, real estate, stocks, etc.
CAB	Civil Aeronautics Board	Government agency having regulatory powers over civil aviation	Government
	Caveat emptor	"Let the buyer beware" (Latin)	Business
CBE	Computer-based education		Education
CCTV	Closed-circuit television		Training, education

CD	Certificate of Deposit	A fixed-income debt security, issued by chartered banks. Terms run for a specified minimum time. If money is withdrawn before time is up, penalties ensue.	Banking
CEO	Chief executive officer	Person who heads up an organization and who generally makes final decisions as to its business direction	General business
CFA	Certified Financial Analyst	Designation used for people who have taken and passed specific finance courses at the graduate level	Finance
CFO	Chief financial officer	Person in an organization who determines its financial direction and oversees all other financial people	Business
CIF	Cost, insurance, and freight		Insurance
	Circular file	Slang term for wastebasket (where most résumés end up!)	General business
CLU	Chartered Life Underwriter	Professional designation awarded to life insurance agents and brokers who pass a series of comprehensive exams	Insurance
	Comptroller	An alternate spelling of *controller* (derived from Middle English). Usually an officer of an organization possessing accounting skills who is responsible for administration of day-to-day financial matters	Accounting, finance
	Consumer packaged goods	Term to describe companies that manufacture products that are marketed directly to consumers	Business
COO	Chief operating officer	Person responsible for the day-to-day operations of an organization	Business
CPA	Certified Public Accountant	Professional designation awarded to a person who has passed a series of comprehensive exams in accounting	Accounting, finance
CPI	Consumer Price Index	A monthly measure, compiled by the government, of changes in the prices of selected goods and services consumed by individuals	Government, general business
CPM	Critical-path method	A planning method or technique for analysis that shows the interrelationships in sequence of all activities involved in a project	Business
CPU	Central processing unit	Computer part that performs calculations and processes data according to instructions specified by the software. CPU is sometimes used interchangeably with "computer."	Computers

CRT	Cathode-ray tube	Picture tube, including the video screen that displays prompting instructions, computer responses, and reports generated by the computer	Telecommunications, general business
	Distributive education	A program of occupational instruction in the field of distribution and marketing	Education
DM	Department manager	Person who manages a group of people	Business
DM	Direct mail	Marketing method used to reach a large population in order to inform, sell, or conduct research. A control method of measurement in a live, statistical setting	Marketing, sales, advertising
DM	District manager	Person who oversees a particular geographical area and several employees	Sales, general business
DOT	*Directory of Occupational Titles*	Publication of the U.S. Department of Labor (DOT can also mean Department of Transportation)	Government
	Down time	The time required for setup, overhaul, or maintenance, or lost time attributable to idleness. Originally a computer term	General business
DP	Data processing	The assembly, classification, recording, analysis, reporting, and storage of information by manual, mechanical, or electronic means	Computers
	Draw against commission	One method used to pay salespeople. Under this arrangement, the person is advanced a specific amount per pay period, which will be deducted from future sales commissions.	Sales (particularly in insurance, real estate, personnel agencies)
DSM	District sales manager	Like district manager, except this designation is specific to sales positions only	Sales
EDP	Electronic data processing	Interchangeable term with Automatic Data Processing or Data Processing	Computers
EEO	Equal Employment Opportunity	Organizations over 25 people in size and engaged in any government work must be EEO employers (they must hire qualified women and minority employees at all levels).	Personnel, government
	Entity accounting	Accounting for an entity, independent, or predecessor or controlling organization	Accounting
	Entrepreneur	A person who, on his own initiative, establishes and operates a business enterprise	Business

	Equity	The residual interest of an owner after all relevant debts have been paid	Accounting, finance
ERISA	Employee Retirement Income Security Act (1974)	Imposes obligations on employers having employee benefit plans to include their employees.	Personnel, government
ESOP	Employee stock ownership plan	An incentive type of retirement plan funded with employers' shares of common stock	Insurance, finance
	Exempt	An employee who is exempt from the provisions of the Fair Labor Standards Act. Not eligible to be paid overtime	Personnel
	Experience rating	Basing premium rates on past history of losses	Insurance, personnel
	Factor analysis	The transformation of statistical data into linear combinations of variables that are usually not correlated	Statistics, finance
FASB-5	Financial Accounting Standards Board	Statement of the Financial Accounting Standards Board establishing criteria for accruing certain liabilities	Insurance, finance
	Fast-track	Slang for any employee viewed as a high potential management candidate	General business
FCC	Federal Communications Commission	Independent government agency that regulates interstate and foreign communications	Government
FDA	Federal Drug Administration	Government agency responsible for the testing and safety of food, drugs, and medical devices marketed to the public	Government
FIFO	First in, first out		Accounting
	Flowchart	A diagram of symbols and connecting lines showing step-by-step progression through a complicated procedure system	General business, computers
FLSA	Fair Labor Standards Act	The federal law requiring employers to pay overtime for work performed beyond 40 hours in any week to nonexempt people	Government, personnel
FMCS	Federal Mediation and Conciliation Service	The federal service that attempts to settle labor disputes between management and organized labor	Government, labor relations
FOB	Free on board	Shipper is responsible until goods have been placed on board vessel, car, or truck, after which the consignee assumes the risk.	Insurance, business
	Fortune 500	A list of the top 500 manufacturing companies identified annually in the May issue of *Fortune* magazine; listed according to gross sales	Business, stock brokerage

	Fortune 1000	A list of the second top 500 manufacturing companies identified annually in the June issue of *Fortune* magazine; listed according to gross sales	Business
FT	Full-time		Personnel
FTC	Federal Trade Commission	A quasijudicial administrative agency of the federal government charged with the general responsibility of maintaining the freedom of business enterprise	Government
FX	Foreign exchange	A transaction involving the exchange of currency of one country for currency of another	Business, finance
FY	Fiscal year	A period of approximately one year for which financial statements are prepared on a regular basis. A fiscal year usually consists of twelve consecutive months, but sometimes covers fifty-two or fifty-three consecutive weeks.	General business
G&A	General and administrative	Refers to operating expenses identified in someone's budget.	Business, finance
GAAP	Generally accepted accounting principles		Accounting
	General ledger	A ledger book or computer printout containing accounts in which all the transactions of a business enterprise or other accounting units are classified	Finance
GMP	Good manufacturing practices		Manufacturing
GNP	Gross National Product	The value of all goods and services produced by the economic system in one year	Business
	Grievance	A complaint against an employer by one or more employees alleging a breach of a collective agreement	Labor relations, personnel
	Ground zero	Military term used in business to mean "from the beginning"	Business
	Group dynamics	Interpersonal dynamics that comes out of a group of people based upon certain conditions established by a seminar leader within a seminar context	Training and development (personnel)
	Hands-on	Slang term for style of management in which the manager gets directly involved in doing part of the work, through close supervision and frequent follow-up	Business, from manufacturing, education

	Hardware	In computer language, the mechanical, magnetic, electrical, and electronic devices, components, and equipment of a computer system	Computer
HBA	Health and beauty aids	Term used by that part of the Consumer Products Industry which markets health and beauty aids (toothpaste, cosmetics) to consumers	Marketing
	Headhunter	Slang term for an executive search consultant	Business, personnel
	Human resources	The 1980s term for the personnel function. Its mission has been expanded beyond hiring and firing to encompass the full development of employee potential. Areas of responsibility usually include compensation, benefits, wage and salary administration, training and development, and employee and labor relations.	Personnel, business
HVAC	Heating, ventilation and air conditioning	Technical term used in companies that manufacture and/or market these products	Engineering
	In-house	Work that's done within the organization versus having it contracted to an outside source	Business, publishing
	Interactive computer programs	Programs performed on a computer that requires mutual action on the part of the operator and the computer	Computers
	Interface	To be the liaison between different groups of people; originally a computer term referring to adaptive gear	Business
IR	Industrial relations	Rules and regulations governing the relations between a labor union and management	Business
	Jobber	Someone who buys from a producer and sells to a retailer. A middleman (wholesaler)	Business
	Keyed ad	Advertising coded so the advertiser can know which publication or mailing piece generated responses	Direct mail, marketing, sales promotion, advertising
LIFO	Last in, first out	A method of inventory valuation or a personnel policy	Accounting, personnel
	Logo	A distinctive symbol used by an organization to identify itself	General businesses, advertising
	Matrix organization	A method for planning and controlling an organization's structure. Frequently used on project management	Business

M.B.A.	Master of Business Administration	Advanced degree in business (very "in" now)	Education, general business
MBO	Management by objectives	A management technique designed to achieve overall and individual objectives with all levels of management and staff participating	General business
	Media buyer	A person who buys space or time for advertisements in various media (TV, radio, magazines)	Advertising
	Microfiche	A sheet of microfilm containing rows of micro-images of pages of printed matter	Business
	Microfilm	A film bearing a photographic record on a reduced scale of printed or other graphic matter.	Business
MIS	Management information systems	An all-encompassing term for those systems within an organization, especially the computer center, that provide data to management	Business, computers
	Modem	A device that couples a computer to a terminal via a telephone unit. Used for transmission of data over a distance.	Computers, telecommunications
MRP	Materials requirements planning	Integrated system that includes the computer-directed flow of inventories and lots to be processed through manufacturing	Manufacturing
	Multimedia methods	All-encompassing term referring to all the audiovisual devices and methods of presenting information	Training, sales, advertising
	Nielsen Report	Competitive sales information provided by Nielsen through auditing of product categories (and some services) by sampling the points of distribution of these goods. Provides a behavioral measure of brands within categories.	Market research
NLRB	National Labor Relations Board	A government group that hears labor complaints and determines if any U.S. labor law was violated	Labor relations, personnel
	Non-Exempt	A category of employee not exempt from the federal government's Fair Labor Standards Act. They are eligible to collect overtime pay. Hourly employees	Personnel
NYSE	New York Stock Exchange	One of the two exchanges that buy and sell the securities of publicly held companies	Stock market
OEM	Original equipment manufacturer	Company that built a specific piece of equipment	Business, manufacturing

OFCCP	Office of Federal Contract Compliance Programs	Part of the Equal Employment Opportunity Commission in D.C. that monitors the hiring practices of organizations having federal contracts	Personnel, government
OSHA	Occupational Safety and Health Act	A federal law establishing safety and health standards in the workplace nationwide	Government, personnel
OTC	Over the counter	A market where brokers can buy and sell the securities of smaller publicly held companies. Also term used for nonprescription drugs	Stock market, pharmaceuticals
PBX	Private branch exchange	A type of switchboard	Telecommunications
PCB	Printed Circuit Board	A piece of equipment on which electronics hardware is wired.	Electronics
P/E	Price/earnings ratio	What you look at before you buy a company's stock!	Finance
	Perks	Short for perquisites; special benefits or privileges provided as an additional, indirect form of compensation in lieu of salary	Business, personnel
PERT	Program Evaluation and Review Techniques	System under which an activity (such as factory production) is organized and controlled on the basis of the sequenced time periods required for each operating step. Usually represented in chart form	Business, manufacturing
P&L	Profit and loss		Business, accounting
	Platform skills	A personnel term referring to a person's ability to instruct in a classroom setting	Training
	Programmed instruction	Instruction utilizing a workbook, textbook, or mechanical and/or electronic device that has been "programmed" to help participants attain a specific level of performance	Training, education
	Project management		Business
PT	Part-time		Business
QA	Quality assurance	Process by which a product that has been tested is given approval to be released to the public	Manufacturing
QC	Quality control	Method or function that audits and inspects manufacturing production	Manufacturing
RAM	Random access memory	Semiconductor chips within a computer serving as a scratch pad. The CPU enters and retrieves information from RAM almost instantaneously, but unlike	Computers

		data in external storage, the contents of RAM are lost when electrical power to the computer is turned off.	
RBO	Results by objectives		Business, sales
R&D	Research and development	Activity in organizations that takes place to discover and then develop new products and services	Business, science, medicine, etc.
	Real time	A real-time computation is one that is performed during the actual occurrence of the physical event to which the calculation pertains.	Computers
ROI	Return on investments	The annual profit resulting from an investment, usually expressed as a percentage of the investment	Finance
ROM	Read-only memory	Semiconductor chips that are like a printed book whose information cannot be erased. System software is often stored in ROM. (ROM is pronounced either as a word or letter by letter.)	Computer
RSM	Regional sales manager		Sales
SAMI	Sales Areas Marketing, Inc.	Company that provides data on grocery and drug products to supermarkets. Audits the flow of goods from warehouse to the retail outlet.	Market research
SEC	Securities and Exchange Commission	The government agency charged with regulating the issuance and trading of securities (stocks and bonds)	Government, finance
	Sell-thru	Selling 100 percent of received merchandise or products and having no leftover inventory	Retailing, consumer products
	Service bureau	A company that runs programs for a client for a fee. The customer need not have any computer equipment on his own premises, although a remote terminal and a modem are often used for convenience (and become necessary if time-sharing is involved).	Computers
	Skills assessment	A technique by which the level of workers' skills is determined in any organization. It can be accomplished usually in only four ways: (1) direct observation of a worker's behavior, (2) interviews, (3) questionnaires, and (4) research through existing records.	Training (personnel)

SMSA	Standard Metropolitan Statistical Area	A geographic area defined by census data, such as traffic patterns, product use, etc., not one defined by legal boundaries	Marketing
	Software	The programs, or instructions, that tell the computer how to respond to specific user commands	Computers
SOP	Standard operating procedure	Military term now used in business	Manufacturing, business
SPI	Standard practice instruction		Manufacturing
	Succession planning	The method by which an organization identifies and develops its future managers	Business, personnel, management development
	Switch premium	The amount of money it costs a company to get an individual to switch jobs from one company to another. This is especially common with high-technology firms.	Business, personnel
TA	Transactional Analysis	A concept of interpersonal actions, reactions, communications, and noncommunications popularized by Dr. Thomas Harris in his book *I'm OK, You're OK*	Personnel, training, psychotherapy
10K	Ten-K	A formal business summary of a publicly held company or corporation done by outside auditors and submitted annually to the SEC. Also can mean ten thousand dollars (as in salary)	Finance/ business
	Terminal	A point of input or output. Many terminals have a keyboard plus a printer and/or a video display electronically linked to a computer.	Computers
	Time-sharing	Simultaneous access by several users to one central processing unit	Computers
	Track record	As in "successful track record." Employee who has done very well. (Sports term meaning record of past accomplishments)	Business
TRASOP	Tax Reduction Act Stock-Ownership Plan	Created in 1975, it allows employers to claim as credit against taxes an amount equal to one percent of their capital spending if the money saved is used to buy company stock for employees (who pay nothing for it).	Insurance

	Turn-around	General business term used to refer to those business situations that have gone from losing money to making money	Business
VTR	Video tape recorder		Training, communications
	"You" attitude	The quality all successful direct mail letters have (whether the word "you" is used or not)	Direct mail marketing

Most definitions of these jargon words we did ourselves, with a little help from our friends. We also used Leon A. Wortman, *A Desk Book of Business Management Terms* (American Management Association, 1979); Eric H. Kohler, *Dictionary for Accountants* (Prentice-Hall, 1970); J. Lyman MacInnis, *A Handbook of Business Terminology* (General Publishing Company, 1978).

Index

242

group members, 227–228; for
women, 226–227
Flanders, Russell B., 47
Food service occupations, 19–20
Forbes, 57
Foundry occupations, 15

General Foods, 72

Harvard University, 224; Law
School, 43
Health occupations, 28–30, 47
High school graduates, tips for, 43
Homemaking, 7
Homequity, 166
Hospital occupations, *see* Health
occupations
Hudson Pharmaceutical Corporation,
72

IBM, 166
INC. magazine, 163
Industrial production and related occupations, 15–17
Instructing, 168
Insurance occupations, 18
Internal Revenue Service (IRS), 205,
218–220
Interviewing: developing skill of,
168; for information, 218
Interviews, job, 52, 183, 207; attitudes before, 184; four stages of,
184–186; proper dress for, 195;
stress-oriented, with questions and
answers, 196–202; tested questions for "structured," 186–195

Jargon: defined, 146; importance of,
146; used in job-hunting letter,
63, 64
Job(s): best, in 1980s, 9–10; not re-
quiring B.A. or B.S. degree, 40;
prospects, by region, 43–45.
See also Occupational employment
outlook
Job campaign, questions frequently
asked about, 214–217
Job hunting: determining strengths
while, 50; hours spent, 50–51
Job market: hidden, 117, 203, 208–
211; successful penetration of,
203–208

Labor, U.S. Department of, 9, 13,
161
Lawyers, decreases in job openings
for, 43
Letters, action, 70, 81, 96–97,
102–103; analysis of typical,
172–175; dos and don'ts of,
175–179; examples of, 6, 94,
145, 170, 171–172, 175–178,
180–182; formula for, 169–172;
portfolio of, 179–182; strategies
for overcoming weaknesses in,
100–102
Letters, cover, 70, 80
Library occupations, 21
Life science occupations, 26
Los Angeles Times, 133

Machining occupations, 15
McKinsey & Co., 10

Management: personnel; 41–42;
succession planning, 41
Management consultants, 10
Managing/supervising, 168
Marketing, 12–13
Mathematics occupations, 26
Mechanics and repairers, 27–28
*Mechanix Illustrated Guide to Per-
sonal Computers,* 39
Medical practitioners, 29. *See also*
Health occupations
Medical technologist, technician,
and assistant occupations, 29–30.
See also Health occupations
Merchant marine occupations, 23
Merrill Lynch, 42
Miami Tribune, 133
Middle Atlantic states, job prospects
in, 44
Midwest, job prospects in, 44
Military service, obtaining technical
training in, 43
Mobililty, competition and, 37
Mountain states, job prospects in,
44

National Center for Educational
Brokering, 223
National Center for Education Sta-
tistics (NCES), 9
National Commission on Working
Women, 57
National Personnel Associates, 163
Nelson, Herbert, 12
Networking, 217–218
New England, job prospects in,
43–44
Newspaper reporters, 10
New York, University of State of,
222
New York Times, 133, 204;
National Recruitment Survey of
(1981), 43–43
Nielsen reports, 12
Northwest, job prospects in, 45
Northwestern University, 224
Nursing occupations, 30. *See also*
Health occupations

Occupational employment outlook,
15–33
Occupational Outlook Quarterly
(1980), 9, 13, 41, 47, 225
Office occupations, 17–19; shortage
of skilled workers for, 42
Oil companies, salaries of secretaries
at, 12

Pennsylvania, University of, Whar-
ton school at, 224
Perception, of abilities, 7–8
Performing artists, 32
Perry, Robert L., 39
Personal service occupations, 20
Physical scientists, 26
Political scientists, 13
Pond, Samuel A., 224
Printing occupations, 15
Private household service occupa-
tions, 20
Problem-Action-Result (P-A-R) for-

mat (paragraphs), 55, 56, 99, 117;
in action, 58; constructing, 58–
65; gaining credibility through,
98; portfolio of sample, 65–68; in
résumés, 76, 81, 82, 96–97;
summary of, 65
Procter & Gamble, 72, 166
Product manager, ad for, 69, 72
Profits, as primary goal of organizations, 72, 97–98
Protective and related service occupations, 20
Publications, selected list of, on
financial aid, 225–28; for minority group members, 227–228; for
women, 226–227
Public speaking, 168

Railroad occupations, 24
Reading resources, useful in career
planning, 228–229
References, avoiding mention of, in
résumés, 78, 80
Rehabilitation and therapy occupations, 30
Repairers and mechanics, 27–28
Reporters, newspaper, 10
Resignation from present job, notice
required upon, 208
Résumé(s), 114; avoiding chronological gaps in, 148–149; avoiding
list of references in, 78, 80;
avoiding mention of salary in, 80,
99; chronological, 76, 104–105,
109–111; combination of
chronological/functional, 76, 107–
108, 113; conflicting philosophies
about, 80–81; examples of, 4,
48, 95–96, 104–113, 118, 120–
121, 147, 150–151; formats, 76–
80; functional, 76, 106, 112; as
introduction, 71–72; as marketing tool, 72–76; personnel departments' view of, 69–71;
preparation services, 52; reference, with examples, 82–97,
102–103; strategies for overcoming weaknesses in, 99–102; strategies for using, in career
campaign, 102–103; telling truth
in, 52–53
Robotics, 43
Robots, displacement of factory work
force with, 43

Salary: avoiding mention of, in résumés, 80, 99; decrease, accept-
ing, when switching positions,
164; issue, handling, 99; questions
about, in job interviews, 198–
199; shrinkage, calculating,
161–162
Sales Executive Club, 224
Sales occupations, 21–22, 33–35
Sales representative, qualities of
successful, 34
SAMI reports, 12
Scheele, Adele M., *Skills for Success,* 5
Scientific and technical occupations,
24–27